The S U P E R M E N

. . . .

*The Story of Seymour Cray
and the Technical Wizards
behind the Supercomputer*

. . . .

Charles J. Murray

John Wiley & Sons, Inc.

New York · Chichester · Brisbane · Toronto · Singapore · Weinheim

Copyright © 1997 by Charles J. Murray
Published by John Wiley & Sons, Inc.

Library of Congress Cataloging-in-Publication Data:

Murray, Charles J.
    The supermen : the story of Seymour Cray and the technical wizards
    behind the supercomputer / Charles J. Murray
        p.   cm.
    Includes bibliographical references and index.
    ISBN 0–471–04885–2 (cloth : alk. paper)
    1. Cray, Seymour. 2. Computer engineers—United States—Biography
3. Cray computers—Design and construction—History. I. Title.
TK7885.22.C73M87   1997
338.7'6100411'092—dc20   96-36448

Printed in the United States of America
10 9 8 7 6 5 4 3 2 1

To my wife, Pat, for her undying patience

To Tim, Erin, Joe, and Dan, for all the weekends lost

CONTENTS

· · · · · · · · · ·

PREFACE

. . . .

This book is about engineers. Specifically it is about the founders of a particular branch of computing that eventually became known as supercomputing.

The idea for this book grew out of a simple observation during a visit to Cray Research in 1989—that is, that Seymour R. Cray experienced the same travails encountered by all corporate engineers. Despite his reputation as one of the best engineers of the twentieth century, he continually battled corporate bureaucracy and constantly struggled for funding. The difference between Cray and most other engineers is that he often won those battles. His success was attributable to his existence in a postwar culture where engineers were valued. He was also part of an extraordinary industry where revolutionary developments were encouraged, and even necessary. Lastly Cray was blessed with rare technical ability and with managers—Bill Norris, Frank Mullaney, John Rollwagen—who understood that creative freedom was critical to success in supercomputing.

Obviously this book could have covered the works of many other talented engineers in the supercomputer industry, at such places as IBM, Sperry, Burroughs, Texas Instruments, Silicon Graphics, Thinking Machines, Intel, Convex, Fujitsu, Hitachi, NEC, and the University of Illinois, among others. The companies and people portrayed in this book are by no means the industry's only significant figures. They were, however, the most prominent individuals in the industry's history. And their contributions will be remembered after the illusory line between supercomputing and the rest of the industry has long since disappeared.

April 5, 1996

If a man can write a better book, preach a better sermon, or make a better mousetrap than his neighbor, though he build his house in the woods, the world will make a beaten path to his door.

—RALPH WALDO EMERSON, 1871

Thank heaven for start-up companies or we'd never make any progress. People who get unhappy with structure in companies can move on and start their own, take big risks and occasionally find the pot of gold. I think that's just wonderful.

—SEYMOUR R. CRAY, 1994

PROLOGUE

. . . .

At the Crossroads

On a sunny spring day in 1989, Steve Nelson looked up from his desk to see his company's founder leaning quietly against his office door. Nelson, a high-ranking engineer with Cray Research Corporation, knew instinctively that there must be good reason for the visit. This particular day—May 14, 1989—was a Sunday. Most of the offices in the Lowater Road facility were dark; the halls had fallen silent; the computers hummed quietly. The majority of the engineers rested at home, trying to take a mental break from their current projects.

Yet here, lingering in Nelson's office doorway, was Seymour R. Cray. He was no longer the dark-haired engineer with the starched white collar pictured in so many newspaper accounts. Now sixty-three years old, his hair was gray and slightly thinning and his once smooth face had given way to subtle lines of age. Still, Cray's quiet way with people hadn't changed. His legendary desire for solitude was the same. He wasn't one to roam the halls in search of idle chatter. So Nelson waited patiently for Cray to deliver his message.

"There's a going to be a major announcement at tomorrow's shareholders meeting," Cray said. "Les and I have talked about it. And we've decided that it's best for everybody." Then he left.

The visit was vintage Cray—brief, stoic. In his own way, Cray was extending a courtesy to a trusted friend and colleague. He was sharing a major piece of company news so that Nelson wouldn't have to hear it through the grapevine or, worse, through the

/ 1

media. True, Cray had tiptoed around the subject, but that only suggested that it must be too emotionally charged to fit the normal nuts-and-bolts pattern of office patter. Besides, Nelson would learn the nature of the announcement soon enough.

When the news broke the following day, however, Nelson realized that their brief conversation hadn't really prepared him for the announcement. Seymour Cray was leaving. The visionary, the icon, the father of the supercomputer industry, was departing from Cray Research. Though the company's board of directors and its management deeply respected Cray, they had concluded they could no longer support his latest supercomputer project. The project, they said, was too costly and too risky. With corporate earnings slipping, a failure of this magnitude could wreck the company, they said. It could mean the loss of hundreds of jobs—jobs for people with families to support. Their logic was hard to dispute.

Still, it seemed impossible. This was, after all, *Seymour Cray*. He had designed the world's first "supercomputers," a name that referred to their status as the speediest machines on earth. His computers were routinely used by the National Security Agency for codebreaking and by the national weapons labs for nuclear bomb simulation. Automakers employed them for crash tests and air flow studies; aircraft builders used them to design wings and fuselages; oil companies applied them to petroleum exploration. Programmers knew that Cray's machines could process huge chunks of data in hours, whereas conventional mainframes might take weeks to do it. His supercomputers were so fast that a man with a handheld calculator would need more than a thousand years to accomplish what one could do in a single second, yet Cray could already foresee the day when his machines might be a hundred times faster. But now he was leaving, his ideas deemed too risky for the industry that he had founded.

For Nelson, Cray's departure was particularly painful. To him, Cray was both a mentor and a friend. Answering a tiny ad in the *Minneapolis Star* in 1976, Nelson had joined Cray Research as its seventy-sixth employee. Cray, who was two decades his senior, had taken Nelson under his wing and helped to advance his career. But now, Cray Research was choosing Nelson's project, eventually to be known as the C90, over Cray's more risky CRAY-3. It was an ironic turnabout from which Nelson could derive no personal satisfaction.

Around the company, many of the engineers were equally astonished. To them, Cray was an almost mythic figure. In the 1950s and 1960s, he had put Control Data on the map by fashioning the company's first computer from a reject load of 37-cent transistors. Later, he established Cray Research as a Fortune 500 company by introducing the CRAY-1, another machine of his own design. The company's culture—its corporate attitude toward personal freedom and creativity—was built around Cray's own legendary work habits. Even now, in 1989, he still kept odd hours and worked in his own unorthodox ways. It wasn't unusual for Cray to work straight through the night, or to show up at his lab at lunchtime, or to toil for weeks on end in seclusion. Up until recently, he had operated out of a lakeside "lab" in northern Wisconsin. In truth it was a cottage—a three-bedroom unit with a kitchen, living room, screened porch, and fireplace. But, incongruously, it also housed a Data General mainframe computer, a dozen or so PCs, a powerful air conditioner to cool the mainframe, and a backup power unit to handle the large electrical loads. There, in his own unusual setting, Cray laid out the most complex aspects of the CRAY-2 and CRAY-3 computers. In any other company, his behavior would have been regarded as odd. But at Cray Research, management had not only grown accustomed to it, they'd built a corporate culture around it. Understandably, it was a culture that was unusually tolerant of the creative process. That was one more reason why the company's engineers were now so stunned to see Cray leave.

As word spread about Cray's split with his company, scientists around the country wondered aloud what it meant. What would this do to national defense? How would the United States now compete with furious Japanese efforts to surpass its supercomputing programs? Defense authorities feared the implications; computer experts worried where their next generation of machines would come from. To programmers, Cray was a towering figure, and had been so for many years. After a rare speech at the National Center for Atmospheric Research in Boulder, Colorado, in

1976, programmers in the audience had suddenly fallen silent when Cray offered to answer questions. He stood there for several minutes, waiting for their queries, but none came. When he left, the head of NCAR's computing division chided the programmers. "Why didn't someone raise a hand?" he asked. After a tense moment, one programmer replied, "How do you talk to God?" *That* was the computing world's view of Cray. He was no mere mortal in their eyes.

Yet, now, the tide was turning. Cray's latest project, the CRAY-3, was openly questioned by many engineers. Cray wanted his new machine to employ circuits made from a material called gallium arsenide. Gallium arsenide had achieved limited success, particularly in satellite communications and military electronics. But no one had succeeded with it in anything so complicated as a computer. In the computer industry, engineers had developed a saying: "Gallium arsenide is the technology of the future," they would say. "And it always will be."

That was why Cray Research was now backing away from Cray's project. Nevermind his past successes. Cray Research was the biggest supercomputer company in the world, selling three times as many machines as its nearest competitor. It sold more machines than the combined total of *all* of its Japanese competitors. But it was also a prisoner of its own success. It had stockholders to satisfy and jobs to maintain. At Cray Research, there was no longer room for large-scale risks. That was the domain of smaller, more agile, companies.

The decision to eliminate Cray's program had been a heart-rending one for Cray Research's managers. John Rollwagen, the company's chief executive officer, had risen to his position largely through Cray's help. And Les Davis, the company's chief technical officer, was a close friend of Cray's for nearly three decades. Yet now they felt cornered by a harsh form of fiscal reality: The industry was changing. The market was transforming itself into something they barely recognized. Fewer customers could afford $30-million supercomputers. In this market, Cray Research's managers could not afford to take risks, even if the risk taker was a friend and a mentor.

In a few months, international politics would reinforce the wisdom of their decision. Giddy East Germans would mount the Berlin Wall to chisel away the final remnants of the Cold War. It would be an extraordinary moment in world history—one that would have a profound effect on the future of supercomputing. The Cold War had been mother and father of the supercomputer industry. It had supplied much of the funding for the development of Cray's revolutionary technology. Without it, engineers would be far less daring.

It was ironic that Cray should now be set back by the industry's new aversion to risk. Cray's strength, after all, had been his willingness to take risks. He was well-known for his penchant to build revolutionary, rather than evolutionary, products. He had forged a reputation as an engineer who tackled tough projects, then made them work against all odds. In a rare speaking engagement during 1988, he was introduced to the audience by a Los Alamos National Laboratory scientist who joked that he couldn't decide whether to call Cray the "Albert Einstein of supercomputing," or the "Thomas Edison of supercomputing," or the "Evel Knievel of supercomputing."

Now, however, Cray Research needed to steer clear of the Evel Knievel mentality. So Rollwagen arranged an extraordinary deal: The company would send Cray on his way to a new facility in Colorado Springs with $100 million in cash and $50 million in assets. Cray's project would no longer be part of Cray Research. His new firm would be an independent entity. It would be a competitor.

Cray agreed to the deal. He understood. There were jobs at stake, stockholders to satisfy, he knew. Cray was not one to confuse his own goals with those of the corporation.

But industry analysts couldn't help noticing that he was not backing down from the risk, either. Yes, he admitted, gallium arsenide was risky. And, yes, the market was changing. The *world* was changing. But he believed he could make his machine work. He still wanted to be an engineer, to build computers, to feel them go together, to breathe life into them, to beat the odds. For Cray, that was his life's calling. So he quietly packed his belongings and spoke one-by-one to his old friends and colleagues.

There would be a new company called Cray Computer Corporation, he said. It would launch the next generation of supercomputers. It would beat the odds and make gallium arsenide work. And the engineers of Cray Computer Corporation would share in the success.

Maybe the industry was growing risk averse elsewhere, but not at Cray Computer Corporation. Seymour Cray was looking for another miracle. And although most of the reasonable engineers in the industry doubted he could succeed, there was always an unshakable urge to look over their shoulders. So within weeks, a new expression emerged in the halls of Cray Research: "We wish Seymour luck," the engineers would say. "But not too much luck."

. . . .

ONE

The Codebreakers

For six days U-66 poked and prodded the gray water of the Atlantic Ocean, frantically searching for a place to surface, but the ships were always there. At any time of day or night the planes and ships would close in, and the crew of the U-boat would flee for their lives, hoping to find a safe haven.

Now they were surfacing again. Kapitänleutnant Gerhard Seehausen, the U-boat's commander, would have preferred to come up at another time, in another place, but he was running out of options. Here in the mid Atlantic on the moonlit night of May 5, 1944, U-boat life was dangerous, but *this* was incredible. Everyplace U-66 went, it was hounded. It could barely surface without being stalked. Time was running out. Seehausen's U-boat could go no further without running its power generators, which provided electricity and light, and it needed to rendezvous with a refueling sub.

With his U-boat at the water's surface off the Cape Verde Islands, Seehausen quickly sent a message to the radio room. The radio operator typed the message into a machine called Enigma, which scrambled its text; then he broadcast it to Berlin by tapping it out in Morse code: "Refueling impossible under constant stalking. Mid Atlantic worse than the Bay of Biscay." The message included the sub's location, a standard practice for all German U-boat transmissions. Seehausen never worried that Allied forces would intercept the message and crack the code during his hour at the water's surface. If they found him, as he knew they might, it would be by some means other than cracking the code. Never by cracking the code. No one could crack the German Enigma code *that* quickly.

Minutes after U-66 surfaced somewhere near the African coast, a teletype clattered to life in a Washington, D.C., laboratory. The machine rattled away, sending the lab's operators into a frenzy. One grabbed the teletype's paper output and frantically keyed its message onto punched paper tape. Another fed the tape into a 7-foot-high, 5,000-pound calculating machine. Inside the machine, primitive logic circuits examined U-66's message. Outside, the lab's codebreakers anxiously awaited its response.

Seehausen could never have imagined the scenario taking place halfway around the world. To think that someone was intercepting his message, then sending it across the Atlantic, where a 5,000-pound machine was stripping away its encryption codes would have been beyond the bounds of the most dedicated science fiction fans.

For that matter the activity in the Washington, D.C., laboratory was beyond the imaginative scope of almost every U.S. government official. Other than President Roosevelt, few knew of the effort, mundanely titled Communications Supplementary Activity—Washington (CSAW). The decryption activity was cloaked by such secrecy that its highest ranking officials required Ultra Secret clearance—a security level even higher than that of the Manhattan Project.

Roughly a thousand codebreakers worked at the navy's Nebraska Avenue facility—a tidy, red brick, former girl's school located in a quiet section of the city. These codebreakers were about as diverse and unconventional as any task force ever marshalled by the U.S. military. They had backgrounds in mathematics, physics, engineering, astronomy, and just about any discipline requiring intuitive pattern recognition. Some were chess experts, bridge champions, and musicians. Many had Ph.D's; a few were world-renowned scientists.

When the war began, they had decrypted messages like those of U-66 without the benefit of machines. To do it, they had quietly labored over volumes of coded messages, searching for patterns that departed from pure randomness. When they had stumbled upon a pattern, they had conferred, discussed, debated, bickered, and fought among themselves until groups of them had finally arrived at a consensus. Sometimes it had taken as long as six hundred hours.

As the war progressed, they developed machines to do the job. Following the lead of British scientists, a naval group in Dayton, Ohio, struggled to construct the machines, which they called Bombes. At first the Bombes were like 1930s adding machines, which used little electrical relays that clicked and clacked as their wheels spun furiously. By the end of 1943 the Bombes were far faster and more complex than electromechanical adding machines. By now they incorporated advanced circuits with more than fifteen hundred vacuum tubes.

When technicians entered a coded message into its circuits, a Bombe could buzz through a decryption in about the same time as it took a thousand cryptanalytic clerks. It was uncanny. Somewhere in the Atlantic a Nazi technician would tap the keys of the Enigma machine and scramble a message in such a way that a codebreaker would have to try millions of permutations to crack it. And yet the machines could, in some cases, blaze through that code in a few minutes.

Now the Bombes were cracking U-66's coded message—and it was about time. Since early in the war U-66 had done more than its share of damage. American intelligence blamed it for sinking the *Allan Jackson*, a 435-foot oil tanker owned by Standard Oil of New Jersey. They'd also blamed U-66 for sinking the *Lady Hawkins*, an ocean liner with 212 passengers on board, mostly civilians including women and children. Many sinkings were ugly: Victims swam through thick black smoke and layers of floating fuel, often burning to death after the fuel was ignited by signal flares.

But the tables were turning. The cryptologists at the Nebraska Avenue lab had cracked the code of U-66's message: "Refueling impossible under constant stalking. Mid Atlantic worse than the Bay of Biscay." Then came the most important information: "17 degrees, 17 minutes North; 32 degrees, 29 minutes West."

Through a series of channels, the cryptologists relayed their information to the destroyer USS *Buckley,* which steamed through the mid Atlantic toward Seehausen's U-boat.

Seehausen suspected that it was only a matter of time before Allied carriers and destroyers found him. They had been hounding him since April 29, and it was nearly midnight on May 5. Now he could see the USS *Buckley* about twenty-five hundred yards away. It was far too late to dive—an emergency dive could take as long as twenty minutes. He would have to face the *Buckley,* and he knew he had no chance of surviving.

Seehausen would never know the truth about his sub's sinking. He would never hear about the red brick building or the cracking of the Enigma code. And he would never suspect that his sub's real nemesis was the ancestor of a machine that would one day be called the digital computer.

During the last of his four years at the navy's Nebraska Avenue facility, Lieutenant Commander William C. Norris started thinking about other uses for the codebreaking machines. Surely, he thought, there must be business applications for machines as fast as these.

Bill Norris knew that the war would end soon and wondered about his options after he left the service. Unlike some of the other navy men, Norris *had* options. If he wanted, he could return to his family's farm in southern Nebraska, or he could go back to the Westinghouse Corporation in Chicago, where he had worked before the war selling X-ray equipment. A more staid personality might have done just that. After all, most of the country dreamed of little more than settling back into their prewar lives. But Norris wanted more, and he prided himself on his willingness to take risks to get it. A genuine, callous-palmed, Dust Bowl farm boy, he had traded his overalls for a slide rule thirteen years earlier, and at age thirty-five he wasn't anxious to go backward.

At the red brick school Norris methodically worked his way up in rank, despite being surrounded by some of the country's best scientists. Unlike many of the other codebreakers, he didn't hail from a posh eastern college or have a distinguished track record of scientific achievement, but he was a quick study who was forceful and direct, almost to the point of bluntness. With his wide face and high cheekbones, he looked a little like the tough-talking character actor Sheldon Leonard. Though he was an average-sized man, he had an air of intimidation about him. When the occasion called for it, Norris could, as the saying went, curse like a sailor.

Prior to joining the codebreakers, his crowning achievement had been in cattle farming. He'd grown up on a grassy spread of about a thousand acres along the Republican River in southern Nebraska. His life was classic midwestern Americana: small towns, rolling pasture lands, even a one-room schoolhouse.

He had been a bright student, but because he'd attended a school with only seven or eight other children in the tiny town of Inavale, Nebraska, it was difficult to know just how bright. Life on the farm had made him practical, an improviser. He had a strong mechanical aptitude and a passion for radio technology. His bedroom was strewn with vacuum tubes and copper wire and he was a ham radio aficionado. After he finished high school, Norris went on to the University of Nebraska at Lincoln to study electrical engineering.

Decades later, after Norris had achieved overwhelming success, the stories of his early years on his family's cattle farm would still be recognized as his defining moments. He returned home from the University of Nebraska in 1932, an electrical engineering degree in hand, and was hit with three crushing blows at once: His father had passed away a month earlier; the country was mired in the depths of the Great Depression; and the Midwest was wracked by the worst drought in the nation's history. The soil was so thin that it was being whisked away by the wind, and people in neighboring states were afraid to hang out laundry for fear it would be coated with brown dust while it dried.

Cattle owners, too, were besieged by difficulties. Without crops, they had no feed for cattle. The corn on the Norris farm— which had always been used to feed the animals—was coming up in pathetic little stalks that rose about knee high and then wilted.

Most of the other cattle farmers faced the same problems. Livestock buyers, recognizing the farmers' plight, were taking advantage of the situation by doling out painfully low prices for cattle.

Norris refused to sell at distressed prices. The twenty-two-year-old college graduate consulted his mother and decided to feed the cattle Russian thistles. About eight inches long, soft, and green, the Russian thistles were young versions of tumbleweed—the kind that always seem to be blowing down the dusty street of some Western movie set. But Russian thistles weren't regarded as cattle food, and most farmers believed they would kill the cattle or, at the very least, lead to the birth of deformed calves.

When Norris announced his plan to the neighbors, they as much as said he was crazy, but he ignored them. When they refused to help him stack the Russian thistle "crop" that covered his land, Norris hired vagrants at the nearby Red Cloud, Nebraska, railroad station to do it. And the cattle lived—for not one, but for two more winters—before he sold them at higher prices.

Norris liked to repeat the story because he believed that it demonstrated his willingness to take risks. More than that, though, it showed that he was profoundly confident and had good instincts. What may have looked like big risks to others weren't risks at all in Norris's mind.

Having been educated as an engineer, however, Norris wanted to try his hand in the technical world. After two years on the farm, he interviewed for engineering jobs. Westinghouse offered him two positions: part-time engineer for $80 a month or full-time salesman for twice that much. Having survived the Great Depression, he opted for the logical choice and soon began working out of a Chicago sales office, traveling to accounts in various parts of Illinois, Iowa, and Nebraska, selling medical and industrial X-ray equipment.

Despite success in sales, his heart was still in engineering. When the war broke out, Norris jumped at a chance to break into a hardcore technical position. He took a job as a civil servant with the Bureau of Ordnance, where he hunched over a drafting board in a bullpen with about a hundred other engineers who worked on fire control for antiaircraft guns. Eventually he signed on with the Naval Reserve, ending up at the red brick school in Washington, D.C.

At the Nebraska Avenue analytical center Norris was in his element. Though he wasn't in an intellectual league with the scientific theoreticians, he was technically proficient, and his managerial style was well suited for the navy: smart, gruff, and practical. While working at the red brick school, he was promoted to lieutenant commander.

At CSAW (pronounced "Seesaw" by the codebreakers) Norris made more technical contributions than at any other stage of his career. At one point he discovered a method for identifying the source of German radio messages: Transmissions from each individual U-boat, he said, had their own set of peculiar characteristics. If he was right—and if they could identify the U-boat that was sending the message—they would crack the codes far faster. Scientists, however, questioned Norris's unproven theories and balked at the risks involved in using them. The characteristics, they said, were peculiarities of the ionosphere—the weather—not the U-boat. When they questioned his idea, Norris simply bypassed them and put the technique into effect. If he was wrong, he said, they could call him on the carpet. He wasn't wrong.

Three years later when Norris again pursued a risky course, he would change the face of technology. But at that time, the idea he pursued seemed downright absurd.

No one was sure who first raised the concept of commercial applications for the codebreaking machines. But Norris occasionally found himself sitting around one of the research labs at the Nebraska Avenue building, idly brainstorming with some of the other technical people. During those sessions, they often wondered aloud about other uses for their machines. In the beginning it had seemed like a joke. He and Commander Howard Engstrom, a former Yale University mathematics professor who headed the research operation, lobbed ideas at each other and at some of the other men in the lab. What about flight reservations? Air traffic control? Guided missiles? Flight simulators? The old

Link Trainer, a flight simulator for military pilots, was stiff, slow, and unrealistic. Digital electronics, they reasoned, could make the Link Trainer smoother, faster, and more flexible.

But all of them knew that the new technology needed more development. Sure, they could replace the electromechanical relays in the Link Trainers with digital circuitry, but the cost of the system would skyrocket. Same for air traffic control and flight reservations. Even though digital technology offered the potential for scorching speed, it wasn't yet economically viable.

Still, their pipedream grew. It started to appear so real that they stopped thinking of it as a joke. One evening during their ramblings Engstrom mused about the looming end to the war, "I, for one, don't want to go back to Yale, so I'd like to think in terms of something else."

Norris, Engstrom, and the others briefly considered continuing their work in a government lab after the war, but they were unanimous in their disapproval of that prospect. Next they discussed setting up a private company and working for the navy on a contract basis. A good idea, they all agreed, but it still wasn't enough. Cost-plus-fixed-fee government work was hardly a road to riches; in fact, it was barely a living. Someone proposed that they find companies to sponsor or invest in their start-up. Though their technology wasn't yet ready for industry, it could be with enough capital for development. Their game plan evolved, eventually calling for Norris, Engstrom, and the others to own half of the proposed company, while outside investors owned the other half.

In an extraordinary display of entrepreneurial wisdom, high-ranking navy officials drummed up support for the idea. The navy's rationale was simple self-preservation. The war's end was looming and the Cold War was on the horizon. Cryptanalytic work would be as crucial as ever, even after the war, yet navy officials would be unable to order their codebreakers to remain at the Nebraska Avenue facility. Most of the codebreakers had already dismissed the idea of continuing their effort in civil service positions, so the navy had little choice: Either keep the existing group together or start again from scratch.

Convincing the captains of industry to buy into their proposal, however, was another matter. In their own minds they could see how the technology might give a boost to, say, an airline company. A reservationist might talk to a business executive who wanted to fly from Chicago to Omaha. By punching a few keys, the reservationist could send the electrons zipping through bundles of spaghetti wiring, jumping across vacuum tubes, speeding through the logic circuits and electronic memory, where the information on the Chicago-Omaha flight would be stored as little magnetic bits of information. American Airlines at the time used "card boys," who dashed around the reservations office with little three-by-fives on which were scribbled the number of available seats for a flight. Given the state of the art, the need for electronic machines seemed obvious.

Still, it was a hard sell. Norris and Engstrom polished their shoes and donned their aristocratic-looking white naval officer uniforms with their shiny gold buttons. Through their navy contacts, they managed to get audiences with presidents of companies such as American Airlines and Western Union. But their pitch—replete with references to electrons, logic circuits, and bits of magnetic information—sounded like voodoo to the baffled company executives. The executives sat politely and listened and their ears perked up every now and then at the thought of the potential corporate efficiency, but their answers were always the same.

In the end it was simply too unrealistic. When it came to discussing reliability or past experience, Norris and Engstrom were handcuffed. They couldn't talk about past experience: All that information was classified and it was a felony to discuss it. They couldn't say how they'd used the machines, or for how long, or what their reliability record was. One of the few things they *could* say was that the machines existed.

Worse, Norris or Engstrom could offer no business savvy. They were a mathematician and an engineer proposing an entry into a foreign domain, and the time simply wasn't right for taking on such a program. As the war drew to a close, most companies were reorganizing and rethinking their business plans. One after another the executives listened, then politely declined. It was a fine idea, an idea with great potential, they said. But the war had just ended, their company was reorganizing, funding was difficult to come by, the risk was too great.

The navy, however, wouldn't let Norris and Engstrom quit. Determined to keep their cryptological programs afloat, naval officials arranged for the two to visit with James V. Forrestal, secretary of the navy and former Wall Street financier. Forrestal helped set up interviews with still more firms, including New York investment banker Kuhn Loeb & Co. But even there they met with resistance. Executives at Kuhn Loeb flatly concluded that there was no commercial future for their . . . electronic calculators.

Norris had never heard of Northwestern Aeronautical Corporation. Northwestern, formed in conjunction with Twin Cities–based Northwest Airlines, made wooden gliders for the war effort. Allied forces used the unpowered gliders at the Normandy D-day invasion and at other battles to silently carry troops into enemy territory. The company assembled fifteen gliders a day in a huge plant on Minnehaha Avenue in St. Paul, Minnesota.

Nor had Norris heard of John E. Parker, owner of Northwestern Aeronautical. Parker was a Naval Academy graduate, a social hobnobber, and an entrepreneur. A jovial, round-faced man with an amazing recall for names and faces, he was universally liked. Parker and his wife lived in Washington, D.C., about three months a year and spent the other nine months at the Commodore Hotel in St. Paul, a ritzy little hotel with a rich, dark wood decor and big, luxurious rooms. Despite his apparent wealth, John Parker was facing a potential financial crisis. As sole owner of Northwestern Aeronautical and part-owner of the Toro Company, much of his capital was tied up. Northwestern Aeronautical had a dim future, because with the war's end there would be no imaginable need for wooden gliders.

For Parker, the disintegration of Northwestern Aeronautical would be a giant loss. He liked to claim that Northwestern was the second- or third-largest contractor to the war effort, and now his company was about to collapse with a suddenness that few businessmen ever experience. Parker was desperately searching for a solution to his problem when a high-ranking navy official called him. Through channels, the official said, he had heard that the navy was looking for an investor. He knew little about the opportunity because the information was classified. *Highly* classified. He told Parker to go back to Washington and to talk to naval officials there.

Parker did, and was stunned to find that the first naval official they wanted him to meet was Admiral Chester W. Nimitz, former commander of the Pacific Fleet. It was clear that the navy was pulling out all the stops in its effort to find an investor. Parker was escorted into Nimitz's office, where the admiral shook his hand and jabbed a finger in his chest. "I've looked into your background and there's a job that I'd like you to do," Nimitz told him, "and it may be more important in peacetime than it is in wartime." Nimitz then made a fleeting reference to a particular naval group, saying that it was important to keep the group together. And that was it.

Being an Academy graduate, Parker had the proper respect for naval authority. "Aye, aye, sir," he said, though he had no idea what he was agreeing to. Later Parker was ushered into the assistant secretary of the navy's office and then into the office of the judge advocate, who gave him legal advice on the matter. By the time Parker finally met with Norris and Engstrom, he was only aware that the navy thought that this proposed venture was vitally important. Or at least he was aware that the navy was trotting out its biggest names in an effort to woo him.

Norris and Engstrom made the same pitch to Parker that they'd already made to a dozen other potential investors. They told him that they'd been involved in highly classified work and would like to continue it on a private basis, but that they needed an investor to pick up half the tab for their new venture. They promised at least three years of service and laid out a few of the potential business applications for the technology.

After they finished, Parker still knew almost nothing about the proposed venture. Nimitz hadn't given him a shred of information about it, and had said only that it was of great importance to the country. Norris and Engstrom had provided a little bit more, but even their information was sketchy. They apologetically explained that it would be a felony to reveal any more, and Parker accepted their explanation. By the end of the fourth meeting they still hadn't told Parker who his new customers would be.

Parker had grown wealthy as an entrepreneur and was far shrewder than any of the navy men suspected. No, he didn't understand digital electronics or vacuum tubes, and he couldn't assess the technical capabilities of Norris and Engstrom. But he *could* read between the lines. He implicitly understood that the company's main customer would be the navy—that was plain enough—and he knew that the navy had already assessed the capabilities of Norris and Engstrom. If Norris and Engstrom had come up short in its estimation, he wouldn't be here. It was a roundabout way of evaluating the situation, but it was all he had. Parker liked to tell his friends that it was a little bit like taking on a symphony orchestra without knowing a note of music, but that didn't worry him.

Besides, there was this issue of Northwestern Aeronautical. Parker had already declared the glider factory as war surplus and had liquidated his inventory. The company was clearly on the verge of collapse—that is, unless he could pull off a last-minute miracle. And this new venture certainly fell into the category of a last-minute micracle. If he could pull it off, he knew that the new company could potentially offer jobs for his current employees. Whatever machines the navy men planned to make, machinists and assemblers would be needed to build them.

Parker considered everything: the fate of Northwestern, the loss of jobs for all the machinists at his plant, the risk of investing in a project he didn't understand. But one image kept coming back to him—Nimitz jabbing a finger in his chest and saying, "There's a job I'd like you to do." In 1945 most of the country still felt a sense of common purpose and patriotism, and an order from someone the stature of Admiral Nimitz was almost impossible to resist, especially for a Naval Academy man. So Parker sold his $300,000 stake in the Toro Company to fund the new venture.

Then he called together Norris, Engstrom, and Captain Ralph Meader from the Naval Computing Machine Laboratory in Dayton, Ohio. They and their wives met for dinner—in grand Parker style—at the Metropolitan Club in Washington, D.C. The navy men agreed to sign a contract binding themselves to three years of service to the new company; Parker agreed to head a group that would purchase a hundred thousand shares of the company stock at ten cents each. Pooling their resources, the navy men bought the other hundred thousand shares, and the deal was complete. Parker then returned to the St. Paul glider factory and announced to a band of cheering machinists that their jobs had been saved.

In January 1946 the group incorporated the new company, calling it Engineering Research Associates (ERA). The navy men immediately hired forty members of the "Seesaw" staff, and Parker arranged for the new company to share his cavernous glider factory with Northwestern Aeronautical. Sharing quarters with Northwestern was critical because ERA wasn't yet qualified to carry out a major government contract. Although most members of its staff had worked for the navy during the war, ERA didn't have a corporate track record. Northwestern Aeronautical, however, *did* have a track record. So by setting up shop in the glider factory, ERA could work on major contracts that had been officially awarded to Northwestern Aeronautical.

As far as the navy brass was concerned, Parker had saved their codebreaking operation. The machinists in St. Paul also considered Parker a savior—his last-minute heroics were responsible for saving their jobs. Norris and Engstrom were the only ones with an inkling of the business potential that could emerge from the new enterprise, but even they had more personal concerns. Parker's cash influx was helping free Engstrom from a life as a Yale math professor, and Norris no longer faced a return to his job as an X-ray machine salesman with Westinghouse.

Everyone was pleased. They had taken an obscure military technology and transformed it into a private enterprise. They wanted to congratulate themselves for their foresight and steadfast determination, but Norris and Engstrom knew that their victory was not born of their own resolve. The real reason for the formation of Engineering Research Associates was that the U.S. Navy wanted it that way, and had pushed the company into existence through the bony finger of Admiral Chester W. Nimitz.

. . . .

The Incubator

To outsiders Engineering Research Associates looked like a branch of the military. Its main compound on Minnehaha Avenue was surrounded by a six-foot chain-link fence topped by barbed wire. A uniformed guard watched the main gate around the clock. The compound's architecture invoked military images: Its vast glider factory had the outward appearance and charm of an armory, and the smaller structures (used mainly for offices) were of the temporary construction variety favored by military bases.

Inside, ERA was decidedly noncorporate. It had the look, feel, and musty smell of an antiquated manufacturing plant: Its furniture was unmatched and shabby; the walls, mostly unpainted; the floors, uncovered. A corner of one of the buildings housed a Naval Computing Machines Lab, and its director, Captain Creasor, maintained strict surveillance over the work of the company's engineers. Creasor carefully watched their expenditures and often peeked over their shoulders as they worked. He said little about their technical designs, but engineers felt his presence, and heard his frequent "hrrumphs" as he passed.

None of this, however, bothered Norris or any of the engineers in the least. Norris felt that it was a magnificent stroke of luck to have a customer—the Naval Computing Machines Lab—on the premises. He was elated to have a regular patron that paid its bills and paid them on time. For all he cared, his company could have been called "Seesaw" West.

ERA's new engineers were equally unfazed by the military atmosphere. The vast majority had just been discharged from the navy, so they were accustomed to taking orders and suppressing their curiosities. If the navy wanted to build machines for cryptologic work and keep the engineers in the dark about their specific operations, it was fine with the engineers. ERA was a huge improvement over the military, if for no other reason than an engineer could go home at night and could resign if conditions grew intolerable.

Besides, most of the engineers who passed through the front doors of the glider factory had few preconceived notions about their profession. For most, engineering was a way to improve their lot, to do better than their fathers had done. Most came from middle-class families, families who rented small houses or two-flats during the Great Depression and World War II. Their parents were rarely doctors or lawyers; rather they were farmers, machinists, industrial laborers, or any of a variety of mechanically handy individuals who knew the call of the factory whistle.

For them the glider factory was an introduction to civilian engineering. After the war ended, they wandered into ERA's office looking for work, hoping to find the kind of job that would allow them to use their technical backgrounds and to make enough money to buy one of the neat little postwar homes that were sprouting up around the Twin Cities. Within a year after its founding, ERA had grown to about sixty employees, mostly engineers.

They were, in general, happy to have *any* jobs. After surviving the Depression and the war, they thought a civilian job seemed like a luxury. During those lean years they'd lived with few amenities, so they thought little of the conditions at the glider factory.

The glider factory was a strange mix of overwhelming size and austerity, of informality and military rigidity. Its main building was about two blocks long with ceilings that rose up almost thirty feet. Along the aisles Sheetrock partitions reached a third of the way to the ceiling, acting as pseudowalls to break up the drab pea green decor and to give the engineers the sense that they had offices.

The partitions didn't make much of a difference, though. The place was dirty, and the doors were open, so the wind always seemed to be whisking the dirt one way or the other. It created a phenomenon that the engineers called the "self-emptying ash tray." The open doors also invited birds—sparrows or some other little species—to fly inside. The sparrows perched atop the partitions or up in the rafters and left little deposits around the office. Tiny dishes of rat poison were placed in strategic locations on the concrete floors, though no one ever claimed to have seen a rat. In the northeast corner of the main building was a machine shop with a cadre of Bridgeport mills, grinders, and lathes. Near the center of the building was a wooden mezzanine that housed a disorganized library. Books were difficult to find without the help of the librarian, Debbie, who coded them not by subject or author but by color.

Many of the engineers had accepted their positions without fully comprehending the nature of the work. ERA recruiters, who traveled the Midwest in search of bright young talent, were not allowed to share the details of the job until the recruit had the proper security clearance. And that never happened until weeks—sometimes months—after the recruit was hired.

When a short, wiry, aeronautical engineering graduate named Willis Drake interviewed for a position with ERA in 1947, he was simultaneously attracted and baffled. The interview, in one of the engineering buildings on the Purdue University campus, was upbeat, even alluring. The interviewer, an ERA engineer named Bill Windget, described a company staffed by former navy men. It operated like a consulting firm, he said, taking on projects for companies that lacked the engineering power to do the work themselves. He described ERA as a growing company, a multi-discipline firm that had its own aeronautical group and worked hand in hand with Northwestern Aeronautical. Windget expressed a need for a technical manual writer—a position unlikely to stir visions of glory in a young man's mind.

But Drake was intrigued: He liked the idea of working for a fast-growing company. He felt comfortable surrounded by former navy men, since he had also served in the navy. And he delighted in the prospect of returning to St. Paul, Minnesota—the town where he'd grown up. By the end of the interview he'd been offered the position and had accepted. Soon afterward he called McDonnell Aircraft Company in St. Louis to turn down an offer that they'd made to him.

Drake began his engineering career atop a balcony in the glider factory, seated on an old metal chair with three wobbly casters. He and two other young engineers were assigned the task of writing incredibly detailed technical manuals that described *exactly* how ERA's computing machinery worked. Drake had no idea what the computing machinery was used for, and ERA wasn't telling him. So he sat in the balcony every day, scribbling page after page for the manuals, which often exceeded ten thousand pages in length. Drake was baffled: He'd been told about their aeronautical group, but he wasn't working on any airplanes, or aircraft subsystems. At first he was deeply disappointed. He'd spent time at a naval air station in Jacksonville, Florida, and had studied hard for his aeronautical engineering degree.

But as time passed, and as Drake earned his security clearance and spoke with the company's other engineers, he began to notice something unusual. Amid the aisles and labs of the glider factory, there was an almost inexplicable sense of energy. The cynicism that often pervaded corporate life was absent. Engineers worked nights and weekends, came in early on weekdays, and expressed no resentment. Among some of the key people there was a creative fire, a sense of urgency. The navy gave them specifications to build the machines, but it let them carry out the design according to their own insights. The projects were not so much owned by the navy as by the engineers themselves. The machines were their designs, their ideas, their responsibilities, and they breathed life into them right there on the factory floor.

Whether the engineers understood it or not, such freedom to create was rare in their profession. In general, American firms shaped new products through collaborative efforts involving people from marketing, manufacturing, financial, and research departments. In corporate America, products weren't so much defined by individuals as they were by executive committees. That was the way it was in the biggest and most powerful companies, such as Ford, General Motors, and Boeing.

But the glider factory was different. ERA engineers didn't need marketing studies to identify their customers; they didn't need manufacturing experts to show them how to build their products; they didn't even need financial people to tell them if their ideas were economically feasible. Their customers were government agencies—one of whom was on the premises. Their products were handcrafted, one at a time, so volume production never crossed anyone's mind. And their financial arrangement was cost-plus-fixed-fee.

It was, in short, an engineer's paradise. As a profession, engineers always wanted the kind of freedom that ERA was now offering. In most universities, engineering students worked at a frantic pace—professors typically expected a minimum of fifty hours a week of study *outside* the classroom. Students went on this way for four years, immersed in a world of textbooks, equations, and unsympathetic professors. That was why, by most accounts, engineering was among the toughest curriculums offered in the American educational establishment. So by the time these young engineers had toiled for four years in the university, filling their minds with electrical circuit theory, thermodynamics, fluid mechanics, and the like, they thought as engineers, not as businessmen. They'd finished their hazing and were dedicated to their new discipline—maybe even more so than they were dedicated to their employers.

At the glider factory the engineers never had to worry about choosing between their profession and their employer. Out of necessity the engineers there operated more like researchers. They were building revolutionary, not evolutionary, machines. They had little or no written documentation to follow. They were blazing a trail—molding science into a product. That was the one element of their existence that distinguished them from researchers. The navy, in its wisdom, saw to it that ERA's machines worked—and worked reliably.

The freedom to create was extraordinary, and the engineers loved it. Some actually said that they couldn't wait to get up in the morning—that's how excited they were. They were unrestrained by the realities of normal corporate life. It was engineering in its purest form. That's the way they thought it *should* be, and the way they thought it would always stay.

Willis Drake never imagined that corporate life would operate in this way. At the time, postwar American manufacturers characterized themselves in stiff black-and-white photos depicting their engineers hard at work. The engineers always looked neat and clean: white shirts, dark ties, high-waisted baggy slacks, horn-rimmed eyeglasses, short military-style haircuts. All of it was part of being a happy, humming, prosperous, postwar American manufacturing firm.

But at ERA Drake saw none of that. It was as if the company's chain-link fence separated them from the conformist style of corporate America. One of ERA's chief assets was a wonderful sense of informality, Drake thought. It had no dress code, written or otherwise. Drake rarely saw suits, sport jackets, or ties. Some of the engineers wore the kind of gray pants favored by laborers. They donned open-necked sport shirts, sweaters, sweatshirts, and jackets—which were necessary because of the glider factory's open doors. On a hot, sticky summer day it wasn't even unusual to see some of the men toss their shirts aside. The atmosphere of informality stretched all the way to the front offices and into the personnel department, which consisted of a man, a secretary, and a dog.

In the strange excitement of the new atmosphere, Drake's initial disappointment over the lack of aeronautical work was waning. For Drake, that in itself was a surprise. He'd gone off to college via a special navy program midway through the war, hoping to earn an aeronautical engineering degree. After the war, he'd served at a naval air station in Jacksonville, Florida. Throughout his service and his studies, he had always planned to stay close to airplanes. That had been his biggest reason for taking the ERA job—the company was supposed to be working closely with Northwestern Aeronautical. But Drake now suspected that something more exciting than airplanes was being built here. It came to him more as a feeling than as an intellectual thought, but he sensed a buzz of excitement in the air.

In fact ERA's recruiting pitch to Drake had been absolutely accurate, even if it had left a few details out. The company *was* doing engineering work for other firms. Its consulting projects included the design of analog recorders, microfilm selectors, ultrasonic machine tools, and instrumentation for "Project Boom," an underground explosion testing program. ERA also did, in a minor sense, delve into the aircraft business: It designed "honey wagons" to clean out airplane septic systems. But the truth about ERA's most important business—design of calculating machines for cryptologic work—still hadn't dawned on Drake. Oh, he knew that ERA was working for the military. That was clear enough; he'd seen the Naval Computing Machine Laboratory. But having been a navy man, he knew enough not to ask questions.

As he plodded through the task of writing the massive manuals—each manual took up as much as four feet of library shelf space—he began to comprehend the inner workings of ERA's calculating machinery. With each new task, Drake absorbed the technology. He found that it was the one awe-inspiring aspect of his job. Even at Purdue he had never seen anything like this. The machines had a strange hodgepodge of names: Goldberg, Demon, and eventually Atlas. But the truly impressive aspect of them was their size—one of these monsters could fill the entire first floor of a small house. Then there was their mind-boggling speed: They could perform a series of basic arithmetic operations in far less time than it took to blink an eye. The performance was almost incomprehensible to Drake.

Equally mind-boggling was the technique they used. A few years earlier, adding machines had been simple, so simple that a person could actually *watch* them work: Electrical current passed through a circuit and entered a relay. The relay closed and the electrical current passed through it and energized a motor. The motor turned a wheel or a dial and . . . click, click, click, the machine added its numbers.

But these new machines were different. Their parts didn't spin or click. The familiar visual and tactile elements of machinery were gone, replaced by vacuum tubes that metered the flow of electrons. By configuring the vacuum tubes in certain ways, engineers could create a logic circuit capable of performing any basic arithmetic function. The advantage of building machines in this way was speed: A typical logic circuit could handle many thousands of inputs in one second.

Some of the engineers who built the electronic calculators had come to St. Paul from the red brick building on Nebraska Avenue in Washington, but more and more were trickling in from the Twin Cities. Drake was amazed at the similarity in their backgrounds. An inordinate number were former navy men. Many were electrical engineers, and a high percentage were graduates of the University of Minnesota, which was less than ten miles away. The most striking similarity was that they were almost all radio freaks. Ask any of them to describe their childhood bedrooms, and they'd say that they were jammed with circuit boards and vacuum tubes. Low-voltage vacuum tubes were the backbone of radio receivers and the backbone of their social lives. When they'd gone on to high school, most had joined the Radio Club. When they'd gone on to college, many had worked at radio stations or had received amateur radio licenses.

Vacuum tubes were once again at the core of their existence. For many the job at ERA was a natural extension of their hobbies. They were like overgrown high school boys, playing with electronics in their bedrooms. Only now, they had a two-block-long bedroom and an unlimited supply of vacuum tubes.

None of the engineers at ERA used the phrase "start-up company." Most of them, Norris included, wouldn't have attached any special meaning to the term and wouldn't have known what an entrepreneur was. But Norris, more than anyone else in the company, was an entrepreneur. Since his days at "Seesaw," Norris had stubbornly clung to his conviction that computing machinery had vast commercial value.

Norris had never stopped believing. He still thought that airlines could apply computers to their reservations systems, that airports could use them for air traffic control, that flight simulators could be vastly improved by incorporating them, and that thousands of businesses could apply computers to such mundane chores as payroll computations. He also knew that his company's original arrangement with the U.S. government put it in a perfect position to move into the commercial market. The patents on their jointly developed computer technology were held by ERA, not by the U.S. government. The government's only proviso was that it be allowed to license the technology on a royalty-free basis. The contracts had been set up that way for the good of both parties: Under the arrangement ERA was free to make additional revenue off the technology, and the taxpayers' financial burden for development of the computers would be lessened by spreading the cost out to interested members of the business community.

So now, in 1949, Norris again wanted to begin reaching for commercial markets. True, he'd failed in 1946 when he and Engstrom traveled around the country in their officers' uniforms, trying to preach the gospel of computer technology. But now he had more to work with.

For starters Norris had a device called the magnetic drum, an extraordinary invention. In ERA's newer computers it served as the external memory and was an enabler of a concept called the "stored program." For the computer industry, realization of the stored program was a critical step toward building a general purpose computer. A few years earlier, calculating machines had been dedicated to single tasks, which were hard-wired into their circuits. In contrast, the stored program enabled a computer to perform a variety of tasks. All the user needed to do was change the program.

During a five-year period, the magnetic drum underwent many changes, but in its later iterations it looked like a washing machine tub with spark plugs sticking out of it. The "tub" served as an outer enclosure; a memory drum resided inside. Magnetic read/write heads—the spark plugs—were threaded through the tub. About forty-five heads were positioned so that they came within two thousandths of an inch of the drum's moving surface. While the drum slowly turned, the read/write heads would change the machine's electrical signals to magnetic pulses, then store those on strips of magnetic tape glued to the drum. Working this way, the drum could hold up to one million bits of data.

When ERA engineers first built the magnetic drum in 1947, the process of writing information was excruciatingly slow: One full turn of the drum took nine minutes, and bits of data were stored at a rate of ten per second. But the inventors of the system—

engineers Arnold Cohen, Bill Keye, and Bob Perkins—had created a concept that would last for decades. The drum was the earliest ancestor of the personal computer hard drive.

By industry standards fifty years later, magnetic drum technology would seem crude. Read/write heads on modern machines
would be roughly a hundred times closer to the source, and personal computer disk drives would retain a thousand times more
information in a fraction of the space. But drum technology was
momentous for its day and Norris recognized its value. Machines
with magnetic drums could *randomly access* data, meaning that
they no longer had to hunt through reels of tape to find chunks
of information. Magnetic drum memory also was *nonvolatile,* so it
didn't lose everything when the machine was turned off. And
with the drum, stored programs were *alterable,* meaning that users
could change programs with the results of their own computations. The alterable, nonvolatile, random access, stored program
machine was taking the industry beyond the realm of electronic
calculating, and into the world of general purpose computing.

ERA started its marketing efforts by placing tiny ads in technical magazines. The company then set up the drum along with an
electric typewriter in booths at trade shows. ERA salesmen
demonstrated the drum's abilities by tapping the typewriter's
keys, storing its output onto the drum, then playing it back moments later. Showgoers were astounded. They'd slowly mill
around the booth, then stop and stare at the strange contraption
that swallowed data from the typewriter, then spit it back out intact. Though they didn't know it, booth visitors were viewing the
future: Together, the drum and the typewriter formed a crude
word processor.

ERA's drum demonstration was a stroke of marketing genius.
It was easy to comprehend and made people think about the storage of digital data. Salesmen explained that the drum was an alternative to the task of storing programs on tens of thousands of
punched cards or on reams of punched paper tape. On the
strength of the demonstration, their words hit home. Showgoers
left business cards and telephone numbers.

Norris identified two target groups to which he wanted to license the technology: the first, communications companies, included AT&T, Automatic Electric, and ITT; the second involved

ERA's competitors—National Cash Register, Burroughs, IBM, and Remington Rand.

Engineers at Remington Rand quickly recognized the value of magnetic storage and told ERA salesman William Butler that they were interested in learning more. Butler and Norris traveled together to Norwalk, Connecticut, where they met with a crew from Remington Rand, but from the moment they arrived, Norris and Butler were on unsteady ground. Electronic calculating technology was so new that it was hard to put a value on it. For all ERA knew, its drum might be worth $500 or it might be worth $1 million. For Remington Rand the new technology might be the missing link in the construction of a general purpose computer.

From the outset Remington Rand's engineers seemed to sense Norris and Butler's trepidation and they quickly started hammering away: "How much for the magnetic read/write heads?" Norris, unsure how to answer, simply avoided the question; instead, he launched into a description of the advantages of magnetic drum technology. He explained how the system worked, then told them how it could eliminate the use of punched cards and punched paper tape. The engineers listened politely for nearly an hour before one interrupted. "All we want to do is buy these heads," he said, pointing to the drum's read/write heads. "Now, how much are your heads?"

The heads. That was a development for which Norris hadn't prepared. No one in ERA had considered selling the read/write heads separately. For that matter, they weren't sure how to price the magnetic drum technology. When they'd been approached earlier by Automatic Electric, someone had arbitrarily suggested a sale price of $5,000. But the read/write heads? They'd never even considered it. Norris managed to avoid the question through the rest of the morning and through lunch. After lunch, however, Remington Rand's patent attorney pinned him down. "Well, Mr. Norris," he said. "if we did buy a system, how much would it cost?"

Norris was still at a loss. As far as he was concerned, putting a value on the technology was nearly impossible. In frustration, he turned to Butler, who knew no more about pricing than Norris. "We sold a very nice system to Automatic Electric Company for $5,000," Butler said. Norris turned back to the Remington Rand group: "Well, we could give you a good demonstration unit for about $5,000."

Norris and Butler managed to sell the entire system—heads and all—for $5,000. It was a beginning. With this sale, and with the earlier sale to Automatic Electric, they started to count themselves as believers. It was one thing to say that industry *should* invest in computer technology; it was another to see them do so.

Some of the engineers at ERA began to approach Norris with the idea of building a specialized business computer. Sometime during 1950, as the company's engineers worked on the design of a machine called Atlas, it began to dawn on them that these machines, which were being used by "Seesaw" through the navy's Bureau of Ships, had commercial possibilities. A couple of years earlier, IBM had introduced the Selective Sequence Electronic Calculator, a mammoth business machine measuring 120 *feet* long and using a combination of vacuum tubes and electromechanical relays. Because it was a hybrid—mechanical and electronic—the machine's future was dim, but its existence sent a signal to the industry that IBM, the reigning king of calculating machinery, recognized the commercial value of electronic computing. Up to that time, IBM had been profoundly resistant to the concept of electronic computing. Its engineers had preferred the electrical relay over the vacuum tube, but now they acknowledged the value of the vacuum tube—if only in a roundabout way.

The engineers at the glider factory saw those signals. They looked at their own machines and their magnetic drum technology, and it dawned on them that they were building something very close to a general purpose computer. With Norris's blessing, they set to work on the development of a machine called the 1101, their first computer designed specifically for commercial applications. Their idea was to make some minor adjustments to Atlas to make it more viable for the business computing market. Atlas was a monstrous machine that took up about four hundred square feet of floor space and used twenty-seven hundred vacuum tubes, but it was far smaller than IBM's Selective Sequence Electronic Calculator. And it could use the stored program concept.

ERA engineers knew that they had competition. Burroughs, National Cash Register, Raytheon, RCA, and Westinghouse also were building electronic calculating machines, and a tiny company called Eckert-Mauchly in Philadelphia was widely credited with launching the electronic age in 1946 with a machine called ENIAC. But like its competitors, Eckert-Mauchly had had no luck venturing into the commercial market.

But ERA engineers thought the time was right. After its initial successes in building classified machines, such as Goldberg, Demon, and Atlas, ERA had ballooned to more than four hundred employees. It now had the staff to pursue commercial applications without losing its cryptologic customers at "Seesaw." What's more, its success with the magnetic drum was proving that there *were* customers out there. More than ever, ERA engineers had reason to believe.

Few, if any, engineers at ERA knew that John Parker was planning to sell the company, so on a chilly afternoon in December 1951 when Parker let word slip that the company had been sold to Remington Rand, the reaction was shock. In the offices and aisles of the glider factory a sudden seething form of disappointment was brewing. Engineers hustled from office to office, discussing the sale in hushed tones. Over and over again, they repeated, "They can't do this." "What are we going to do now?" For more than a year ERA engineers had looked forward to taking their products to the commercial market. Now their plans would be shifted to a holding pattern, while their rich new parent decided what ERA had to offer.

In theory, the purpose of the sale was to eliminate the company's debt and give it access to the funding it needed. Parker, president and majority owner of ERA, had made the deal. For several months he had shopped ERA around to potential purchasers, including Honeywell, Raytheon, National Cash Register, and IBM. He'd had good reason: Though the company was profitable, its debt hovered around $300,000. Every week it struggled to pay salaries and to lop a few dollars off the debt. Other companies were jumping into the computer business, and Parker knew that ERA needed capital to invest in research and development to stay ahead of them.

When Remington Rand approached Parker late in 1951, he sold his majority stake in ERA. He explained to an angry Norris that the deal was in ERA's best interest. It would now have money for research, and all of the founding partners would make *eighty-five times* their initial investment. Parker said that Norris could expect to move quickly up the corporate ladder—acquisitions, he explained, often had that effect.

Norris and the rest of the crew at the St. Paul glider factory were incensed over the sale. Although it was true that Remington Rand made tabulating machinery, its effort was a distant second to IBM. Remington Rand was biggest in typewriters and shavers—areas that obviously held no interest for the engineers at the glider factory. Worse, Remington Rand seemed to view ERA in terms of one particular product: a device called an antenna coupler. A by-product of one of ERA's many consulting contracts, the antenna coupler was an important device for the aircraft industry, which needed a new antenna tuning device in the wake of its new interest in jets. But to view the entire company in terms of that one product was incomprehensible to ERA's engineers.

Remington Rand attempted to learn more about its new acquisition by sending executives to St. Paul to talk to ERA's engineers, but the get-to-know-you sessions quickly broke down into an executive grilling, which made the engineers even more resentful. At one point Arnold Cohen, a gentle professorial engineer who'd earned a Ph.D. in physics, turned the tables on the Remington Rand executives by saying, "Well, now, we've answered your questions about ERA, suppose you tell us a little about Remington Rand. We know you make shavers and typewriters, but what else do you do?" It was an extraordinary moment—the precocious child standing up to the domineering parent. The crowd of engineers in the room, stunned by Cohen's uncharacteristically bold rebuttal, broke into spontaneous applause—and the chasm between the two companies grew even deeper.

The saving grace of the acquisition was Remington Rand's earlier purchase of Eckert-Mauchly Corporation. A young firm much like ERA, Eckert-Mauchly was best known for the introduction of ENIAC in 1946, a feat that etched it into the minds of many Americans as the inventor of the electronic digital computer. Juxtaposing their acquisition against that of Eckert-Mauchly, ERA engineers thought they saw a pattern: Maybe this was all part of an effort to add digital capabilities to Remington Rand's tabulating machinery.

What ERA engineers didn't realize was that many people believed that Eckert-Mauchly had the real digital expertise. Eckert-Mauchly's leader, J. Presper Eckert, was a genius-level engineer from the University of Pennsylvania's Moore School of Engineering who had constructed his first radio at age five and was regarded as the single most brilliant computer designer in the world. Though still a young man at thirty-three, the balding Ivy Leaguer had already made his mark in the world of technology by heading development of ENIAC, a stunning accomplishment. ENIAC covered 1,500 square feet, weighed 30 tons, and used thirty thousand vacuum tubes. Designed for the U.S. Army Ordnance Corps, it replaced two hundred women who punched numbers into mechanical calculators eight hours a day.

A few months after the ERA acquisition, Eckert and his partner, John Mauchly, added to their already prodigious fame when their UNIVAC I (Universal Automatic Computer) predicted the outcome of the 1952 presidential election on CBS News. The machine's prediction that Dwight Eisenhower would defeat Adlai Stevenson in the electoral college by 438 votes to 93 was so incredible that CBS executives balked at using it. When the actual count came in at 442 to 89, few television viewers knew how close the machine had come, but that didn't matter. In the eyes and minds of the television-viewing public, UNIVAC I had been a stunning visual success. Prior to the election coverage, a group of CBS technicians wired the machine with flashers and incandescent bulbs, which could then be made to flash on and off like Christmas tree lights. Viewers remembered the visual display and forever related it to the UNIVAC I.

So by the time ERA was officially welcomed into the Remington Rand fold, a pecking order had already been established. Remington Rand's executives already knew about the technical prowess of J. Presper Eckert and his staff. Eckert was the genius who built election forecasting machines for CBS News and his position in the technical community was unparalleled.

The purchase of ERA was a curiosity to the engineers at the old Eckert-Mauchly facility. They were unsure what ERA did. They'd heard something about ERA making cryptologic equipment for the navy, but they were unclear how the objectives at the St. Paul glider factory fit in with those of Philadelphia. Most of the engineers in Philadelphia were openly disdainful of the St. Paul crew. Eckert told Norris he thought ERA was in "the Dark Ages." In Philadelphia they referred to the St. Paul facility as "the factory." When that reference trickled back to the engineering crew in St. Paul, it rankled them. *The factory?* It was true that the ERA crew referred to their own facility as "the glider factory," but when Eckert-Mauchly engineers said it, it had a distinctly different feel—as if it pictured a band of steelworkers building automobile crankshafts. Whether it was reality or paranoia, or a combination of both, the ERA crew began believing that Eckert-Mauchly engineers looked down their Ivy League noses at them. Every slight was remembered and repeated. Someone had referred to them as "the farmers." *The farmers.* Of their state-funded, prairie school educations, someone else had coined the term "Moo U." With each slight the gap between the sister divisions grew deeper.

If the Philadelphia group was disdainful of ERA, however, the St. Paul band returned its condescension in trumps. True, they grudgingly admitted, the Eckert-Mauchly crew was more innovative. Some of the features on the UNIVAC I had required astounding leaps in engineering, but the crew's record of reliability proved that they were far better scientists than engineers. That was the one element of justice in it all. In a perverse way ERA was gratified that the Philadelphia theories weren't always successful. ENIAC had been plagued by downtime, and UNIVAC I was lucky if it could sustain a ten-minute run without going down due to a bad vacuum tube or some such thing. In contrast, ERA's Atlas had an extraordinary run of five hundred hours in which it required only sixteen hours of unscheduled maintenance. The technological gap that emerged between the two groups centered on the practical versus the theoretical. It was Ivy Leaguers versus the farmers, and the debate never ceased.

What galled the ERA engineers about the debate was that the theoreticians from Philadelphia never seemed to acknowledge the importance of the practical side. It was as if Philadelphia's job was to explore theory, leaving the issues of building workable designs to lower forms of life. Eckert bluntly told Norris that ERA's creative capabilities simply didn't exist.

The tension between the two groups reached a peak when Eckert visited ERA to discuss new ideas for a commercial machine called the 1103. The engineers in attendance were quizzical at first, wondering how Eckert could discuss a design that was so close to completion. When he proceeded to spend an entire morning and part of an afternoon lobbing brilliant ideas at them, the ERA engineers were appalled. They sat in stony silence on their metal folding chairs, wondering how he could possibly expect to incorporate new theories in a nearly completed machine. Eckert, who was known for his blustery ego, sensed their reticence and exploded. "What's the matter with you people?" he barked. "I've been standing up here all day throwing out new ideas, and no one's said a word." But the farmers sat quietly, eyeing him with their stony midwestern stares. Afterward, they privately confided to one another that Eckert's outburst served as a metaphor for all his company's problems: Brilliant as they were, the engineers in Philadelphia wanted to keep the design unbuttoned until the last tense moment, and in the process Eckert-Mauchly had eventually ruined their reliability.

When Norris took the helm as general manager of the Univac Division, he learned that the differences between the two operations went beyond petty name-calling; they reflected profound disparities in philosophy. "The difference," he told the Philadelphia group, "is that you people run a laboratory, and ERA runs a business." The principals in Philadelphia were interested in raw speed and didn't particularly care about reliability. Worse, they had put themselves in a financial tangle by bidding less than one-fifth what it cost to build the UNIVAC I. Later when building a computer called the LARC, they would spend $19 million on a project for which they had bid $2.85 million.

The navy had forced ERA to toe a financial line by setting up a cost-plus-fixed-fee arrangement and then planting itself on the premises in the Naval Computing Machine Laboratory. With Eckert-Mauchly now answering to Norris, the intimidating farm boy from Nebraska, the brilliant theoreticians from Philadelphia were forced to toe the financial line, too.

⊕

In mid-1953 Bill Norris asked Willis Drake to go to Louisville, Kentucky, for two weeks to oversee installation of the world's first on-site commercial computer, the UNIVAC I. For an engineer who'd begun his career in St. Paul, as Drake had, it was a strange request. The UNIVAC I was designed and developed in Philadelphia, and in a sense it was a winner in the race to be the first commercial machine—and a St. Paul employee was being asked to oversee its installation. But Drake understood that the walls between the two organizations must one day collapse, and he agreed to go.

When he arrived in Louisville, Drake was first dazzled by the accommodations that had been made for the new machine. General Electric, the first customer, intended to proudly display UNIVAC I in a special site at its Appliance Park facility. GE planned for tremendous news coverage—the machine was purchased as much for public relations as for real computing. As a result, it built a gleaming new showplace for UNIVAC I: floor-to-ceiling glass walls, multicolored drapes, huge potted plants, and spotlights, all designed to solidify GE's image as a technological leader.

But the real surprise that awaited Drake went far beyond the building's decor: much of the UNIVAC I was missing. The UNIVAC I, dark and quiet, sat in the middle of its vast new showplace, surrounded by cardboard boxes. And inside the boxes was . . . nothing. Remington Rand had delivered a box of electronics and little else. There were no input or output systems, so GE's programmers would have no way to put in data or take out data. The card-to-tape reader, the tape-to-card reader, the high-speed printer—all were missing.

Drake was perplexed. Here he was with only half of a UNIVAC I to install. A whole machine was a rat's nest of wires and contained thirteen thousand vacuum tubes. GE had spent millions of dollars on it and had already orchestrated substantial press coverage. And after the press coverage died down, GE would expect the machine to work. Its users were already putting together programs for business applications: payroll, inventory control, production scheduling.

Drake called Remington Rand's Philadelphia offices, but was told that none of the missing equipment was ready. For several weeks he worked with GE managers, explaining the problems involved in the installation, and in the beginning the managers waited patiently. He pushed the operation dates back, and GE reluctantly accepted the new dates. Still, the parts failed to arrive.

Drake meanwhile called John Parker, who now worked as a vice president in one of Remington Rand's New York facilities, urging and begging for the missing parts. The situation was becoming awkward, he told Parker. There'd been mountains of publicity. The press wanted to see UNIVAC I in operation; GE wanted to run its payroll and production programs. Parker seemed surprised. "Gee, the card-to-tape was due to ship last Wednesday," he explained, "but there was a last-minute change and they felt it would enhance your liability if they put that change in before they sent it. And as long as it's this late anyway ..."

Drake was appalled. Each week there was another problem with the delivery of the card-to-tape system, or the tape-to-card system, or the printer. And each week the engineers in Philadelphia seemed to be tweaking the design just a little bit more. The original two weeks had now stretched to three months.

Finally GE's Appliance Park manager, whose patience was at an end, called Drake on the carpet. "Either this equipment is going to be here on this date, or all this stuff is going to be out in the middle of the street, and I'm not kidding you," he said. Panicked, Drake purchased a plane ticket with his own money and boarded a flight to Philadelphia. He entered Eckert-Mauchly without an appointment and introduced himself, asking to see the card-to-tape converter and the high-speed printer. He showed them a letter from John Parker, promising a delivery date that had long since passed.

The engineers shot glances at one another, gazing at Drake as if he were speaking Italian and they'd forgotten their Italian-English dictionaries. One of them led Drake to a Ping-Pong table with electronic parts scattered across it. "That," he said, "is the card-to-tape converter." The printer was even farther behind schedule. "I don't know where in the hell you got any dates like that," he said. "This isn't going to be ready for a year." The Philadelphia engineers, Drake thought, acted as if the input-output devices were mere details, that they'd already completed the important part.

Drake hustled out of the Eckert-Mauchly facility and boarded a flight to New York, where he cornered Parker. He told Parker about the card-to-tape converter, the printer, and the Ping-Pong table. He explained the position he was in, the waning patience of GE management, and the lack of any concrete solution. Parker listened in disbelief. Then, to Drake's amazement, he responded, "You're wrong." Parker stood up, ambled across his office, and pulled a letter from a file, showing Drake that the systems were supposed to be ready. Drake was incredulous. As far as Parker was concerned, the memo said the parts would be ready, so they must be ready. It was as simple as that.

For Drake, it was the ultimate learning experience. The fiascoes continued, deadlines were missed again and again. Drake remained in Louisville two years before his two-week project ended. Ultimately, the machine worked, and GE obtained years of use from it.

The lessons were obvious: The years at the glider factory, under the guidance of the navy, had taught ERA engineers how walk a fine line between evolutionary and revolutionary product development. They knew how to use research without becoming researchers. They were engineers, and as engineers they'd learned to build machines that worked—reliably and on time. For that, they didn't need a giant conglomerate or a rich parent company.

The problems at Appliance Park were an example of how far the engineers at the glider factory had come. If this was the state of the art in the commercial market, carving out their own niche wouldn't be difficult.

THREE

. . . .

Seymour

The metal frame of a computer chassis lay on a wooden table in one of the glider factory labs, surrounded by loose parts. An engineer hunched over it, pulling part by part from the chassis, then squeezing his hands through the frame to click new ones into place.

Frank Mullaney, one of ERA's top engineers, stood a few feet away, watching curiously. He was a tall, slender, bespectacled man who was respected by the technical staff for his easygoing but knowledgeable approach to his work. After only four years at ERA, Mullaney was regarded as a veteran staffer and therefore oversaw development of some of the company's new machines. Ordinarily he liked to yield to his engineers, to give them the freedom to make decisions, but as he watched the engineer remove and replace parts, he scratched his head. The machine the engineer was working on—the Atlas II—was already deep into its development cycle. As far as Mullaney knew, no one had authorized any changes, so he tapped the engineer on the shoulder and asked what he was doing. The engineer answered matter-of-factly, "Well, Seymour thought this ought to be changed."

Seymour. Mullaney immediately recognized the name. Seymour Cray had started only two weeks earlier but, despite his being fresh out of college, had quickly taken charge. Cray was a skinny twenty-five-year-old who had come to ERA after graduating from the University of Minnesota. He had a thin, reedy voice that shook a little bit when he talked. His colleagues noticed immediately that Cray always chose his words carefully; he spoke slowly, and the inflections in his voice had an almost melodic quality to them. Around the glider factory he was usually quiet, but behind his restrained exterior was a profound sense of confidence. When he saw something he considered inefficient, or just plain wrong, Cray spoke up immediately. That, of course, wasn't unusual for a young grad. Many engineers left college assuming that they knew everything, but the odd thing about Cray was that the *other* engineers thought he knew everything, too. Something about him—his knowledge, his demeanor, his overall confidence—suggested that he was more than just a raw kid.

Mullaney stared in wonder as he watched the engineer replace the parts in the chassis in front of him. Cray, he thought, wasn't even assigned to this part of the Atlas II project, yet had somehow felt a sense of responsibility . . . to what? The machine? The company? For some reason Cray had felt that the flaw that he'd seen must be corrected, and he'd had the confidence to tell more experienced people that they'd made a mistake. Most amazing of all, Mullaney thought, Cray was right: The new parts were better than the old ones.

As time passed, Mullaney noticed again and again that this skinny young engineer was separating himself from the crowd. Once or twice a week Mullaney taught special classes in Boolean algebra for the engineers. Boolean algebra was critical for computer designers because it taught them how to manipulate information in a binary, or base-two, number system—that is, a system made up of only ones and zeros. In the classes engineers learned how to perform basic algebraic and arithmetic operations in base two. Using these skills, they could then set up electrical circuits to operate in binary fashion. The ones and zeroes represented high and low voltages traveling through a computer's wires. For some of the engineers, binary thinking was difficult; it felt unnatural, especially after spending an entire lifetime immersed in the base-ten number system. But when Cray enrolled in on-site Boolean algebra classes, Mullaney was amazed. Some employees were faster than others at grasping Boolean, but none that he had seen were like Cray. Cray could pick out errors on the blackboard; he could answer any question; he could find faster and simpler ways to attack any problem. In short, he was a step ahead of the instructor.

Part of Cray's talent was undoubtedly a result of his background. At the University of Minnesota he'd earned a bachelor's degree in electrical engineering and a master's in applied mathematics. With his background in applied mathematics, he quickly absorbed the theoretical side of Boolean algebra. And with his practical grounding in electrical engineering, he easily understood how Boolean related to circuits.

In the lab Mullaney noted that Cray's hands-on proficiency matched his theoretical ability. Cray was initially assigned to design pulse transformers for the computers. Combining theory and practice was unusual for a recent grad—most were good at one or the other, but not at both. Cray exhibited a knack for both. He worked diligently at his bench, asking few questions and quietly focusing on his work. When he did pose a question, he absorbed the answer almost immediately and never made the same mistake twice. Seeing this, Mullaney eventually assigned him a larger and more difficult task—design of the control system for a new machine known as the 1103, a commercial version of the Atlas II.

For most engineers fresh out of school, designing a control system for something like the 1103 bordered on the impossible. In 1951 the subject was so new that little or no guiding information existed and library books on the topic were not yet written. While some engineers had documented their efforts, their work was almost impossible to follow. Engineers, in general, didn't like to write; they preferred to roll up their sleeves and work. Their disdain for writing showed in their documentation.

Lack of documentation made little difference to Cray. Years later when Mullaney asked him whether he had seen a report on a new circuit from MIT, Cray responded, "Yeah, I saw it. But I didn't read it because I figured that if I spent the same amount of time thinking about it from scratch, I probably could do better." In 1951 Cray took the same approach: He'd figure it out himself.

Designing the 1103 control system from scratch was one of the first major proofs of Cray's innate talent. A complex device, the control system analyzed each software instruction and built a sequence of operations to execute it. An instruction might say, for example, to add two numbers and then put the result back in the computer's memory. To accomplish that, it had to place the first number in memory, place the second number in memory, then move them to an accumulator circuit that would add them, and finally move the result back to the memory. Breaking down that series of operations required a knowledge of sequencing, circuitry, and algebraic logic. It also required the designer to know almost everything else that was happening in the computer at that moment, because the control system's role was to receive and send signals to various parts of the machine. In short, designing a control system was a job for a smart, experienced engineer. Cray was inexperienced, but smart enough to make up for it.

To the engineers around Cray, none of this seemed the least bit unusual. They knew, of course, that it was unusual for an engineer to ascend to such levels of responsibility within three months, but they didn't think of Cray as a new employee or an inexperienced college grad. From the day he'd walked through the glider factory's front door, he had seemed like a veteran engineer. On those rare occasions when they thought about it, and realized that he'd been toiling away in college only a few months earlier, they could only wonder where all his knowledge and engineering instinct had come from.

When he graduated from college in the spring of 1951, Seymour R. Cray hadn't heard of Eckert-Mauchly, ERA, or the old glider factory. What's more, he knew almost nothing about computers. But he knew about vacuum tubes. In between his studies at the University of Minnesota, Cray worked as a radio and television repairman. He toiled away in a dim little shop, replacing burned-out tubes in tiny-screen televisions and old electric radios. It wasn't a glamorous job, but it brought home a few extra dollars to help support his two toddlers at home.

Cray and Verene Voll had married four years earlier. She worked as a nutritionist at a local children's hospital and brought home most of the family's income, but both of them had high hopes for Seymour's future in engineering. He was an exceptionally bright engineering and math student, and his professors at the university noticed his uncanny knack for problem solving almost immediately. His grades were good and he'd earned a B.S.

in electrical engineering and a master's in applied mathematics. On the surface Cray's future appeared bright.

But by the time Cray graduated from college, he'd begun to worry about his future. Now nearing twenty-six, he had spent all the money allotted to him by a World War II veterans education program. He had no job prospects and the university offered no placement services. A few of the grads found job leads posted on bulletin boards around the campus, but he had found none. So when one of his professors stopped him on the street, wanting to discuss jobs, Cray was glad to oblige. Hearing that Cray had no prospects, the professor suggested that he apply for a position at an old glider factory in St. Paul. At the time any job lead was a good one, so Cray trekked to the St. Paul glider factory and filled out an application.

To the personnel manager there, Cray looked average in every way. Youthful and fit, and with close-cropped dark hair, Cray at first glance looked like any of a hundred other former soldiers at the glider factory. He was also an electrical engineer, a University of Minnesota grad, and a kid at heart with a passion for radio technology. That made him even *more* like the engineers at the glider factory—so much so that they hired him.

But Cray's real strengths—his relentless drive and unswerving concentration—were not obvious during the company interviews. Those qualities, products of a disciplined upbringing, would surface later. Cray's father (whose name was also Seymour R. Cray) was a smart, tough, disciplinarian who'd brought up his two children as mirror images of himself. The elder Cray was also an engineer and a University of Minnesota grad. Like his son, he'd found his first job through a lead from an admiring professor: He had been strolling across the University of Minnesota campus when a professor had leaned out a window and called to him. Based on the professor's lead, he'd gone to work for Northern States Power near the tiny town of Danbury, in the far northwest edge of Wisconsin. Northern States needed civil engineers like Cray to help them build a dam there.

During his first few months with Northern States, the elder Cray provided a glimpse of the mental toughness that he would pass along to his children. Living accommodations near the dam site were nearly nonexistent, so the newly married Cray lived with his wife, Lillian, in a tent in the northern Wisconsin pine forest, cooking canned food over a kerosene stove. They persevered there throughout the first summer's hot, muggy weather, battling mosquitoes and wood ticks, and scraping every bite of food out of of each can. It was hard work, but Cray had worked even harder to make it through the University of Minnesota's civil engineering program. During college he often pulled all-night study sessions hunched over his books in a canoe in the middle of Lake Harriet near the university campus, straining to read by moonlight. His moonlight study sessions were his modus operandi, mainly because the lake afforded the peace and quiet he needed for deep thought.

At Northern States Cray turned out to be a tough and knowledgeable taskmaster. When surveying crews bragged that they would "walk his legs off," Cray responded by taking their truck away, and making *them* walk six miles to the job site and another six miles back. Crews quickly grew to respect him. Eventually Northern States put him in charge of an effort to build a dam across the Chippewa River in Chippewa Falls, Wisconsin. There officials took a liking to the tough youngster and offered him a position as city engineer. He accepted the post, which gave him the opportunity to settle down and raise a family. He and Lillian had their first child in 1925 and named him Seymour R. Cray. Five years later the Crays had another child, a daughter whom they named Carol.

From the beginning, young Seymour followed in the footsteps of his father. Captivated by technology, he found an avenue for expression in photography at age ten. He built a darkroom in the basement, snapped photos in his yard, and developed them himself. His sister helped him in the darkroom, holding up black-and-white prints and hanging them on a line with clothespins.

Before long, young Seymour's interest turned to electronics. He ran wires through the Victorian woodframe house that his parents rented. The wiring enabled him to set up a special alarm system in his bedroom that signaled the entrance of family members. He drilled holes through the closet floor, then ran the wires to the basement so that the alarm could alert him while he worked in his basement photo lab. His sister and parents grew accustomed to the sound of young Seymour's voice echoing up from the basement whenever someone entered his room.

Once the technology fire was lit, young Seymour branched off into a variety of areas. While still in elementary school, he wired the house so that he and his sister could send Morse code messages to each other. He encouraged her to learn Morse code, then tapped out messages to her room after his father had declared "lights out" at ten o'clock each night. When his father learned of his late night transmissions and ordered him to cease, young Seymour simply replaced the beeping of the conventional Morse code system with a silent, flashing light.

By most measures his teen years were ordinary. He spent summer days at a little cottage his father built along the Chippewa River, swimming and boating with his sister and occasionally with high school friends who dropped by. He kept a pet rooster at the cottage, liked to fish in the river, and developed an intense interest in kite flying, which lasted into his adult life.

The one element of Cray's life that distinguished him from other teens was, of course, his passion for science. When his father bought him a chemistry set for his birthday, Cray got so excited that he stayed up late for several nights, eventually losing so much sleep that he grew sick. In his last two years of high school, other students began to take note of his scientific and technical leanings. He served as electrician for the junior prom and in physics class acted as substitute teacher when the regular one called in sick. In the Chippewa Falls High School yearbook, *The Monocle*, a classmate wrote: "As science is becoming more and more important each year, many students are needed in this field. Seymour Cray has received the science award. He has been very much interested in this work through high school days. If anyone were to predict his future, I dare say it would be along the science line."

After graduation Cray applied his technical expertise in the army, where he worked in radio communications. Though he talked little about his role in the war, he lived for a short time in Europe, where he set up a communications center in a castle, and hid under a baby grand piano during bombing raids. He later landed in the Philippines, where he operated his radio equipment from a cave in a remote area.

About a year after being discharged from the service, Cray married. Like his mother, Cray's wife, Verene, was the daughter of a Methodist minister. Though the marriage wasn't arranged in a strict sense, both families expected it. As they saw it, Seymour and Verene's backgrounds were strikingly similar and they'd known each other since childhood, so it seemed a natural pairing. The two had only dated a short time when they married in 1947. After the wedding, Cray and his wife moved to Madison, where they enrolled in the University of Wisconsin. They lasted there only about a year before he decided that the University of Minnesota would have a better engineering program.

Cray felt more comfortable at the University of Minnesota, though he later complained in tongue-in-cheek fashion that his circular slide rule had given him social problems. As Cray told it, "real" engineers packed straight slide rules in leather cases that hung from their belts. Because he was unable to wear his circular slide rule in this fashion, he believed that it failed to distinguish him as an engineer. By the time Cray graduated in 1951, however, he had bigger concerns. Family expenses were rising and his government support was gone. The couple's hope for the future hinged on his offer from the new company at the St. Paul glider factory.

For Cray the next few years at the glider factory passed quickly and his reponsibilities expanded. After his success on the 1103 control system, Cray worked his way up to senior engineer, then project engineer, then supervising engineer, in charge of some of the company's most important undertakings. At each level, his superiors noticed his confidence, his attention to detail, and the breadth of his knowledge.

For most engineers, working under Cray was both inspiring and trying. He was an extraordinary worker, typically laboring well past midnight. He was also committed to his projects in a way that few engineers had ever witnessed before. For some staffers, however, Cray's intense commitment had a downside: He quickly lost patience with engineers who made haphazard decisions or who asked foolish questions. As a supervisor, he had a habit of taking over work if he saw insufficient progress. Engineers began to live in fear of being "scrayed"—that is, reassigned to oblivion for some decision they'd made. On two occasions engineers asked Mullaney or Norris to be moved away from Cray; in both cases they returned a day later to say they'd changed their minds. "Forget what I asked you yesterday," said one. "I decided that I'm learning so much from him that I'd be a damned fool to switch."

To many of the engineers Cray was an enigma. He could be scorchingly sarcastic or impatient. Sometimes he would walk the aisles of the glider factory, lost in thought, oblivious to those around him. He could also be downright charming and sincere. For the most part, Cray was decent to those who worked for him; for the employees he valued most, he was protective and took pains to provide freedom to create.

Whatever their personal dispositions toward Cray, engineers were universally in awe of his focus and determination. Cray felt that no job was below him. If it were for the good of the project, he would perform the tasks of a supervisor, engineer, technician, or laborer. He was not recognized as a workaholic, however. Once a week during Minnesota's hot summers, he joined colleagues for a round of afternoon golf. And because he kept his desktop scrupulously clean—fellow workers couldn't recall seeing so much as a scrap of paper on it—he often gave the appearance of a man who had little to do. Yet his work binges produced extraordinary results, both in volume and quality. His designs were elegant in their simplicity and they worked reliably. As a result managers at the Univac Division of Remington Rand asked him to play increasingly more prominent roles on a computer for Naval Tactical Data Systems, among others.

It was a little-known project in 1954 that helped launch Cray and his colleagues to computing's next level. By this time the crew in St. Paul had been using vacuum tubes in its computers for eight years, but users in government circles were now looking for alternatives. Although vacuum tubes offered sufficient speed, they were unreliable and there was no easy way to weed out the bad ones. At the University of California Radiation Laboratory, one scientist had devised a "tube cooker" that culled out the duds but required two hundred hours of cooking for each set of tubes. Even then, some tubes burned out prematurely on the job. Worse, many tubes failed due to faulty electron emission, a phenomenon that was almost impossible to predict.

The first concrete effort to replace the vacuum tube began in November 1954. Arnold Cohen, by then one of the top technical people in the Univac Division of Remington Rand, attended a classified U.S. Air Force meeting in which he learned that the air force was building a device called the Inter-Continental Ballistic Missile (ICBM). Plans were for the ICBM to carry a nuclear warhead at supersonic speeds. By design, it would follow a ballistic trajectory for thirty-five hundred miles after its launch. The idea was to provide a counteroffensive to the USSR, which was believed to be building the same kind of missile.

Reaching remote targets with an unmanned ballistic missile was a task requiring sophistication. A ballistic missile, by definition, follows a trajectory determined by gravity. Using an inertial navigation system, it makes small corrections to the path to keep itself on course. Building a guidance system for such a missile required new technologies. To more accurately determine trajectory, the air force wanted to develop a computer that could be used to remotely control the ICBM's guidance system.

Univac bid on the project, but even as it did, its engineers were unsure how to build such a computer. The problem was reliability—the last thing the air force wanted was to rest the fate of an ICBM on the performance of a faulty vacuum tube.

Engineers in St. Paul thought they saw two technological candidates to solve the problem. The first was the magnetic switch. Invented by Cray for another project, the magnetic switch used a tiny torus of very thin magnetic ribbon wound around a stainless steel bobbin. Magnetic switches offered advantages over vacuum tubes; namely, size, reliability, and power consumption. The second candidate—the transistor—was less well known. It had been quietly developed at Bell Laboratories in Murray Hill, New Jersey, in 1947. Invented by John Bardeen, William Brattain, and William Shockley, it was designed to improve telephone switching systems and long-distance voice transmissions, and it held great promise in the computer industry as an alternative to the vacuum tube.

Cray, who after three and a half years was a supervising engineer, assigned two of St. Paul's best project engineers to build computers based on both candidates. Jim Thornton headed the "Magstec" team; Dolan Toth led the "Transtec" team. The team leaders were exceptionally young: Cray was twenty-nine, Thornton was three days older than Cray, and Toth was about to turn thirty-two. Toth and Thornton were assigned to build dueling prototypes, identical down to their instruction sets, with a single exception: Thornton's would use magnetic switches while Toth's incorporated transistors. Cray gave the engineers initial guidance, then left them alone to carry out the designs.

Management moved the engineers to the basement of a warehouse on Pryor Avenue, about a quarter-mile from the glider factory. In the beginning the engineers scratched their heads and tried to put a set of defining equations on paper, but after a few days, Toth's team realized it was going in circles. No one had built solid-state machines before. Building a vacuum tube computer was still considered a major technical achievement. Yet here they were, already trying to build something better. They had almost no supporting research, because little was known about the performance of transistors in computers. The company's research department had previously studied the concept, but the results of its work were so inconclusive that Cray had grown impatient and had cut it off from the project.

The lack of conclusive research made the design of the new computers mind-numbingly difficult. Toth's crew struggled with the design of a logic circuit, trying in vain to apply the results of earlier research, but each time they solved one problem, two more cropped up. After three days Toth and the other engineers trekked back to the glider factory to meet with Cray. Cray led them to a small conference room with a blackboard. Chalk in hand, he jotted down the transistor's performance characteristics. "Suppose you had a circuit like this," he said, sketching a logic circuit on the board and plugging numerical values in for the resistors and other components. In about fifteen minutes he had diagrammed the machine's entire logic system. "Try that out," he said. "It'll probably work."

Unlike the researchers—who had tried to replace vacuum tubes with transistors in a one-for-one exchange—Cray recognized that transistors had their own performance characteristics. He struck vacuum tubes from his mind and started from scratch, rather than try to reverse-engineer a vacuum tube system. In fifteen minutes he had solved a problem that baffled the research department for weeks and eluded six electrical engineers for several days.

Toth soon found that transistors offered almost every imaginable advantage over vacuum tubes. Each of the little cylindrical devices took up about a half of a cubic centimeter. Vacuum tubes, on average, consumed about *five* cubic centimeters. The transistors were also faster, smaller, and far more reliable. The only downside was cost: While the Philco transistors that Toth used cost approximately $6 each, vacuum tubes ran about a dollar apiece. But that, too, would soon change.

Still, the transistor was no shoo-in. Magnetic switches showed nearly the same advantages, plus a few that the transistor didn't have.

When the prototypes neared completion, Cray called a meeting in the basement of the glider factory. The goal was to select the better technology, then pursue it in the ICBM design. One engineer stepped to a blackboard and scrawled the pros and cons of each technology. Clearly both alternatives offered advantages over vacuum tubes: They were superior in size, weight, speed, reliability. The magnetic switch offered more uniform performance and was better understood, so from a purely logical standpoint the magnetic switch appeared to be the winner. But the engineers at that meeting had spent months on the project, and most had developed a gut instinct about transistors. Transistor technology was in its infancy, they said, and was destined for dramatic improvement. They couldn't prove that assumption to a board of directors, but they didn't need to. So after members of the group finished scribbling the logical pros and cons, they followed their instincts. The consensus turned, and they bet their future on the transistor. Seymour Cray, sitting quietly at the back of the room, nodded in concurrence. In the ultralogical profession of engineering, seat-of-the-pants instinct had won out. To the engineers in the basement of the glider factory, the decision was a minor event—just one of the little workaday choices that engineers made all the time. They had no way of knowing how it would affect the company, or the industry, or the design of computers in general.

In Philadelphia, J. Presper Eckert and his crew faced the same decision, and they selected magnetic switch technology. Their design, known as the 409-3, became the air force computer.

But for Seymour Cray, the transistor was the winner. Two years later when he and others in that room would embark on a new venture, Seymour Cray would remember why they had chosen the transistor and would prove that the transistor had been the right choice all along.

By 1956 virtually every technology giant was considering dipping a toe in the digital water. General Electric, RCA, Philco, Xerox, Bendix, Honeywell, Burroughs, National Cash Register, Raytheon, and others were trying or had already dropped out. Most intimidating of all was the presence of IBM, which had started by building machines that combined relays and vacuum tubes in the late 1940s and was currently positioning itself for industry leadership in electronic computing.

Bill Norris knew that the herd was fast approaching, but he believed Univac, with proper funding, could hold off its competitors. A year earlier Remington Rand had merged with Sperry Corporation to become Sperry-Rand. Remington Rand executives said the motivation behind the merger was cash: The company needed additional capital to support its core businesses. Sperry was a huge company that was respected by Univac engineers, and at first the merger buoyed their spirits. Sperry had a solid reputation in the military equipment field, making such items as gyroscopes and aircraft radios.

The technologists at the glider factory also liked Sperry's chief executive officer, Harry Vickers, an old-time engineer and inventor. Vickers's presence as CEO was a breath of fresh air. For years the engineers in St. Paul had all been uncomfortable with the stuffy atmosphere of Remington Rand, which treated its executives like royalty, staging elegant luncheons for them at its Rock Ledge mansion in Rowayton, Connecticut. A few years earlier the company had named the legendary General Douglas MacArthur as the chairman of its board of directors. Meetings at Rock Ledge then became an odd mix of elegance and militarylike ritual, with MacArthur entertaining the troops by telling battle tales of World War II. The tales sometimes ran deep into the afternoon, and some of the managers, Norris included, often accompanied Mac-Arthur back to his permanent suite at the Waldorf-Astoria Hotel in New York City, where they listened to stories for hours on end.

What any of this had to do with running a computer business was beyond the engineers in St. Paul. That was why, with Vickers in charge, they believed the firm's focus on technology would return. At first all of their hopes seemed to come true, particularly when the company named Norris to succeed John Parker as head of the Univac Division. In a sense the move proved Parker a prophet: He had once told Norris that mergers had a way of fostering quick promotions. At the time, however, he hadn't realized that Norris's quick promotion would come at his own expense. ERA engineers thought they would finally gain access to their share of development funds.

Norris was one of the first to buttonhole Vickers, explaining that the Univac Division needed more development capital if it wanted to keep pace with IBM. Vickers encouraged him to do whatever was necessary to keep Univac in the lead. But the truth was, Vickers was nearing retirement, and most of the company's resources were still controlled by the crowd who attended the meetings at the Rock Ledge mansion. So while Norris was telling his engineers to get going, the managers at Rock Ledge were busy blocking their funding.

The problems came to a head over such issues as the Tucson research and development facility. Norris had told Willis Drake to find a suitable site for a new R&D facility in another town. Drake found one in Tucson, Arizona. But a Sperry-Rand executive, newly assigned to oversee the crew in St. Paul, had flatly rejected the idea, as well as others they'd proposed. The fact that executives made such hard-nosed decisions all the time made little difference to Norris and the others. ERA had been *their* company. They'd called the shots. *They'd* had control. And now here was some corporate creature, who'd probably never started a company in his life, telling them how to run the business. The executive's obstinacy was considered a devastating head-on assault, not only by Norris but by the engineers in St. Paul. Increasingly they watched the Sperry-Rand executives muscle Norris out of the picture, and they felt the sting of their own diminished roles and grew angry.

As frustration built in St. Paul, Frank Mullaney met with a former ERA employee named Arnold Ryden at the Minneapolis Athletic Club. Ryden had an idea for a new company, to be staffed mainly by former ERA employees. A Harvard business school graduate, Ryden said he knew where he could get initial capital to launch a business. A couple of years earlier Mullaney couldn't have imagined considering such an offer. Back then the engineers had been provided with proper funding and had been given the freedom to create, but the realities of the corporate world were closing in, and Mullaney and the others felt those realities in the most profound ways. The engineer's paradise was gone. So Mullaney listened to Ryden, then reported back to Norris, who reacted in typically stoic fashion, making no comment.

A few months later, however, Norris called Mullaney for lunch. He'd given Sperry-Rand a chance, he said, and he could see that nothing would change. The business he'd founded eleven years earlier had been absorbed, wrapped up inside the monstrous tentacles of a big conglomerate, and swallowed. The time had come to make a change—he was interested in Ryden's idea.

Norris and Mullaney met Ryden. In the new company, Ryden said, Norris would be president and chief executive officer; Ryden would serve as chief financial officer; Mullaney would direct engineering; Willis Drake would head marketing. Norris listened, offered some vague ideas for the company's product line, and agreed to pursue it.

Unlike eleven years earlier, however, the U.S. Navy would not help them launch their business. They would have to do it themselves, and despite their experience with ERA, most were naive in the ways of starting a business. Ryden knew that the new company must have a business plan to begin raising capital, so seated at Drake's kitchen table, he and Drake wrote out a prospectus for the new organization. Ryden's idea was to raise $600,000 by selling shares of stock in the company, based on the prospectus. To Drake, who was trained as an engineer and had no feel for business matters, Ryden's idea seemed feasible. Drake quit his job at Univac to sell stock in the new company.

On July 26, 1957, Norris resigned, too. Stunned Sperry-Rand executives frantically approached Mullaney, offering him Norris's position. Mullaney rejected their offer, resigning a few hours later. Almost immediately the halls of the new Univac facility on the banks of the Mississippi River were abuzz with talk of a new company. Drake had left, Mullaney and Norris were leaving, and several other employees were rumored to follow.

Drake took it upon himself to sell shares in the new company. Meeting with other prospective employees, he managed to garner about $15,000 in promises to buy stock, but that still put them about $585,000 short of their goal. Norris promised to invest $75,000 of his own money, most of which he had earned in the sale of ERA. He also convinced a physician friend in Iowa to invest $25,000, though the physician didn't even vaguely understand the nature of the business. The company was still far short of its goal. Drake planned to fill in the remainder by selling individual shares of stock at a dollar a share. In truth he had no idea if it was possible to raise half a million dollars through a public underwriting based on a prospectus written on someone's kitchen table.

Drake grabbed a notebook and a copy of the prospectus and drove down to the Minnesota State Securities Commission to register for the sale of six hundred thousand shares of common stock. The representative at the securities commission was incredulous: "You don't have any products; you don't have any plant; you don't have any machines; you don't have any money." And you want to sell stock—in what?" Drake tapped his finger on the prospectus and answered, "Here's our business plan—that's what we want to sell shares in."

Another meeting ensued, in which the man from the state securities commission gently explained to Drake that his proposal was . . . unusual. "You seem like nicer people than that," he said, implying that Drake's proposal smelled of snake oil. "Obviously you don't know what you're doing." When Drake persisted, the man handed him a stack of special subscription forms that were to be signed by buyers of the stock, and which stated that the sale was a highly risky affair.

Undeterred, Drake grabbed the forms and set out to sell stock. In the beginning he sat in his station wagon, a block from Univac's new Mississippi River facility, and as employees filed by, he would fling open the car's door and offer them stock at a dollar per share. He also arranged one-on-one meetings with ERA employees at Mrs. Strandy's Tea Room, a little snack shop a couple of blocks from the plant.

At first Drake found it difficult to raise capital. The people he talked to weren't the types to play the market. Most were engineers with wives and kids at home. Many hadn't saved much from their ERA salaries as they struggled to raise families. Because they were new to the stock market, they didn't ask questions about business plans or products; they simply asked Who are your people? When he made his first stock sale, Drake's customers—a husband and wife—never knew that they were the first.

Eventually Drake moved his sales office from the tea room to a full-fledged restaurant, the Parker House in Mendota, where over meals he succeeded in selling more shares in blocks of about $500 each. But he found the one-on-one capitalization process too slow. To step it up, he called a meeting in his home one night, inviting twelve people. He was using a sales technique that would one day be common in the Tupperware business: Draw groups of people into an informal setting, then lure them, one by one, into the sale. There in his living room, Drake made a brief presentation, then asked, "If there are no more questions, who would like to subscribe?" One hand went up, offering to buy twenty thousand shares, then two more offered.

Drake repeated his meeting the next night, attracting thirty more people and doing a brisk business. By the time he ran a meeting on a third consecutive evening, word had spread. Curious parties came from all over the Twin Cities. Cars parked for two blocks in every direction. Inquisitive investors filed into Drake's house one after another, until his entire home was wall-to-wall people. Neighbors called, asking if they could invest. One speculator phoned from New York. Drake had requests for 1.2 million shares of stock.

Drake returned to the state securities commission and convinced them that it *was* possible to sell stock for the company, which was still unsure of its business plan. Ten years later the stock would reach $110 a share. Norris's original investment would balloon to $8.25 million; his total investment to over $40 million.

The new company, Control Data Corporation, set up shop in an old warehouse at 501 Park Avenue in downtown Minneapolis. The warehouse, owned by one of Control Data's stockholders, shared space with the *Minneapolis Star* and *Tribune,* which stored their paper rolls there. Drake ordered a telephone and a typewriter and drove down to the facility. Up to that moment he and the others had felt that they'd won the war. They'd beaten Sperry-Rand; they'd successfully raised their cash; they'd escaped. But as Drake slid the key into the warehouse door for the first time, he was overcome with a new sensation: *Now what do we do?*

The locale an hour's drive east of San Francisco featured sandy soil, ideal for growing grapes and roses. It also offered an abundance of fog-free days—the highest in the country. As a result the navy had constructed a naval air station there in the small town of Livermore during World War II. In most respects it was a beautiful area for aviators—sunny, warm, and dry.

A decade after the war, the old naval air base was reemerging in a new role. Abandoned in the late 1940s, it had been resurrected by famed physicist Edward Teller, who had insisted on starting a government lab there for the purpose of building a hydrogen bomb. Teller was a giant in the physics community. He'd been a fringe member of Manhattan Project, which had developed the infamous Fat Man and Little Boy atomic bombs that were dropped on Hiroshima and Nagasaki. In the dusty mountains of New Mexico, Teller and other noted physicists had created a one-of-a-kind stockpile of scientific talent. They were the country's most important defense resource, managing in a single grotesque stroke to end the war in the Pacific. Teller felt that not enough effort was being directed to the country's next big weapon—the so-called Super Bomb project at the Los Alamos National Laboratory in New Mexico—so he convinced government officials to start this new, competing lab.

In the beginning the new lab featured the same isolated, rat-shack, military atmosphere as Los Alamos. The base's run-down buildings regularly felt the lash of the desert wind, and sand crept into all the crevices inside. The walls were unpainted; desks were old; air conditioning and heating were nonexistent. Scientists worked in the dispensary, the ready room, and the enlisted men's barracks. They converted the bedrooms in the officers' quarters to offices, and changed the air base's control tower to a security room. Desk lamps and phones were prized commodities, reserved only for the highest ranking of the lab's two hundred or so employees. It felt a lot like the early days of Los Alamos. Early on, Teller had foreseen a unique defining characteristic of this effort at the old naval air station: More so than Los Alamos, it would rely heavily on electronic digital computing.

The new lab, to be known as the Livermore Branch of the University of California Radiation Laboratory, hired physicists to work as computer "coders," or programmers. It typically found degreed individuals who could act as liaisons to the world-class physicists who built the bombs. The lab's managers felt it was important for the coders to have an understanding of the math behind a nuclear chain reaction so they could convert it to computer code without losing anything in the translation.

The Livermore coders were led by a smart, energetic physicist named Sidney Fernbach. Fernbach, one of the lab's first employees, arrived in 1952. He was a short man who wore thick eyeglasses and a bow tie. Fernbach could have been mistaken for the clichéd image of the introverted scientist, but in fact he was a tough urbane man who had grown up in Philadelphia.

Fernbach came to the lab as a theoretical physicist, a brilliant young student who'd earned his Ph.D. at the University of California at Berkeley, where he'd been a disciple of J. Robert Oppenheimer, leader of the Manhattan Project. But Fernbach's Ph.D. thesis at Cal-Berkeley was criticized by the technical elite, and his ties to the upper echelon of science were tenuous. As soon as he stepped onto the scene at Livermore, Edward Teller asked him to funnel his prodigious energy into the lab's computing efforts, and Fernbach complied.

The coders who arrived at the beginning typically waited in the lab's cooler (waiting area) for security clearance for three months. Once cleared, they were given a set of notes to read—notes explaining the programming, or coding, procedures for the UNIVAC I, the lab's first computer.

Even for the rawest of the new scientific recruits, the need for computing quickly grew obvious. Unlike other scientific endeavors, where experimentation was the key to understanding, nuclear weapon construction was different. Weapons builders had little in the way of experimentation available to them, especially with regard to nuclear detonation. During the war the scientists at Los Alamos had tested a weapon in a remote area of New Mexico; after the war they'd tested in Nevada and at places like Bikini Island in the South Pacific.

But for obvious reasons the bomb builders couldn't explode nuclear weapons at will. Testing was not only undesirable, it took tremendous logistical support. Besides, experimentation couldn't answer all questions, even if scientists had unlimited access to it. They could hardly stick a temperature probe or pressure gauge into the core of a nuclear reaction. Scientists estimated that the temperature at the point of detonation was tens of millions of degrees and that pressures were *tens of billions times* atmospheric. The release of energy was simply beyond the bounds of human imagination. Being anywhere near a nuclear blast was probably the closest thing on earth to hell itself. That knowledge had, in fact, been one of the driving forces behind the formation of the new lab. Legend held that on his deathbed, world-renowned mathematician John von Neumann had called for a greater push in the area of computational study of nuclear weapons. "Never let the lab be like the aircraft industry," he had said, "building, crashing, and then fixing."

The concept of computing was not new to nuclear scientists. Those at Los Alamos National Laboratory—or more accurately, their wives—had used primitive calculating machinery to work through the mysteries of Fat Man and Little Boy. The simplest problems had been fed into electromechanical punch-card machines, but the difficult ones were saved for the wives. There had been more than two hundred wives in all, seated along a computational production line, hacking away at hand-calculating machines. The scientists had turned it into a competition—the wives against the punch-card machines—with the cheering wives along the production line frantically trying to hold the lead. By nuclear physicists' standards it was a crude way to generate knowledge, but there was little choice.

The equations that governed nuclear chain reactions were so complicated that they defied many of the analytical methods that mathematicians tried. First of all equations were nonlinear—physicists couldn't just plug in values at the low end and high end of an equation, then draw a line between the two points. A nonlinear function could go almost anywhere, and it was in everyone's best interest to know exactly where it was going.

The best way to do that was to plug in values for, say, the temperature, pressure, velocity, and a few other variables in an equation, and then solve for the internal energy, for example. To get a complete picture, this would be done for each of the variables. That didn't sound bad, until one realized that this technique only provided solutions for one tiny, tiny point within the nuclear chain reaction. There were many of these tiny points, called *cells*, which contained a group of equations to solve. To fully understand an "event," as the scientists stoically called a nuclear implosion, they would have to solve for *all* of the variables at *each* of the cells.

Even that, however, was not the big problem. The big problem was speed of reaction. During a nuclear implosion, pressure and temperature could change spectacularly in the tiniest sliver of a second. To deal with it, Los Alamos scientists divided each second into one hundred million parts, called "shakes," supposedly because they were faster than the shake of a lamb's tail. For accuracy's sake, they had to re-solve all the equations, at all the cells, at least every ten shakes.

On the Manhattan Project, scientists had computed in small numbers of cells—between fifty and one hundred—mainly because they didn't have the machines to do more. But on the hydrogen bomb project, they needed more cells. To solve the equations at so few points, they said, would be coarse. And they didn't want to be coarse with a hydrogen bomb.

To do it right, they needed to raise the number of cells dramatically. Instead of calculating one hundred cells in one dimension, as they had done in the 1940s, scientists wanted to do their calculations in two dimensions. *That meant 100 times 100, or ten thousand cells, each containing as many as ten mathematical variables, and each being recalculated one hundred thousand times per second.* The need for mathematical operations was growing so fast that the concept of hiring scientists' wives to punch the numbers in by hand was now laughable.

The new breed of electronic calculating machines, such as the UNIVAC I, could handle these mathematical operations. Sure, the machines were expensive, but what choice did the scientists have? Even a fairly slow computer could churn out a hundred thousand calculations per second. In contrast, they would need millions of people operating at the speed of a calculation per minute to keep up with *one* of those machines. In 1953 they could have hired everyone in the state of California—men, women, children, infants, pets, *everyone*—and still not have kept up.

For that reason Livermore's scientists needed a scorchingly fast computer. Their need was such a desperate one that they were willing to accept almost any conditions. Assembly of their first UNIVAC was extraordinarily difficult, gobbling up almost thirty days. Incredibly the machine's tape drives were strung together by pulleys and fishing line. During assembly, Univac engineers had to be on hand to thread the fishing line through the pulleys in just the right way to keep the machine operating properly. Many of its five thousand vacuum tubes also lacked reliability, and Livermore engineers were left with the task of weeding out the "gassy" tubes. Eventually Livermore engineers invented a giant rack that they called the "tube cooker," which passed electrical current through the tubes for a couple hundred hours until the bad ones burned out. Yet they persisted—and did so virtually without complaint.

The task of making the hardware work was small by comparison to the job of programming. Decades later every cheap desktop computer would come equipped with operating systems. (The Disk Operating System, or DOS, would be the best known.) But in 1953 computers were little more than huge electronic boxes. Breathing life into them was a job for the coders.

Led by Fernbach, the coders addressed the enormous task of writing programs for the UNIVAC and for every machine that followed. It was an incredibly labor-intensive task. A single line of code could take an hour to write and verify. On a good day a smart coder might produce ten lines of code; a novice, four or five. A large program—depending upon the user's needs—might require more than a hundred thousand lines of code.

All of it was uncharted territory. Colleges offered no degree programs in computer science—indeed, they were years behind industry. And coders' manuals were merely sets of notes handed down from one to another. The coders had no choice but to learn on the job. They scribbled programs on special Univac coding paper, then handed it to assistants who typed the coding symbols onto small metal oxide magnetic tapes. Line by excruciating line they developed the routines for mathematics, data handling, displays, and input/output. A separate group of coders learned to convert the physicists' equations into *macros* or procedures to solve them in an orderly manner.

None of this deterred Fernbach in the least. Starting with the UNIVAC, the lab ordered a string of computers, including IBM's 701, 704, 709, 7090, 7094, and 7030. The machines came so fast, one after another, that when an IBM 7094 toppled off a truck and over a cliff during delivery, legend had it that a new one was delivered before the old one had hit bottom.

For computer manufacturers the needs of the bomb builders created an incredible opportunity. Throughout the early and mid-1950s, Livermore and Los Alamos stepped up their computing efforts until a friendly competition formed between the two labs. They vied for prestige; they vied for funding; they vied for access to the first of every kind of computer. For both labs computers emerged as status symbols, much as they had for giant corporations such as General Electric.

The makers of scientific computing machinery now saw an extraordinary opportunity to cash in. The government labs had such a dire need for the machines that they were willing—even *happy*—to accept machines with almost no user amenities. By any other standards reliability of the machines was woefully inadequate. And because user programs and operating systems were handled by the labs, manufacturers were freed from the laborious task of writing these instructions.

In the mid-1950s the lot of the user was a simple one: Accept the machines and work around their inadequacies. By 1957, after five years at Livermore, Fernbach had formed two theses: First, greater speed required bigger machines; second, small computers weren't worth the lab's attention. The lab's philosophy was simple: *Bring us your biggest and fastest; cost is not the issue.*

Ultimately the lab's scientists felt a need for a machine with extraordinary performance capabilities, one that could offer a hundred times more speed than any other. But even if such a machine could be built, Fernbach and the other bomb builders knew they would need another, and another. Their craving for speed was an unending spiral—each time they reached it, a newer, bigger problem surfaced. Fernbach knew that they would always need a bigger, faster machine. What they needed most was to find a company that could build the world's fastest computer and, when it finished, build another that was even faster.

Control Data's founders moved into the 501 Park Avenue building at the end of 1957, and led by Frank Mullaney, the engineers set up shop. Not even the most spartan of ERA's engineers had ever considered the glider factory luxurious. With its self-emptying ashtrays and the sparrows in the rafters, the glider factory had smacked of postwar bare-bones austerity. An engineer could be stoic about that sort of thing, but no one in his right mind would describe it as luxurious.

But compared to the new facility at 501 Park Avenue in the middle of downtown Minneapolis, the glider factory was beginning to look downright elegant—a real palace. The Park Avenue building was actually a warehouse that the *Minneapolis Star* and *Tribune* used to store blank paper rolls. The place was big and dark, with ceilings about twenty feet high and few windows.

Propane-powered forklift trucks routinely zipped through the warehouse—spitting exhaust right into Control Data's engineering department while stacking and unstacking the giant paper rolls, each about four feet in diameter. They placed the rolls on wooden pallets, then piled the pallets high atop one another. At night Control Data's engineers could hear the wooden pallets creaking under the weight of the rolls. They all feared that one day, the wooden blocks beneath the pallets would crack, and the rolls, one by one, would come thundering across the warehouse and crashing into the walls. All of it made for great coffee-time tales, as long as no one was killed in the process.

The poor conditions were offset by the full-throttle pace of Control Data's partners. It was, after all, *their* firm. Had it been someone else's company and someone else's money, they might have been more inclined to complain, but given their current financial status, no one so much as raised an eyebrow.

The Control Data engineers performed tasks that no other self-respecting engineers would consider. They grabbed push brooms and swept away years of caked dirt from the concrete floor. When they learned that test benches were cheaper unassembled, they bought the unassembled models, and each engineer stayed late into the night, screwing together bench legs, tightening nuts and bolts, then dutifully sweeping up afterward.

Seymour Cray arrived at the warehouse nearly two months after Drake first opened the door. The navy's Bureau of Ships, fearing that Cray would leave Univac, had called Norris and asked him not to take employees from key navy projects. Cray was their prime concern. "If Seymour leaves, our project will collapse," they told Norris. But Norris faced a similar problem: Without Seymour Cray, he had a gaping hole in his technical staff.

Norris approached Cray (whom he still barely knew) and asked him not to come—yet. If Cray left now, Norris explained, there might be no new company, because the navy could blackball Control Data. Cray, disappointed over lack of funding for his pet projects at Univac, reluctantly agreed to hang on there until his navy project was completed.

After two months, with his project nearly finished, Cray called Norris and said he was coming to work. Norris, fearing that Cray's move hadn't yet been cleared by the navy, appealed to his new star to wait just a little longer. "Seymour," he begged, "I don't want to upset the navy."

"I don't care about the navy," Cray responded. "Do you want me or not?"

Having to choose between the wrath of Seymour Cray and the navy, Norris opted for the navy. "Look, Seymour's coming, and I can't stop him," he pleaded with a navy officer. To his surprise, the navy agreed to let Cray leave.

By the time Cray arrived in late 1957, the metal benches stood sturdily in the warehouse. The question was What would they build on those metal benches? Some of the company's partners, including Norris, talked about building products other than computers. In the beginning, talk turned to point-of-sale machines—electronic cash registers. They also considered building digital gasoline pumps and a machine they called the "production data recorder." Norris and Drake believed that the production data recorder, which would digitally record everything that happened in certain parts of a factory's floor, would be one of the company's best prospects. Drake even visited Chrysler to discuss its idea with manufacturing engineers, only to have the idea shot down.

But when Cray arrived, the company's focus tightened. "All I know how to do is build computers," Cray told them, "so I'll do that." Within days of walking through the doors at 501 Park Avenue, Cray was hunching over the work benches, scribbling logic equations, and trying to build breadboard circuits for a machine he called Little Character, which was intended solely as a demonstrator. The idea was for Drake to show the unit to potential customers, who would then better understand the concepts for the full-fledged machine, which, it was hoped, they would buy later.

All of the partners had tacitly understood from the beginning that computers were their best choice, but they all knew that computers were costly to build. And they didn't have much money. Until the navy or another government agency ordered a computer, they hesitated to build one. Cray, however, wasn't waiting. He immediately began working on the logic circuit for a new machine. His big problem, of course, was money. When Control Data had been formed in 1957, everyone had assumed that its revenue source would be government contracts. After all, that was the way it had always been since the founding of ERA in 1946. But Control Data had gone through 1957 and early 1958 without a single government contract, and its $600,000 bankroll was dwindling fast.

Knowing finances were tight, Cray set to work on the new computer in the most frugal way possible. He knew he needed transistors—no state-of-the-art computer could be built without them. But transistors were costly, unless you could find some kind of special deal. So Cray hiked over to an electronics shop—a 1950s counterpart to Radio Shack. He asked the manager for the store's cheapest transistor, and was given a General Transistor Corporation model that cost thirty-seven cents. Cray liked the price so much that he bought all the store had in stock and toted them back to the dusty warehouse at 501 Park Avenue.

He soon found why the transistors cost thirty-seven cents: Their electrical characteristics were dreadfully inconsistent; they were all over the map. No two offered the same performance. Up until that time, the few computer designers who knew anything about transistors had made their selections based on raw speed. They'd actually tested each transistor, culling through scores of them and selecting only the fastest.

But Cray didn't have that luxury. Besides being inconsistent, none of his transistors were very fast. So he set to work on a new logic circuit that would be more tolerant. With his oscilloscope on one side, his voltmeter on the other, and his soldering iron in his hand, Cray began building and testing circuits for the new machine. The other engineers could see him hunched over his metal bench, left hand trembling as he soldered wires to the transistors and other circuit elements.

Among engineers, the process of building the breadboard circuits often was considered technicians' work. Engineers prided themselves on their ability to think, design circuits, evaluate them, and test them. But at Control Data early in 1958, engineers didn't have such luxuries nor would they have been allowed them. Cray liked to get his hands on the components, to build them, test them, and understand them. It was all part of the Seymour Cray Process. He would have it no other way.

Most days, Cray would leave the warehouse at dinnertime and drive to his lakeside home in Brooklyn Center, about eight miles away. He and his wife, Verene, had three small children and made it a point to eat dinner together as a family each night. Cray would stay at home until about ten-thirty, then hop in his car and drive back to the warehouse, where he'd continue to work on his logic circuits far into the night. There he had the quiet he cherished. In those early morning hours no colleagues would interrupt him, no forklift exhaust would choke him. Deep inside the cavernous warehouse, there was only Cray, his equipment, and the occasional creak of the wooden pallets.

Eventually Cray came up with a basic circuit that used two transistors for every one in a conventional computer circuit. He ganged them up in such a way that the current or voltage gain was always multiplied. As a result, he could use much poorer transistors, and the circuits were still faster than those in conventional machines.

The company's financial woes continued. When Bill Norris struck a deal with the navy to sell Control Data's new transistorized computer to the Bureau of Ships, the engineers saw a ray of hope. To build computers, however, they needed manufacturing facilities, so Control Data purchased a Twin Cities firm called Cedar Engineering, which made gyroscopes. Cedar Engineering had first-class manufacturing facilities, and the purchase gave Control Data one more ingredient for success—but it added another drain to its skimpy revenue stream. What's more, Control Data now needed more engineers to build the navy's computer, and more engineers meant a larger payroll.

By late 1958 Control Data's partners knew that they would have to take large pay cuts to keep the firm afloat. For engineers such as Mullaney, who had five kids at the time, dropping from $16,000 a year to $8,000 was painful.

At the warehouse the situation was no better. Eventually a representative from General Transistor showed up to tell Seymour Cray that he'd been using the "fallout"—the rejects—from the company's transistor line, and that he'd cleaned them out. They had no more fallout. If Seymour wanted additional transistors, the representative said, he would now have to pay twice as much.

The engineering staff tried to deal with the situation in any way they could. They invited other factory reps to the warehouse, usually scheduling visits at lunchtime and finagling a free meal. Then they used the reps' free samples in their new machine. They didn't *plan* to do it that way; it's just that the salesmen *offered* the samples. Eventually some of the salesmen saw a pattern forming. "You always tell me to come at eleven-thirty," one complained to Mullaney, "and I don't mind taking you out to lunch. But I'll be damned if I'm going to furnish enough transistors for you to build your prototype for free."

Somehow the new machine got built. With the additional manpower, Cray was able to parcel out pieces of the design to others. He was still the machine's master architect, but the engineers who surrounded him—people like Jim Thornton—were trusted colleagues from his ERA days.

Although the new machine used transistors instead of vacuum tubes, the transistors performed the same kinds of function as the vacuum tubes. The difference was that the transistors were smaller and far more reliable. Whereas a vacuum tube could be six inches long, a transistor could easily fit in the palm of your hand. Ultimately the engineers would take their little soldered transistor circuits and hand them to a draftsman, who would draw them up. Then they'd give the drawings to a manufacturer who made them into printed circuit cards. An assembled printed circuit card had all the same logic elements—transistors, resistors, capacitors, and such—but the wires were built into the cards. Each measured only about two by three inches and was relatively flat. Hundreds of the logic cards plugged into connectors in the back plane of the machine, thus making up the "brain" of the computer.

The resulting computer was far smaller than the UNIVACs, which had used vacuum tubes. It was about the size of several tall filing cabinets instead of a one-car garage. Had it been named by a 1950s advertising executive, it might have been called the Calc-A-Tron or the Trans-A-Calc, but the 1604 was named by engineers. They named it by adding 1103 and 501: The 1103 was the model number of their last machine at Remington Rand; 501 was their new address. Hence, the CDC 1604 was christened.

Within Control Data, engineers were in awe of Cray's achievement. Though he worked with several other engineers to build the 1604, he had overseen virtually every aspect of the project on a detailed level. At the time computer engineers knew that the construction of a big machine required talented *teams* with individuals who understood processors, memories, power systems, Boolean logic, circuits, coding, and architecture. Theoretically it was possible for an engineer to turn the study of any one of those disciplines into a lifetime project; mastery of all of them was next to impossible. Yet somehow Cray *had* mastered all of them; his instinct in all of those areas was what enabled the 1604 design to work.

As the introduction of the new machine neared, Control Data's fortunes picked up. Norris took a big step toward solving the revenue problems by convincing Allstate Insurance to invest $600,000. Control Data stock traded briskly and its value began to climb. The company's stock soon jumped from $1 to $9 a share, and Norris's biggest challenge was to convince his employees not to sell their stock. Engineers were cashing in—seven thousand or eight thousand shares at a time—and buying luxurious new homes, not realizing that the value of a share would eventually climb to $135 by the decade's end.

By 1960 when the 1604 reached the market, it was the fastest machine in the world, with a clock speed of five microseconds (0.2 megahertz). Control Data sold the first machine to the the navy, for its Naval Post-Graduate School in Monterey, California. In quick succession, Control Data then sold more 1604s to the University of Illinois, Northrop, Lockheed, the National Bureau of Standards, and the State of Israel, reportedly for nuclear weapons design.

Control Data's first big step into its new market occurred when George Michael and Norman Hardy, programmers from the Livermore lab, visited a computer users conference. On a table at the conference they found a programmers manual for the CDC 1604. They picked it up and paged through it, and what they saw stunned them. The machine's instruction sets (the programming directions that made it operate) were extraordinarily clean and simple. They took the manual to one of the machine's users at the National Bureau of Standards, who verified all of their hunches: The machine was clean, reliable, and easy to program, and because it stored data in larger "words" (later to be known as *bytes*), its calculations were more accurate than those of his IBM machines. Most of all, the 1604 was fast—unbelievably fast. Michael and Hardy brought the user's manual back to Sid Fernbach, who purchased a CDC 1604 shortly afterward.

Within the tight confines of the computing business, the story of Control Data's success spread quickly. Suddenly their reputation was growing. Word spread of the thirty-five-year-old computer designer who had fashioned the world's fastest computer from a reject load of transistors. Cray had beaten IBM; he had beaten the geniuses at Sperry-Rand.

Control Data had found its niche. It wasn't going to build point-of-sale machines or electronic gas pumps or production data recorders. Control Data was now a player in the computer market. It was the company that built the world's fastest computers.

FOUR

• • • • • • • • • • •

Engineers' Paradise

Seymour Cray was a force in his industry. At age thirty-five he was recognized as the world's preeminent designer of high-speed computers. The weapons builders at Los Alamos and at Livermore's radiation laboratory looked to him for their next-generation machines. So did the cryptologists from the "Seesaw" group in Washington, who in 1952 had been absorbed into a new organization called the National Security Agency. Cray's business instincts, which had been good before the success of the CDC 1604, were now heightened. He had gained the confidence he would need to follow his instincts, even in the face of corporate dissent.

This was critical, because dissent was already brewing. The company's management—Bill Norris in particular—gazed at the future from a perspective different than that of Cray. Norris foresaw a greater need for *business* data processing, and he wanted Control Data to challenge IBM in that arena. Norris couldn't make himself forget the way IBM had suddenly surged into digital computing's leadership. That leadership role, Norris thought, should have been Remington Rand's. IBM had been a digital neophyte in 1950. It had struggled to leave the realm of punch-card machinery in the late 1940s, and its first entry in the digital market had been the Selective Sequence Electronic Calculator, a 120-foot-long machine that was as clumsy as its name.

By 1955 IBM's president, Thomas Watson, was on the cover of *Time,* and his company's name was suddenly synonymous with computing. The *Time* article itself had been an embarrassment for Norris and Remington Rand: *Time*'s reporter had first approached Remington Rand but received little cooperation, so she turned her attention to IBM. Watson made the cover, and Remington Rand was all but forgotten.

In 1960 IBM was so dominant that the average American believed it had invented electronic computing. IBM's machines not only dominated the business market but also reigned supreme in scientific computing. Over a seven-year period IBM had rolled out the 701, 704, 709, 7090, 7094, 7030, and a machine called Stretch. During that time the bomb builders almost exclusively used IBM machines. The Livermore radiation lab, for example, purchased twenty computers between 1954 and 1961; nineteen were IBM models. Livermore's 1962 purchase of the CDC 1604 finally broke that string.

Norris and the rest of Control Data's management didn't want to be left behind again. They wanted to capitalize on the success of the CDC 1604 and assert themselves in both scientific *and* business computing. To do that, they needed a machine that could appeal to business clientele. They also wanted a machine that would be compatible with the CDC 1604. With compatibility, they could more easily lure existing customers into another sale.

The first source of tension between Cray and the rest of CDC management was that Cray didn't buy into their ambitious new plan. While others looked at IBM and saw monumental success, Cray examined IBM and spotted a flaw. The company's managers, its bureaucracy, had too much control over the design of its machines, he thought. The result of their meddling was embodied in the machine called Stretch, so named because it was supposed to stretch the technological envelope of electronic computing. In Cray's eyes, Stretch was a typical management machine: potentially clean, but bloated and rendered less effective by the wishes of too many individuals. By the time IBM management had finished with it, Stretch was an electronic monument to the art of corporate compromise: Its instruction set—the built-in directives that "tell" a computer what to do and when to do it—numbered 735. That was about ten times as many instructions as Cray thought a machine should have.

Stretch's architecture served as a lesson for Cray. It was a textbook example of how corporate meddling could compromise performance, he thought. Unlike most managers, Cray understood that scientific and business computing were vastly different. Scientific computers needed arithmetic speed to solve equations repetitively, often millions of times each. The needs of American business contrasted sharply with those of big labs. Such companies as American Airlines needed to store and manipulate enormous amounts of data—customer names, flight numbers, reservations, payment information, and thousands of other little tidbits. To accomplish that, the machines needed large instruction sets, which enabled them to easily manipulate alphanumeric data. High-speed operation, while important, was a secondary requirement.

Cray didn't want large instruction sets that sapped a machine's raw performance. Nor did he want compatibility. To him, compatibility was poison. It limited speed because it constrained the overall architecture of the machine. Compatibility, he thought, was just one more compromise, one more drain from the speed he so desperately sought.

Cray wasn't about to compromise. In his mind unconstrained speed was the Holy Grail of computing. His customers—most of whom he knew on a first-name basis—had expressed their insatiable appetite for speed, and Cray had listened. For three years he'd spent his nights alone at the test bench in the cavernous warehouse, building and learning. During that time he'd discovered how to meet the needs of those customers, probably not more than two dozen in all. It was a small customer base, but Cray didn't mind. If he could sell just twenty machines, he would be successful. The sale of twenty machines might be paltry in any other industry, but other industries didn't sell their products for $5 million to $6 million apiece. Cray had found his niche, and he wanted to stay there. Growth was not his goal. He preferred the role of the master craftsman, building his super-fast machines by hand and selling them to his customers for high prices.

That, of course, was not what any corporate managers wanted to hear. Growth—rapid growth—was almost an obsession even in 1960. So the tension at the newspaper warehouse grew as managers tried to find a way to persuade Cray to build *their* machine. They knew they couldn't force him. Even at age thirty-five, Cray was far too stubborn; he simply couldn't be bullied. They talked with him at meetings, gently trying to persuade. They presented the sound business reasons behind their ideas. But their attempts did not work. No, Cray told them firmly, there would be no large instruction sets. There would be no compatibility. His new mission was to build a faster computer. Not just marginally speedier, but blindingly fast—maybe fifty times faster than the 1604.

The gulf between Cray and his management slowly grew. Knowing that Cray would not build a business machine, Norris assigned a separate group to design one. The machine, to be known as the CDC 3600, would incorporate the larger instruction sets that a business machine needed.

In subtle ways Cray and CDC management were parting ways. Cray didn't look, act, think, or dress like his executive colleagues. He disliked virtually all of the things associated with corporate behavior: memos, dress shirts, ties, luncheons, budgets, presentations, office politics, and all of the other little irritations that seeped into everyday business life. It wasn't that Cray was a rebel in the obvious sense. No, he was a conservative-looking fellow whose close-cropped hair was always neatly combed. Nor did he rant and rave; most colleagues had never even heard him curse. But he wasn't buying into the traditional corporate culture. He arrived late for work in the morning, usually around 10:30 or 11:00 A.M., ignoring the normal business hours that ruled the lives of most employees. At work he rarely wore a tie. Slacks and a sport shirt were his regular attire, and he often dressed that way for management meetings.

But Cray's unorthodox methods worked, making him a hero of sorts to the other engineers, most of whom reveled in his handling of routine company matters. Cray often ignored corporate edicts and bristled at the need to write reports. Asked to illuminate management with detailed one-year and five-year plans for his next machine, Cray produced two sentences: "Five-year goal: Build the biggest computer in the world. One year goal: One-fifth of the above." Another time, when company leaders were assigned to write lengthy status reports for Norris, Cray's counterparts wrote twenty- and thirty-page documents. Cray again produced just two sentences: "Activity is progressing satisfactorily as outlined under the June plan. There have been no significant changes or deviations from the June plan."

For Control Data engineers, Cray's attitude was a breath of fresh air. As director of engineering he was actually a member of the management team, yet he did not feel compelled to adopt a corporate stance on any issue. In a sense he served as a shield for those below him—the engineers who typically gave up creative freedom to meet management demands. To have such a leader was rare in the ranks of engineering. For most engineers in corporate America, the relationship with management was an ongoing, energy-sapping battle. Managers seemed never to understand the engineers' travails, or fully appreciate their successes. And too often the engineers who were promoted to management happily jumped on board and forgot those they'd left behind.

But Cray was not such a man. He stubbornly clung to his principles. During his grounding at ERA, he'd come to expect creative freedom. His purist approach might have been regarded as naive or unrealistic if he were working for a big auto or aircraft company, but Cray recognized that there was a profound difference between his job and the jobs of engineers at typical American corporations. Cray was always on the cusp of revolutionary new technology. His machines couldn't be designed by a committee. Committees, by nature, were always conservative, compromising, and fearful of failure. Cray was none of those things.

So Cray ignored his management. Using the extraordinary success of the CDC 1604 as leverage, he bulled ahead. He was going to build a machine fifty times faster than the 1604, and that was that.

Late in 1960 Cray gathered the engineering crew for his new machine and moved from 501 Park to the Strutwear Building, a former underwear factory. It seemed a natural move at the time, partly because the engineers could attribute it to the fast growth of the company. Control Data had outgrown the newspaper warehouse. The engineering labs were crowded; benches were pushed closer together. At the Strutwear Building, Cray's engineers could spread out and have a little privacy—or so they said. Tacitly all of them understood that one of the real reasons for the move was to steer clear of management.

By comparison to 501 Park, the Strutwear Building was a palace. It wasn't nearly as dirty as the newspaper warehouse and it didn't have any forklifts whizzing through it. The engineers set up their benches on the concrete floor in the warehouse, but the building also had office space with tiled floors. Parts of the facility even featured built-up flooring, under which they could run hundreds of yards of cabling.

The plan for the new computer, to be called the CDC 6600, was a grand one. Cray talked about lowering the machine's clock cycle to one ten-millionth of a second (10 megahertz). In any computer—even in the decades that followed—the clock cycle always served as the key measure of a machine's speed. Every calculation began with a clock pulse. The clock pulses shot out from the processor in fast succession, and the machine's logic circuits gobbled them up and used them for their calculations. Calculating required a continuous parade of clock pulses, and the faster they came, the faster the calculations could be completed. None of the logic circuits could operate without them; clock pulses made it possible to carry out all of the computer's actions. So the cycle time—the period between clock pulses—became *the* key to achieving speed.

The 1604—"the old machine"—had a clock cycle of five millionths of a second (0.2 megahertz). If Cray were successful, he would reach the factor of fifty speed increase he'd earlier set out to achieve. Even in 1960, with computer technology advancing in enormous leaps, a fifty-fold speed increase was considered ambitious, maybe overly ambitious.

Up to that time, computer architects had aimed for speed increases of four or five times. A tenfold increase was considered an achievement. Trying for more was viewed in some quarters as foolhardy. Univac's LARC machine, for example, had aimed for a hundredfold speed improvement and had been a spectacular flop, mainly due to reliability problems.

Cray would not be deterred. He and the other engineers began their quest for speed by building a prototype that employed an enhanced version of a logic circuit from the 1604. It was little more than a *multiply unit,* a computer designed only to multiply as a way of demonstrating its circuits. At first the engineers took new transistors—better ones than had been used in the 1604—and assembled them in circuits almost identical to the earlier versions. The 1604's performance was so impressive that engineers often wondered how much faster it *could* have been if Cray had used state-of-the-art transistor technology, instead of 37-cent rejects. Now they could find out.

But when they assembled the circuits with the new transistors and placed them in the multiply unit, they weren't coming close to the desired speed gains. So they stayed with the same transistors, tweaked the circuits a little bit, and tried again. Still no improvement. They kept on this way for months—designing, testing, redesigning—and the results stayed about the same. They had tweaked the processing unit so much that it was now losing reliability; much of the time it just didn't work.

By early in 1962 almost sixteen months had passed, but all Cray and his group had to show for their time and effort was the faulty multiply unit. Meanwhile, the CDC 3600—the machine launched by management—was everything Norris and the others had wanted: It used a larger instruction set and was geared for business use. And *it* wasn't running into any major design snags.

Unknowingly the stakes were silently rising for Cray and his engineers at the Strutwear Building. Though no one talked openly about it, all engineers knew what a failed project could do to a career. At best, it meant that an engineer had wasted time and money yet produced nothing; at worst, it meant that an engineer was contaminated. Failure touched almost every individual on a project and left a mark, as if each member were responsible. Only the lowest level engineers could escape unscathed. For the technical directors, it was like being the director of a movie that bombed. After one major failure a chief engineer would be viewed with a jaundiced eye; after two, opportunities suddenly disappeared.

Cray had stubbornly defied management. He'd resisted their advice and followed his own instincts. Unfortunately his instincts had led him down the hard road, and it now looked as if he were trying to do the impossible. In desperation, he decided to try a new transistor marketed by Fairchild Semiconductor. The transistor was made from silicon, the basic element of sand. Up to that time all transistors had been made from germanium. The silicon device was reputed to offer a long list of impressive electrical characteristics. One of those characteristics—fast switching speed—caught Cray's eye. It was significantly faster than the germanium transistors he'd used on the 1604.

Cray studied the performance characteristics of the new transistor and quickly started designing circuits around it. He soon learned that his new circuits were not only breathtakingly faster than his old ones, they were also much simpler. But the engineering team had already chewed up sixteen months designing a vastly different machine, and somehow they had to make up for lost time. Yet it seemed that they had less time than ever to concentrate on the machine. The business side of the operation was driving Cray crazy. Salesmen always seemed to be towing someone through the lab who wanted to meet him. Most of them were potential customers—businessmen or scientists from various government agencies who either owned a 1604 or had heard of it and just wanted to meet the genius behind it. All they really needed was a smile, a handshake, a few words with the master, little nuggets to bring back to their colleagues.

But Cray wanted silence. As the other engineers were now learning, his concentration was extraordinary. To facilitate that concentration, Cray would clear his desk of *everything* except a pad and pencil. Then he would sit for hours, scribbling Boolean logic equations and thinking. But he couldn't do it without silence. During regular hours, interruptions invariably pulled him from his Boolean world, and when he worked in his lab at home, interruptions were almost nonstop. So Cray began growing vigilant about maintaining the atmosphere around him: When he worked in the lab at night, he instructed others to detour around the halls near his office. When he was home sick, he asked Verene to silence the kids. When he drove with the family in their car, he demanded silence so he could solve design problems in his head.

For the most part, the people around him were not bothered by his demands. At work they'd all seen examples of his ability to get lost in thought. In the halls of the Strutwear Building the other engineers steered around him for fear he'd walk right into them while he concentrated. And colleagues who said hello to him knew that they might receive nothing more than a blank stare in return, while the wheels inside Cray's head worked on something else.

As the company continued to grow, Cray found it increasingly more difficult to maintain his concentration. The phone rang, customers visited, management called him in for meetings. At one point Cray disconnected the phone, then set it atop a cabinet, where it sat for days before anyone realized why it hadn't been ringing. He stepped down from his post as director of engineering, in hopes of eliminating his management duties. Still the interruptions continued.

In 1962 Cray began looking for another new facility. The Strutwear Building was too close. In characteristic fashion he decided he must move even farther from management—to another city. He and Jim Thornton considered possible locales. Redwing, Minnesota (a town known for its shoe factory), seemed a plausible spot. It was a quaint little town in southwestern Minnesota, not far from the Mississippi River. Redwing was the right size, just large enough to satisfy his band of engineers—and it was nearly an hour from Minneapolis.

Cray and Verene drove down one weekend and toured Redwing but came away unimpressed. Soon afterward, they visited Chippewa Falls to see relatives. On the way back to Minneapolis they again discussed new sites for the Control Data lab, and one of them asked, "What's wrong with Chippewa?" Cray spoke with Chippewa Falls's industrial development committee, and his search stopped. The decision was made. For Cray, Chippewa Falls offered every imaginable advantage: It was more than eighty miles from the Twin Cities; it was quiet; it was difficult to reach; it was his hometown. Those reasons alone seemed enough to Cray, but he added another: It was far from a potential target of a nuclear blast.

Early in 1962 talk of nuclear war was escalating. The Soviets had been piling up an arsenal since 1949. Great Britain had had The Bomb since 1952; France since 1960. China was rumored to be working on nuclear weapons, and Israel had purchased a 1604 computer from Control Data a few years earlier for the purpose (everyone assumed) of building its own nuclear weapon. Twin Cities contractors were selling bomb shelters, little square concrete buildings where a man could keep his loved ones and few canned goods after the blast. The shelters' thick concrete walls were designed to keep out the radiation. In the midst of all this, Cray had grown edgy. When The Big One seared the Twin Cities, he wanted to be elsewhere. No one, in his wildest fit of imagination, could imagine the Soviets pointing their weapons at Chippewa Falls.

At Control Data, Cray had given various reasons for wanting to move: privacy, control, distance from management, The Bomb. A few suspected the real reason was merely restlessness. They all knew that Cray had displayed some wanderlust since starting with ERA. He and Verene had rented apartments in Mound, Golden Valley, St. Paul, South Minneapolis. They'd rented a house on 42nd Avenue South in Minneapolis, then bought their first home in a blue-collar neighborhood on 42nd Street. They currently lived in the lakeside home in Brooklyn Center.

But most of the engineers never questioned Cray's need to move. They all knew his working habits: his extraordinary hours and his unusual need for silence. If it came time to follow him, most of them said they would. In their eyes Cray was effective, and engineers asked little else from their leaders outside of effectiveness.

Cray met with Bill Norris and laid it all out: He couldn't work this way, so close to management. He spoke quietly and courteously, but implied that he wanted a remote lab or else. He told Norris that he would arrange everything himself. He would buy the land and take care of the lab's construction. He wanted no interference from the company executive who handled buying and selling real estate. He would make his own deal with the town of Chippewa Falls.

Norris never flinched. Though known for his outspokenness and colorful vocabulary, Norris was sensitive to matters involving the creative process. By 1962 he'd spent twenty years in the pursuit of new technology, working with all manner of individuals. At the red brick school in Washington he'd worked shoulder to shoulder with musicians, bridge masters, and mathematicians. He knew that truly creative individuals couldn't be expected to adhere to the same schedules and conditions as the rest of his staff. Besides, Norris wasn't about to lose the company's technical backbone. Even if Cray's effort failed, the thought of losing him to a competitor was frightening. Norris sat back in his chair and gazed across his big desk at Cray. "Do what you have to do, Seymour," he said.

When word spread that Cray was moving again, a few of the managers rolled their eyes. No one was surprised by Cray's need for privacy, but they were stunned that the flinty Norris had acquiesced. A few days after Norris's meeting with Cray, the executive who handled real estate deals hustled into Norris's office. Cray's going *where?* To do *what?* "Are you gonna let him *do* that?" he asked incredulously.

"Oh, he'll probably do all right," Norris responded. "Anyway, he's moving." Control Data managers knew when not to push Bill Norris. His mind was made up. Cray was going, and he was taking twenty or so employees with him. And that was that.

Cray didn't care what the rest of the company thought about his move. With each passing day, the stakes rose silently. His machine was behind schedule, while the 3600 already verged on success. He'd made a point of resisting management, of following his own instincts. At this point, failure was far worse than any image problems that might be caused by his move. But to succeed, he needed quiet. He *needed* to move. So he bought some land along the Chippewa River in his old hometown, hired a friend who was a contractor, built a new lab and a new house a couple hundred yards from the lab. Then one day in July 1962 he drove to the Strutwear Building, packed up his graph paper and slide rule, and led the caravan down state road 29 to the tiny town of Chippewa Falls, Wisconsin, about eighty miles away.

In 1962 corporate relocation was a common practice. Every day, families were uprooted and resettled, as companies asked their employees to stake out new territories. There was a driving need for the change: a growing customer base; cheap, plentiful labor; gorgeous new surroundings.

But the move to Chippewa Falls fell into none of those categories. No one in Chippewa needed to purchase a $5 million computer. And Cray's new lab didn't need cheap labor—it didn't need *any* labor, with the exception of a janitor. Nor did Chippewa Falls fit into the category of a Shangri La. Those were among the reasons why the move was not financially supported by Control Data Corporation. These engineers hadn't been ordered to relocate—they'd *wanted* to. So when it came time for the move to Chippewa Falls, it was every man for himself. Everyone on the staff of fourteen engineers and four programmers sold their own homes and bought new ones. They handled their own moving expenses, helped one another load furniture into vans, and found out about schools and churches via word of mouth.

For some it was a real struggle. A young Control Data engineer named Lester Davis was unable to sell his home in time for the July move. As a result the Davis family lacked the capital to buy a new home in Chippewa Falls. So Davis moved his wife and two kids into an unheated, one-bedroom fishing cottage on nearby Lake Wissota. They spent the summer of 1962 there, with Davis and his wife sleeping on the porch while their kids used the lone bedroom. All that summer they waited, hoping that their Twin Cities home would soon sell, so they could move out of the cottage before the frigid winter rolled in. They left in October, about three weeks before their water pipes would have burst.

Still there were advantages. An engineer making $8,000 or $9,000 a year might suddenly find that his buying power had increased. In the Twin Cities, he'd be lucky to afford an 1,100-square-foot home in a nice suburb. If he didn't take a management position, that was about all he could ever expect: a little patch of lawn out front; a couple of bedrooms; a patio with a few lawn chairs and a charcoal grill in the yard. If he'd lived through two wars—World War II and the Korean conflict—such an existence seemed all he could ever ask for.

When the engineers arrived in Chippewa, their salaries suddenly looked big. They could now afford 2,000-square-foot lakeside homes—real palaces with vaulted ceilings and two-car garages.

And because land was cheap, they could buy massive tracts of it. What's more, they could now live the country-club life, complete with golf, dancing, and parties. It was a real bonanza. Most of them joined the Elks Country Club, where they were warmly received by the locals.

Even the town itself looked good. To outsiders Chippewa Falls may have been indistinguishable from a thousand other small towns across the northern states. Old two-story brick buildings lined Bridge Street, the city's main avenue. There were a couple of banks, a department store, a bakery, a few taverns, a drugstore, and a cafe. It was a working-class town—law and order, work ethic, low crime, good schools, predominantly Christian. The locals labored at the shoe factories, the plastics companies, or the brewery. Most of those who didn't work in Chippewa Falls made the daily trek to nearby Eau Claire to make automobile tires in the Uniroyal plant. After work, many of them pulled up a stool in one of Chippewa's little neon-lit taverns. It was a far cry from the opera-house culture and rich architecture of St. Paul, but that didn't bother the new residents from Control Data. Opera houses and architecture weren't high priorities for them. There were exceptions, of course, but most engineers would rather spend a Saturday evening milling out a hunk of aluminum for their transmission's valve body. Besides, most were family men and therefore tended to be more concerned with the town's ability to provide a stable environment for their kids—one of Chippewa Falls's strengths.

The real advantage of Chippewa Falls was its effect on the 6600 project. The move heightened the excitement surrounding the project. More than ever the engineers felt they were all playing a vital role in something critically important. Concern over excessive work hours or personal matters now seemed inconsequential. For most of them the work atmosphere was perfect. Despite their rather mundane public image, most engineers were exceptionally inventive people who thrived on creative energy. Without such commitment, many often found themselves switching jobs or pursuing a feverish dream of inventiveness outside the workplace. In Chippewa Falls none of that was necessary. The engineers were working on a critically important machine, and their leader was uncommonly committed to it. The new atmosphere was just what Cray had hoped for: completely detached. In that respect it was an engineer's paradise, a situation that was exceedingly rare in their profession: In the spacious new building overlooking the Chippewa River, the engineers were alone, out of the way, out of touch.

As soon as they arrived at the new facility, the crew began to realize just how detached they were. After ambling through the building's tiny lobby and sitting down in their labs every morning, they suddenly realized that they had *no* interruptions. It was a strange sensation, somewhat like sitting next to a piece of humming machinery for days on end, then having someone turn it off. The newfound peace was striking.

The advantages were even greater for Cray. He had a beautiful Prairie-style home built on the sixty-five-acre site, only a couple hundred yards from the new facility. Cray designed the home himself, and it was an extraordinary piece of construction—no one in Chippewa had ever seen anything quite like it. From the outset Cray had considered what he would need in the event of a nuclear blast, and had designed the lower level of the home as a fallout shelter. Joists in the spacious first floor were made from cold rolled steel, then topped with a four-inch-thick concrete slab. Block walls in the basement were also filled with concrete; doors between lower level rooms were fireproof. A six-foot-deep pool in the basement doubled as a potential source of potable water and a ten-thousand-gallon underground tank held enough oil to last through four winters. Construction workers were in awe of the building, saying that the basement contained more steel reinforcing than the new bank that was being built downtown. Cray also added his own inventive touch, designing an air-conditioning system that would spray water on the roof and cool the house through an evaporative process.

The best part for Cray, however, was the new home's proximity to the Chippewa lab. With the lab only about eight hundred feet away, he could work any hours he wanted. He simply shuttled back and forth by walking through the forest that separated the two buildings.

After Cray and the other engineers moved into the new facility, management intervention ground to a halt. Most of the corporate directors felt that it was too far to drive. Long-distance calling was considered more trouble than it was worth in 1962 because it required operator assistance. If a Control Data manager wanted to call Chippewa, he would have to dial a long-distance operator, give the number, then wait through a little bit of clicking and popping before being connected. In truth, it wasn't all *that* much trouble, but the minor annoyance of operator assistance was enough to discourage chitchat calls. Managers tended not to phone with minor problems or questions.

By early August 1962 the move was finished and the 6600 work effort resumed in full force. Everyone on the project still hoped to achieve massive speed gains. None of their initial goals had changed, but the stakes had grown higher: The 3600 (the compatible machine with the larger instruction set) was already enjoying success. Lawrence Livermore Lab's purchase of a 3600 increased the pressure on Cray to be successful. If he failed, it would look as if management had been right all along. If the 6600 project continued to misfire, Cray would look worse than arrogant. He would look ineffective.

To maintain privacy Cray set up strict rules regarding visitors: no sales calls, no management meetings, no visits of any kind without his permission. In the Wisconsin woods the engineers had pure, blissful, bare-bones isolation. No one—not even Bill Norris—could walk in without an appointment. If Cray was going to finish the 6600, he could have it no other way. He could tolerate no waste of time. All of the excuses for failure had disappeared.

The Chippewa lab was far more elegant than anything Control Data's engineers had worked in previously. There were no birds inside, no dishes of rat poison, no forklifts, no propane fumes, no concrete floors, no rolls of newsprint. The building was small but modern and comfortable. Low-slung, white, and boxy in the style of 1960s office buildings, the lab fit neatly into its surroundings.

Tucked deep in the woods on a bluff a few hundred feet from the Chippewa River, it was almost impossible to find, even for the locals.

Within a month or so, all the staff members settled into their new homes. Personal issues—mortgages, furniture, schools, churches, club memberships, meeting the neighbors—took a backseat to the construction of the new computer. The acclimation period at the new facility was exceptionally short. After a few weeks in Chippewa, Cray and the others came to *expect* their creative freedom. Their attitude was characterized by a feeling that this was the way it *ought* to be, as if total creative freedom were a natural right of engineers. Cray seemed to feel that his only real accountability occurred at the very end of a project, when the machine either worked or it didn't. In the meantime he made his decisions without bothering to consult Twin Cities management.

Not long after the Chippewa Falls facility opened, Cray's unauthorized purchase orders began setting off alarm bells in Control Data's accounting department. Managers were never sure if Cray was deliberately violating company policy, or if he was oblivious to it. On one occasion, he ordered tens of thousands of dollars worth of electronic components and equipment. When his engineering manager, Frank Mullaney, called him on it, Cray laughed, "Sounds like you're having one of those days." Mullaney, who was a close friend, tried unsuccessfully to explain the reasons for requiring special authorization on big orders. Purchases over a certain dollar level had to be monitored for legal reasons, if nothing else. If Cray ordered a million dollars worth of equipment and it didn't perform as agreed, the company had to have some legal recourse. Cray listened, but was still convinced that Mullaney was just having a bad day. "I had a day like that yesterday," he said. "Don't worry about it." To Cray, purchase authorizations were just another form of corporate red tape. After five years at Control Data, he still didn't know or care why such orders required authorization. To him it was make-work, something to keep management busy.

But Cray's obliviousness, his utter lack of corporate savvy, was also one of the keys to his success. It enabled him to maintain his intense focus on the technical problems at hand. As a result, he devoted the proper amount of time and energy when the biggest problems surfaced. That was critical, because the technical team now needed every bit of Cray's energy. After the switch to silicon transistors, they'd been greeted with a whole new set of challenges. The key challenge centered on the machine's new performance bottlenecks. Cray and Jim Thornton, designer of the 6600's central processing unit, found that the machine's faster clock cycle was offset by the new bottlenecks.

The cause of the bottlenecks was a simple law of nature: Electrical pulses could travel only as fast as the speed of light, and no faster. In one ten-millionth of a second, they traversed about one hundred feet of wire. But a big computer like the 6600 had *miles* of wiring. In effect, the faster clock cycle was pointless if the electrical signals spent all their time whizzing around in the wires. So now wiring delays were becoming the real bottleneck.

On the surface the solution seemed obvious: Shorten the machine's wire. But shortening the wires was a maddeningly complex task, especially on this new machine. Engineers estimated that the 6600 would need ten to twenty times as many logic elements, or *gates,* as the old machine, but if they packed all of those extra elements in a machine the size of the 1604, they would *still* have a bottleneck. They needed to pack twenty times as many gates in a machine that was *smaller* than the 1604. To accomplish that, Thornton laid the processor's circuit boards back to back, then mounted the components—transistors, resistors, and such—so they faced inward. That way he could jam sixty-four gates on one little "cordwood" package. It was a huge advance over the 1604, which had had only two gates per circuit board.

But Thornton now had another, more serious, problem: He'd solved the wiring delays by packing transistors closer together, but greater density meant more heat—*much* more heat. Up to that time, all computers had been air cooled, but if they air-cooled the 6600, with its extraordinary density, the circuits would burn up.

To solve the problem, Cray called upon the lab's mechanical engineer, M. Dean Roush. Roush was a quiet, gravel-voiced, native Iowan who had started his career with Amana, working as a draftsman in refrigerator and freezer design. His technical strength was his knowledge of window air conditioners. He knew about refrigerant circulation, air flow, and calculation of thermal loads. Early in the project, when they'd still been working at the Strutwear Building, Roush had designed a hybrid cooling system—a daring one mainly because all computers had been air-cooled up to that time. With the hybrid system, Roush intended to use a combination of refrigerant and flowing air to cool the machine. The method of operation was similar to that of a window air conditioner: Blowing air whooshed across a set of tubes containing cold Freon, then traveled on, cooling the rest of the machine. Roush had been deeply disappointed when the early versions of the 6600 hadn't worked; it meant he would have to re-design the entire cooling system.

After the technical team decided to use the dense new cord-wood packages, Roush met with Cray. Both expected the new design to need a better cooling system, but when they calculated the power in some of the machine's key circuits, they were stunned. The figures were so high that Roush suggested they abandon the hybrid cooling system. He insisted that they needed a powerful, full-fledged refrigerant cooling system, like the kind used in commercial freezers. His idea was to snake refrigerant circulation tubes between the electronics, making a physical connection to the circuit boards. Using this technique, the heat would actually creep through the boards and into the tubes, where it would be carried off by flowing Freon rather than by air.

If the hybrid system had been daring, then this new proposal bordered on science fiction. No one had ever built a computer with anything like this. Cray listened carefully as Roush explained the logic behind it. When he was finished, Roush waited for the inevitable criticism of his groundbreaking idea. He knew, after all, that his idea was complicated and expensive and on the very edge of feasibility. But the criticism never came; Cray merely nodded his head and told Roush to do it.

Roush sat down at the drafting board in his little office and laid out the details for the new cooling system. He pulled together drawings for entire computer, then wedged the cooling system's compressor, condenser, and tubing into the open spaces. After a few weeks, as he constructed a prototype for the system, he began to feel good about its feasibility. Then he received a telephone call from corporate headquarters: The company's chief mechanical engineer wanted to arrange a visit to see what he was doing.

When the corporate engineer arrived in Chippewa, he was immediately drawn to Roush's prototype. Roush explained the workings of the prototype, showing how the refrigerant flowed between the circuit boards, carrying away the intense heat, but he sensed the corporate engineer wasn't listening. The man looked at the prototype, nodded, and frowned, then he launched into a speech about the problems associated with refrigerant cooling. It was an inexact science, he said. It was far too complex, far too unreliable, and worst of all, far too costly. He suggested strongly that Roush find another way to cool the 6600.

Roush was crestfallen. Again, he had apparently wasted weeks building a prototype, only to have the idea scrapped in a matter of minutes. After the corporate engineer left the building, Roush rushed into Cray's lab, told him about the visit, and explained that he had been instructed to look for a new method of cooling the 6600. Cray never blinked. "Don't worry about it," he said coolly.

Roush thought that Cray hadn't understood. He again explained the situation, this time taking care to describe the problems of cost and complexity. Cray listened dispassionately. "Ignore it," he said again; then he shot a look at Roush as if to say that this was the end of the conversation. It was obvious that Cray had no intention of listening to management on *any* matters.

Roush resumed his work on the refrigerant cooling, eventually laying out a system that would be heralded for its innovations. He worked with the machine's other engineers to remove the heat by capping each cordwood package with an aluminum cover that connected to hollow struts on the machine's chassis. That way, when the computer circuits heated up, the heat crept through the aluminum cap to the struts, and into Freon that flowed inside the struts. The flowing Freon then carried the heat away. Roush's technique enabled them to jam more than sixty-seven hundred cordwood packages in the 6600, totaling more than four hundred thousand logic gates.

When engineers put the finishing touches on the machine midway through 1963, everyone in the lab sensed they had succeeded in a way that no team ever had before. Initial tests on the system revealed extraordinary results: They had reached their speed goals; the 6600 was approximately fifty times faster than the 1604. It used an instruction set consisting of only sixty-four instructions. Together, the smaller instruction sets, denser circuitry, Freon cooling, and silicon transistors added up to a computer of unprecedented speed. The 6600 could churn through three million instructions per second. No one had ever seen anything like it before.

Despite the isolation, word of their impending success began to trickle out of Chippewa Falls. Something unusual was happening up there in the north woods of Wisconsin, and the rest of the industry wanted to know what it was. At the time—mid-1963—the computer industry was so small that it was nearly impossible to keep secrets. Cray's self-imposed isolation slowed the normal buzz of information, but word still traveled quickly. Programmers at the Livermore lab were already anxious to buy the Chippewa crew's first machine. Word quickly spread to Los Alamos and to the National Security Agency in Washington. Everyone in the community, it seemed, had a problem that needed the speed of a CDC 6600.

In August 1963 Control Data opened the lab to selected members of the press, including the *Wall Street Journal* and *Business Week* magazine. At the unveiling, Cray sat in front of the machine's televisionlike console, describing its processor, memories, and cooling system. He quietly explained the marketing strategies and the logic behind the move to Chippewa Falls. The press was stunned, not by the computer itself, but by the apparent incongruity of this high-tech machine emerging from such a low-tech setting. A *Business Week* article prominently mentioned the fact that there was "salt lick for the deer" outside the Chippewa Falls lab, then it followed by saying that the 6600 "is several times as fast and powerful as any other computing machine in existence. In fact, nothing quite like it has ever appeared on the market before." But the article saved its highest praise for the small-team effort, saying that "Cray's staff numbers 34, including the night janitor."

Word of the team's success buzzed through the computer industry with extraordinary speed. Within days the *Business Week* article found its way to the highest offices in IBM, prompting a scathing memo from company president Thomas Watson:

> Last week Control Data had a press conference during which they officially announced their 6600 system. I understand that in the laboratory developing this system there are only 34 people, including the janitor. Of these, 14 are engineers and 4 are programmers, and only one person has a Ph.D., a relatively junior programmer. Contrasting this modest effort with our own vast development activities, I fail to understand why we have lost our industry leadership position by letting someone else offer the world's most powerful computer.

In Watson's eyes, it was a classic David-and-Goliath match, and Goliath was losing—worse, he was getting beat, not just by David, but by his janitor.

The power of the 6600 was so great that it affected U.S. foreign policy. Superfast computers now gave the United States an edge in the arms race because they enabled scientists to simulate nuclear tests, while other countries could test their weapons only by detonating them. Knowing that such machines were available, the United States had negotiated a nuclear test ban treaty with the USSR. The CDC 6600, they knew, would enable them to advance the state of the art in weapons simulation as never before. The State Department even blocked export of a 6600 to the French, fearing that they too wanted to use it for their nuclear weapons program.

By the beginning of 1964, the 6600 peaked in ways that no one, including Cray, had ever envisioned. Sales eventually reached more than a hundred, an extraordinary figure for the time, considering that the machines cost about $8 million apiece. For CDC it was a bonanza: In seven years they'd taken their operation from $600,000 in capital to $60 million a year in sales. They'd also spawned a whole new industry—building superfast machines and selling them to the weapons labs and to universities. Ultimately users of the machines coined the term *supercomputers* to describe this new breed of computers and the growing industry around them.

In Chippewa Falls the victory was even sweeter. Cray and his crew had risen to another level. They'd succeeded. They'd proved themselves, not only by building a better machine, but by building it *their* way. It was obvious that Cray was right: The best machines weren't built by committees; they were developed by small groups of talented, committed individuals. To be successful, companies didn't need huge technical staffs or minute-by-minute direction from management; they needed to be focused.

And no group was more focused than Cray's, who were now the masters of this niche business. With the introduction of the 6600, the public knew that the "Ferraris" of the computer industry were no longer developed in Philadelphia or New York, but a few yards away from a salt lick in the chilly forests of Chippewa Falls, Wisconsin.

Engineering Research Associates laboratory scene, 1951. (Photo courtesy of Charles Babbage Institute)

John Parker, president of ERA, 1950. (Photo courtesy of Charles Babbage Institute)

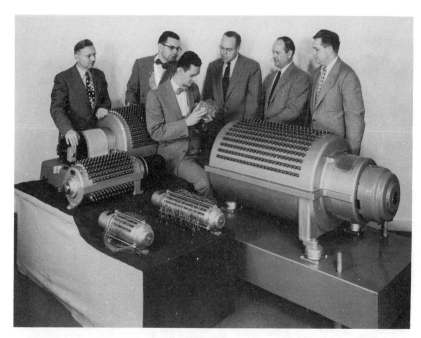

Engineering Research Associates engineers with magnetic drum
memories, an ancestor of today's personal computer hard drives.
From left to right: John Hill, Arnold Cohen, Frank Mullaney
(holding drum), Robert Perkins, Arnold Hendrickson, William
Keye, early 1950s. (Photo courtesy of Charles Babbage Institute)

Artist's rendering of ERA 1103A computer, early 1950s. (Photo
courtesy of Charles Babbage Institute)

Shipment of Control Data's first computer, the 1604, to the U.S. Naval Postgraduate School. Standing on the loading dock of CDC's first headquarters at 501 Park Avenue in Minneapolis, from left to right: William Norris, Frank Mullaney, George Hanson, and a North American Van Lines representative, January 1960. (Photo courtesy of Charles Babbage Institute)

Complete CDC 1604 system, early 1960s. The CDC 1604 had a processor speed of 5 microseconds, equivalent to 0.2 megahertz. By comparison, many desktop computers in 1996 offered speeds of 133 megahertz. (Photo courtesy of Charles Babbage Institute)

William C. Norris, president of
Control Data Corporation, 1963.
(Photo courtesy of Charles Babbage
Institute.)

A complete CDC 6600 system, 1964. The CDC 6600 is often
regarded as the first supercomputer. (Photo courtesy of Charles
Babbage Institute)

Seymour Cray at the console of a CDC 6600 computer at a press conference, August 1963. (Photo courtesy of Charles Babbage Institute)

Seymour Cray with the CDC 7600 computer, 1968. (Photo courtesy of Charles Babbage Institute)

Seymour Cray with the CRAY-1, 1974. (Photo courtesy of Charles Babbage Institute)

Cray Research's Hallie lab, 1982. Located only about two hundred yards from Cray's home, the lab was later used by Steve Chen's firm, Supercomputer Systems, Inc. (Photo courtesy of Cray Research)

Steve Chen at Cray Research, 1984.
(Photo courtesy of Cray Research)

Les Davis in front of a CRAY
X-MP/1 at a ceremony cele-
brating the shipping of the
one hundredth Cray research
system in 1985. (Photo courtesy of Cray Research)

Les Davis (left) and John Rollwagen at the Corporate Cray
Museum in Chippewa Falls,
1990. (Photo courtesy of Cray
Research)

Seymour Cray with Cray Computer's final machine, the
CRAY-4, 1993. (Photo courtesy of Cray Research)

. . . .

FIVE

The Hog Trough

Each morning as Bill Norris slid his beat-up ten-year-old Chevrolet into his executive parking space at the new Control Data complex, he admired the way the campus's modern three-story buildings blended in with the surrounding scenery. Control Data had erected the new office center in 1965 on a semirural site in Bloomington, a suburb of Minneapolis. It was an ideal setting, with rolling cornfields on one side and the Minnesota River on the other. Located only six minutes from the Minneapolis–St. Paul International Airport, Bloomington somehow maintained a rural touch that reminded Norris of his youth on the Nebraska farm.

Though Norris wasn't known as a self-promoter, he couldn't help but feel a twinge of pride each time he looked at the new complex of broad, tastefully designed buildings. He had presided over little of its construction, but had demanded that the site be large enough so that when the company expanded, the new facility would be spacious and comfortable. As a result, the office center aptly reflected Norris's view of Control Data: modern and big.

By 1965 Control Data was, above all else, big. Since its meager beginnings in the newspaper warehouse nine years earlier, Control Data had grown in astonishing leaps. From 1957 to 1959 its payroll had jumped from 11 employees to 325. With the success of the CDC 1604, the company had really taken off, growing to 1,500 employees in 1961, 2,200 in 1962, and 3,500 in 1963. By

1965 Control Data employed more than 9,000 people worldwide, 5,500 of them in the Twin Cities. It had become the third largest computer maker in the world, trailing only IBM and the Univac Division of Sperry-Rand.

Much of Control Data's growth, of course, stemmed from the sale of the CDC 1604 and 6600 computers, but the lion's share sprang from Norris's aggressive business maneuverings. In and around the halls of the new facility, the key phrase was "critical mass." Reaching critical mass was nearly an obsession, especially for Norris. He believed that the computer business would experience frequent peaks and valleys, and that if a company relied on a single product—or even a single *line* of products—the valleys could be devastating, leading to large-scale layoffs and crushing stock market losses. To avoid that, Norris strove to develop a product line broad enough to flatten out the peaks and valleys. That way, if one product failed, the others could pick up the slack.

Norris carefully orchestrated his efforts to attain critical mass. He believed that planning was the key to expansion, and even drew up a typed, twelve-page, single-spaced document to serve as the company's master plan for planning. He asked his fifty top executives to turn in regular short-range and long-range plans, from which the firm created a massive corporate master plan—the guiding light for its acquisition and expansion activities.

In a furious acquisition spree during the late 1950s and early 1960s, Norris fulfilled his desire for critical mass. His effort began with the purchase of Cedar Engineering, a firm that built servo motors, amplifiers, and other kinds of automation equipment. He later added the Computer Division of the Bendix Corporation and Holley Computer Products, a maker of printers and magnetic tape units. Peripheral equipment—tape drives, card readers, paper tape readers, printers and monitors—constituted the biggest area of acquisition. Norris snapped up any willing firm that made peripheral equipment, but he also focused on data and engineering services. In succession he acquired firms with expertise in the distribution of electrical power, gas, oil, and water. He purchased the Control Systems Division of Daystrom, the Control Corporation, and a structural design engineering firm known as

Meiscon Engineers. In all, Norris acquired eight firms in 1963 and twelve more between January 1964 and June 1965.

The point of all the acquisitions was to allow Control Data to offer an all-encompassing package of solutions to scientific and engineering customers. A customer with a need for computing power could purchase a scientific computer, tape drive, paper tape reader, or printer. Or it could buy time on a CDC 1604. *Or* it could borrow CDC's technical expertise to help it write new software programs.

The upshot was that Control Data was now a humming conglomerate, the kind often depicted in snappy 1960s public relations videos with upbeat music and authoritative voice-overs. The firm had a computer division, government systems division, system sciences division, data centers division, research division, peripherals division, and a Chippewa Laboratory. There were offices in Albuquerque, Beverly Hills, Birmingham, Boston, Chicago, Detroit, Dallas, Dayton, Honolulu, Houston, Orlando, San Francisco, Washington D.C., Germany, and Switzerland. Every few months the *Minneapolis Star*, the *Minneapolis Tribune*, or the *St. Paul Pioneer Press* seemed to be running stories with such titles as "Control Data again doubles its earnings," or "Control Data Corp. net income up 210 percent," or "Control Data reports 127 percent net gain." Since the company's founding in 1957, its stock had rocketed from $1 per share to $126 a share in 1961, then to $300 a share in 1964. Control Data was so profitable and its growth so dramatic that its stock performance transformed the lives of its serious investors. Early investors who had plowed $5,000 of their savings into the firm were now bona fide millionaires. Some were able to consider retirement while still in their thirties and forties. Friends and neighbors of Control Data employees who had blindly invested modest sums in the firm in 1957 now had the capital to build bigger homes or to start their own small businesses.

Norris, meanwhile, was taking pains to ensure that the company's growth was not misunderstood. He didn't want Control Data to be viewed as a shooting star, nor did he want to be perceived as an executive who was driving up the value of the company's stock for his own short-term gain. Though he owned ninety thousand shares of stock worth approximately $27 million, he wasn't selling it, nor was he taking an exorbitant salary. By 1965 he still hadn't cracked the $40,000-a-year plateau, and he still drove a beat-up Chevy, an old junker from his mother's farm in Nebraska.

Norris needn't have worried. For the moment all of Control Data's external indicators pointed upward. Its reputation had reached its peak. The local press could find no wrong. And its engineers were among the best in the business. For now, Control Data's problems were only visible *internally*.

In its initial seven years Control Data had enjoyed such meteoric growth that it seemed to everyone it would never end. But in 1965, with each passing day, a disturbing thought began to dawn on the company's executives, from Norris on down: Control Data had grown too fast. At first no one could believe it, but despite all the optimistic outward indicators, the company was sliding toward economic difficulties. Some of its new acquisitions were proving unprofitable; others drained the cash reserves. Many of the new firms requested funding, particularly in the peripherals area, because so many of them were woefully behind the technology curve. Some were still building equipment for vacuum tube computers. To catch up, all of them desperately needed cash.

In addition, some of Control Data's key engineers had grown restless and unhappy. In 1966 four top people—Frank Mullaney, Raymond Whitney, Edward Zimmer, and Robert Kisch—resigned during a tumultuous five-month period. Some had split with Norris over the direction of the company; others simply left for better opportunities.

Worse, the stunning speed of the CDC 6600 had awakened a sleeping giant. IBM executives were deeply troubled by Control Data's success in the supercomputer market. To them, supercomputing was the industry's high ground. It was one thing to let a little company sneak up from the bottom and steal a share of the market in some small peripherals area, but to have a competitor dominate the supercomputer market was another matter. It was offensive, an affront to the name of IBM. At a meeting of the company's officers, IBM president Albert Williams called Control Data's performance a "prestige matter," and demanded development of a machine to knock off the 6600. Pressure grew for IBM engineers to build the machine, and for salespeople to draw Control Data customers back into the IBM fold.

IBM salespeople searched for Control Data's Achilles' heel, and quickly found it. As good as the CDC 6600 was, its first year had been a litany of false starts and flaws. Though Cray's first 6600 had been a scorchingly fast laboratory machine, it hadn't fared well in manufacturing. Moving the manufacturing effort out of Chippewa Falls and into a new facility in Arden Hills, Minnesota, in the mid-1960s had only compounded the problems. CDC engineers in Arden Hills discovered that the 6600 would run for about eight or nine hours and then break down. Despite all the earlier efforts to cool it, high temperatures—up to 170°— were still building up in the memory, and causing parts to overheat and fail. Production of the CDC 6600 quickly fell behind schedule. The Livermore lab had expected a 6600 in February 1964, but didn't receive one until August. It took until early 1965 before Control Data engineers finally exorcised all of the 6600's demons.

The struggles of the CDC 6600 weren't IBM's only competitive ammunition. IBM executives knew about Control Data's economic woes and the executive resignations, and IBM salespeople recited those troubles to their customers. Control Data was struggling, they said, perhaps even facing bankruptcy. The implication behind their words was obvious: Buy a 6600 and it may not work right; worse, there might be no one around to fix it.

Conveniently, IBM salespeople offered an alternative to their customers. They alluded to a new machine called the IBM 360/90, which they said was currently under development. The Model 90, as they called it, would be several times faster than a CDC 6600, and they encouraged their customers to wait for this blazing new machine.

Within IBM, the Model 90 was a hope for the future. Executives believed it would help the company regain its lost prestige. The cost of the machine was no object, they said. If necessary they would sell it at a loss. The important thing was to beat the competition and regain the company's foothold on computing's high ground.

To many customers, waiting for a Model 90 seemed sensible. IBM was, after all, the world's undisputed computing leader. If its sales force said there was a hot new machine in the wings, then there must be one. Besides, there was this issue of Control Data's viability . . .

It wasn't long before Control Data began to feel the competitive squeeze. First, its university market dried up. Government and corporate accounts dwindled. Columbia, Princeton, Johns Hopkins, MIT, NASA-Goddard, Boeing, and a host of other customers signed contracts to buy IBM's Model 90.

Slowly, word of IBM's tactics trickled back to Norris. Control Data's salesmen kept hearing stories from their customers, and soon marched up to Norris's office to pass the word along. Norris listened to the tales and fumed. How could his people sell $8 million computers if their customers believed that CDC was going out of business? And how could IBM dare discourage its customers from purchasing a CDC 6600 by offering them a machine that didn't yet exist? IBM, he heard, hadn't even built a prototype of the Model 90, and here they were, preempting 6600 sales with it. To Norris IBM's tactics were a clear case of unfair marketing practices.

Enraged, Norris assigned a group to begin gathering evidence against IBM. The group concentrated on IBM's claims and its activity with CDC customers. Control Data presented its case to the U.S. Department of Justice, hoping to persuade attorneys there to initiate antitrust actions. But after examining two years' worth of evidence, the Justice Department decided against legal action.

At the same time, IBM engineers struggled with the Model 90. Sparing no expense, the firm poured $126 million into it, only to find it couldn't attain its goals. By the time it came out, the Model 90 was plagued by technical problems and rejected by the marketplace.

For many Control Data executives, the Model 90 fiasco was now finished. The machine was a failure, so why focus on it? Whether it had been unfairly preannounced was now immaterial, they said. Norris, however, wasn't satisfied with the Model 90's failure. He felt that the Model 90 incident had done serious damage to Control Data. Still angry over the whole ordeal, he pushed his board of directors to sue IBM. He was convinced IBM had engaged in unfair marketing practices, monopolization of the market, and violation of antitrust laws. He admitted he was unsure of the legalities, but that didn't matter. He knew right from wrong, he said, and this was just plain wrong. Norris could barely contain himself. He was telling everyone within earshot that the IBM salesmen and executives were a bunch of thugs.

When Norris announced his plan to sue IBM, Control Data's board of directors was stunned. Most felt that IBM's threat died with the Model 90. Besides, no one had ever successfully sued IBM, because IBM had an army of lawyers that could bury a company in paperwork. Control Data's board knew of no one who had ever won a case like this one. One board member flatly advised Norris against it, saying "I think it's a bad idea. They'll kick the hell out of you."

Norris, however, was ready. In a long meeting with the board, he trotted out attorneys and economists who helped him make his case. When the board asked for more authoritative legal opinions, Norris arranged for antitrust specialists to be flown in from New York and Chicago. He convinced the board that IBM had to be stopped, or its salesforce would inflict similar damage on Control Data when its new machine, the CDC 7600, came out. If they didn't address it now, he said, IBM would wreck the company.

The executive board reluctantly agreed. They would not sit idly. They would address Control Data's most serious threat.

While Norris and the executive board braced for the IBM battle, another illness silently grew within the engineering ranks like a corporate case of hypertension. Almost unnoticeable at first, it was silently feeding on itself and spreading throughout the ranks of Control Data's veteran engineers.

Amidst concerns over unprofitable acquisitions, dwindling cash reserves, and IBM's marketing tactics, most of the executives failed to notice growing resentment in the engineering ranks. That resentment was centered in the computer division, which still served as the company's backbone. The complaint was a simple one: Engineers couldn't get enough development money to fund their projects. A decade of dramatic growth had strained the budget in ways that no one had foreseen. During a two-year period Control Data had introduced sixteen new computer products. There was a 900 series and an 800 series, a 6400 and a 6800, and a big new Seymour Cray machine called the 7600. In addition, the company was also funding development of a new machine called the Star and another aggressive new Cray machine called the 8600. Each project called for substantial funding.

The company's management ranks had also swelled. There were now more managers, most of whom reported to Norris. Norris's managers eagerly insulated their leader from requests, especially ones requiring big funding. As a result, the research and development budget was nearly impossible to reach.

The engineers meanwhile found themselves struggling for cash and grumbling amongst themselves. The computer group was irate. Because they saw themselves as the creators of the company's wealth, they couldn't understand why they now had to struggle for funding. Increasingly, their task seemed akin to finding nourishment in a crowded barnyard: Each day the funding trough shrank, and each day more hogs bellied up to the smaller trough. There were people from peripherals, government services, software, and data services—all of which had products *they* wanted to develop, too.

Sadly, the engineer's paradise was fading away. The creative freedom they'd had in the early years was giving way to big company concerns. Budgets were carefully watched; plans were scrupulously laid. Control Data was growing more like IBM and less like ERA. Engineers still wanted to create, to push the state of the art, and to develop revolutionary products, but they now had less control over their own destinies.

On a rational level all of the engineers understood the logical reasons for the budget strains, but for those trying to build the industry's next great machine, the logical reasons were poor consolation. These engineers wanted to finish their machines, and they needed money to do it. But how could they hope to finish their machines while they competed with all the other hogs at the trough?

In the wooded seclusion of Control Data's Chippewa lab, engineers were busier than ever. The initial success of the 6600 had led to the creation of a family of scientific computers that offered tighter packaging, better reliability, and lower cost. For the engineers in Chippewa, that in itself was enough. Let the executives in the Twin Cities worry about diversification, they thought. They were happy to keep cranking out better, faster, cleaner machines.

Most of the computing world now recognized Control Data as the undisputed leader in the production of *scientific* machines. IBM, of course, was still the industry heavyweight. Its sale of business computers was unparalleled, and it still had 80 percent of the world's computer business. But with the failure of IBM's Stretch machine and its Model 90, the scientific computing world increasingly recognized Control Data as king.

Most of that tight-knit fraternity also recognized Seymour Cray as the world's preeminent designer. The 6600 was so fast that many scientific users found they could solve a problem in eight hours that might take a week on another machine. Never mind that the 6600 had developed a reputation for questionable reliability. Many programmers didn't care that its mean time between failures was only nine hours. Nine hours on a 6600, they said, was better than forty on a competitor. The searing speed of the 6600, coupled with the eccentric story of its creator's move to Chippewa Falls, merely cemented Cray's reputation as a genius. In April 1966 a reporter from *Fortune* magazine wrote about Cray, ". . . there is no doubt that, in a field where genius is almost taken for granted, he is a towering figure."

Recognition was a mixed blessing for Cray. It was important for him to be recognized by his customers—what better way to sell his computers? But a by-product of the recognition was Cray's new public persona. Whether he liked it or not, his name was well known in business circles, which meant that he would now be hounded by salesmen, corporate managers, and journalists. Journalists were particularly intrigued by Cray, not only by his success, but by his resistance to the media. Cray was, in a sense, forbidden fruit: The more he tried to resist them; the more they wanted to talk to him. Still, Cray wasn't giving in. He refused visits from all salesmen and corporate managers, and he resisted interviews with the press, both local and national. He had no interest in talking to reporters from *Fortune, Forbes, Business Week, The Wall Street Journal,* or any of the newspapers in the Twin Cities, Eau Claire, or Chippewa Falls. But it seemed that the walls were closing in again. Chippewa Falls was losing its luster as an engineers' paradise. The world had found him.

For the engineers around him, Cray's reticence with the media was an obvious reminder of how different he really was. As a group, engineers had little respect for reporters, believing that most were intellectual lightweights—after all, their articles about "electronic brains" were incredibly superficial and sometimes blatantly inaccurate. But most engineers secretly craved a little bit of public attention—a quote or a mere mention in a newspaper article—just the tiniest scrap of recognition. It would be nice, if for no other reason than it impressed neighbors and relatives. Engineers rarely received such publicity and it was hard to imagine resisting it. But Cray fended off reporters as if they were insurance salesmen. He wanted nothing to do with these people who compared him to Edison and called him a national hero. The question was Would any ordinary person possess the willpower and focus to resist such temptation? Many engineers claimed they were above self-promotion, but in reality most *knew* they weren't.

Cray was oblivious to it all, and not because he was above it— he never made such claims to any of his friends. He simply didn't have time for it. Just as he hadn't had the time to serve on Control Data's board of directors. He had called Norris one day in 1966 and told him that he was resigning from the board. It wasn't a matter of dissatisfaction; it was an issue of time. Driving to Bloomington was a distraction. So he resigned, though he retained his position as an officer and head of the Chippewa lab.

Protecting his time in this way helped reinforce Cray's godlike status among his fellow engineers and gave him more time to do what he wanted most: design computers. By the late 1960s he had already finished his work on the 6000 series, which consisted of spin-offs from the 6600. He then headed development of the 7600, a computer with a clock cycle of twenty-five nanoseconds. At the time, twenty-five nanoseconds was an incredibly high speed, about twenty times faster than any other machine on the market except for one: It was still only four times as fast as the 6600. For scientific labs spending as much as $8 million for a new machine, an improvement of four times might not justify the investment. Over the course of its life, the 7600 would sell briskly, but it would still achieve only about half the sales of the 6600.

For his next machine, Cray had bigger plans, much bigger. The 8600 would stretch the envelope of computer technology in a way that no machine had ever done before. In true Cray fashion, it would offer no compatibility with existing computers, instead, it would provide just one advantage: scorching speed. The 8600 would have a clock cycle of just eight nanoseconds—eight billionths of a second. Decades later a clock cycle of eight billionths of a second would still be considered fast. A 1995 personal computer with a Pentium microprocessor, for example, would have a clock speed of ten nanoseconds, making it a tad slower than the planned speed for the 8600.

To achieve that speed, Cray planned to advance the state of the art on two fronts. The first was an extension of a strategy he'd been using for years: cramming the circuits closer together. By shortening the length of wire between the circuits, he could cut the time needed for signals to go from point to point. But in the late 1960s cramming circuits closer together was a daunting task. Computer circuits consisted of a collection of discrete components—transistors, resistors, capacitors, diodes, and other devices—all of which were soldered together and placed on little circuit boards. Most components were tiny, about the size of a match head, but they were already packed so tight on the boards that it was hard to get them any closer. To achieve the speeds he wanted, Cray would have to find a way to get them closer.

The second part of Cray's technical plan was more radical. Computer makers had traditionally boosted speeds by using faster transistors and by packing circuits closer together, but Cray wanted to add a new ingredient: changing the machine's architecture. Instead of using a single processor, as everyone had in the past, he planned to use four processors working in parallel.

The concept of *multiple processors,* however, was fraught with difficulties, the greatest of which was programming. Cray had always prided himself on the simplicity of his machines. In the 1604 and

6600 his instruction sets had been spare and simple, a fraction of the size of those in competing machines, but with the switch to multiple processors, that would change. The instruction set would inevitably grow more complex, and all existing code, or software, for user applications would have to be completely rewritten.

In theory the concept of multiple processors was a good one. If a user's problem could be neatly cut in half, or in quarters, the machine could simultaneously work on various parts of a problem. But many tasks didn't easily lend themselves to parallel operations; they tended to be sequential—that is, they required the results from one set of operations before they could go on to the next. To make user applications run on a multiprocessor machine, programmers would need to make adjustments.

When he started the 8600 in 1969, Cray was confident that all of the obstacles could be overcome. The team he'd assembled for the project was essentially the same he'd used for the 7600, 6600, and the rest of the 6000 series. The only major exception was the loss of Jim Thornton, who'd been the codesigner of the 6600 with Cray. Thornton was considered an important cog, mainly because his persistence and engineering knowledge had helped make Cray's daring concepts work. But Thornton had returned to Control Data's facility in Arden Hills, Minnesota, where he was assembling the Star-100, a daring machine of his own design.

Even without Thornton, Cray still believed his crew was up to the task. The team included Dean Roush, the refrigeration engineer from Amana who'd designed the cooling system on the 6600 and 7600. He was joined by Les Davis, an engineer with a gift for orchestrating a complex team effort.

From the outset the team realized that the design of the 8600 would be far more difficult than anything it had done before. The project's goals were incredibly aggressive. As Cray saw it, the key to the tighter packaging was the use of larger circuit boards. With larger boards, he reasoned, the engineers could install more components in closer proximity. So they designed each module to use boards measuring about six by eight inches each— about five times as much real estate as they'd had on the little 7600 boards. Then they populated the boards with the transistors, resistors, and capacitors they needed and soldered the connections together.

Not long after they built the first test modules, problems surfaced. There were so many components on each board that the power requirements were astonishingly high, and each module used eight circuit boards. The first module had about three kilowatts of power running through it, power that was dissipated as heat. Three kilowatts was the equivalent of about fifty 60-watt lightbulbs, and all of that heat was contained in a three-dimensional module smaller than a standard textbook.

To solve the problem, Cray again called on Roush's refrigeration background. Roush studied the heat transfer problem, then decided to place sheets of copper inside each board. The copper, he theorized, would absorb the heat and carry it away from the boards. Special wedges attached to each end of the board transferred the heat from the layers of copper to Freon-filled bars, which carried it away.

By the time Roush finished designing the cooling system, it was enormous. It had a refrigeration capacity of twenty tons, making it twice as big as the 7600s and three times as big as the 6600s. The modules were big, too. With all their discrete components, and now with sheets of copper inside each board, they felt like one big lump of cast iron. Though a module was no bigger than a textbook, it took a strong man to lift an 8600 module with one hand.

The real problem, however, wasn't the size or the weight. The real problem was that the 8600 just didn't work right. Try as they might, the engineers could never get it to operate reliably. The modules consisted of a three-dimensional stack of eight boards, each packed with a mountain of components. Any transistor, any resistor—*any part at all*—could fail at any moment. Worse, all of the discrete parts were interconnected by a mountain of solder. Any soldered joint could fail without notice. Add to that the issue of extraordinary heat, and the 8600 looked increasingly like an accident waiting to happen.

Cray, however, wasn't giving up. For two more years he worked nights and weekends, designing, soldering, testing the parts himself. It was as if he expected to make the machine work through sheer force of will.

Midway through 1971, as the crew tried alternatives, Cray received a management memo calling for him to cut his expenses by 10 percent. He was stunned. He was in the middle of a struggling project, and they were asking him to *cut* his costs. He immediately called Bloomington and talked with the manager who'd fired off the memo. Cutting his expenses by 10 percent wasn't possible, he said. He needed more development funds, not less.

The manager explained that the cuts weren't intended to single him out—the entire company was forced to tighten its belt. It was painful, he said, because it would mean cutting his payroll by 10 percent, which would mean cutting staff members. Cray fought the move, explaining that he couldn't possibly cut staff members at a time like this. The staff of the Chippewa lab currently numbered about forty, and a 10 percent cut meant the loss of four people. Still, Twin Cities management wasn't backing down.

Finally Cray gave in. "All right," he said. "We'll cut our payroll by 10 percent, but I'm not laying anyone off. Eliminate my salary. That's about the same as a 10 percent personnel cut."

The manager was stunned. "We can't do that," he said. "It's against the law to make people work without pay."

"So, then pay me minimum wage," Cray replied. Within a few weeks, Cray's pay rate was dropped to minimum wage—about $1.25 an hour.

Cutting Cray's salary, however, didn't alleviate the problem. Nothing in Bloomington was changing, and no one there seemed to care that Cray had sacrificed his salary for the good of the project. The company's executives—Norris in particular—had begun to believe that computer services, rather than computers, were their future. Norris and the other executives were telling the media that the scientific computing market was saturated. "Everyone who needs a computer has one," Norris said.

Cray began to wonder where he and the 8600 stood. He was building a machine that could be the fastest in the world. His past machines had had an extraordinary track record. Sales of his machines—the 1604, 6600, 7600, and others—had accounted for more than a billion dollars. Yet management seemed unsympathetic to the problems of the Chippewa lab.

Cray arranged to meet with Norris. When he arrived in Norris's Bloomington office, he laid it all out: The 8600 didn't work, and if they continued with the existing design, it would *never* work. To take supercomputing to the next level, they would need to start anew. A brand-new design, a new program, more development funds.

Cray's plan was strikingly similar to one he'd proposed ten years earlier. While building the 6600, he'd gotten tangled up in the design of the processor, set it aside, and started over again. When he had re-started, he had chosen a new technology, the silicon transistor, and built the machine around it. The result had been the biggest success in the company's history.

Norris listened quietly, shaking his head. The company simply didn't have the money to fund two supercomputer projects, he said. Jim Thornton's Star-100—an enormous undertaking—was draining funds from the R&D budget. The trough was nearly empty. Besides, Norris had been through all of this previously. He remembered the 6600 all too well. It had been a nerve-racking project, a terrible risk, a real nail-biter. This whole supercomputer business was *extremely* risky, and he just didn't have the stomach to carry two supercomputer projects at once.

He stopped short of issuing a flat no. Control Data didn't have the money *at the moment* (what with all the peripherals and services and other hogs at the trough), but if Cray could wait a year, if he could put the project on "simmer," if he could leave it at a low level of funding, they could probably work it out.

Cray had the instincts of a engineer. He couldn't wait. Though he would never have said it in so many words, he needed to work on something important, something meaningful. He was constitutionally incapable of twiddling his thumbs while Control Data waited for the outcome of Jim Thornton's project.

Cray told Norris he needed some time to think. He would go back to Chippewa and mull it over, then he would let Norris know what his next move would be. But both of them knew that Cray had already made his decision.

While Seymour Cray struggled with the 8600, Control Data fought the biggest battle of its short history. Following Norris's will, it had entered into an extraordinary legal clash with IBM, and Norris and other Control Data executives were quickly learning why ordinary companies didn't tangle with the computing giant. Control Data's lawyers, the private firm of Oppenheimer, Wolff, Foster, Shepard, and Donnelly, anticipated being swarmed by IBM's legal defense. They expected to be buried in evidence, but no one foresaw the scale of what eventually transpired.

From the beginning, the case was an escalating battle of legal maneuvering. Document exchange became the chief mode of evidence gathering, as lawyers on both sides won the right to go through their adversaries' files. One by one, they picked through files, cartons, and crates, looking for the "smoking gun," the irrefutable piece of paper that would win the case for their side. The battle soon reached proportions for which neither side had prepared. The volume of documents eventually grew so great that neither team could read them all. When Control Data lawyers asked the trial judge to force IBM to turn over four thousand documents that they'd shown to the Justice Department, IBM lawyers countered with a request of their own: They wanted copies of *all* of Control Data's files from Bloomington and Chippewa Falls.

The case kept going back and forth this way, with both sides demanding access to the others' documents. In one extraordinary six-week period, Control Data supplied *eighty million* documents to IBM. One by one, a parade of IBM lawyers pulled up in black limousines at the Bloomington doorstep of Control Data, ready to shuffle, scan, read, copy, and microfilm Control Data's memos. In response, Control Data demanded *fifteen million* documents to be turned over by IBM. CDC lawyers worked at IBM facilities from dawn to dusk. On Mondays they flew from Minneapolis to La Guardia Airport in New York; on Fridays they returned home again. They slept in dingy hotels, ate in the IBM cafeteria, and waited in line like schoolchildren for IBM employees to lead them to designated work areas.

Control Data convened a special staff to aid the lawyers in their efforts. Assistants read, copied, and microfilmed documents. Then they coded the copies, typed them onto special forms, and entered them onto magnetic computer tapes with optical character recognition readers. That way, the lawyers could find documents on the magnetic tape simply by performing computer searches for key words. It was the first time that computers had played a major role in the courtroom.

After nearly two years of document exchange, attorneys began taking depositions. Control Data's team traveled to various IBM sites, interviewing executives for weeks on end, listening to a familiar chorus of "I don't know" and "I can't remember." At one point an Oppenheimer lawyer was stunned when an IBM employee, schooled in the tactics of legal evasion, replied "I don't know" when asked his age.

As the case ground on, weary Control Data executives whispered about the wisdom of Norris's decision to battle IBM in the courts. Wasn't this, after all, what everyone had expected? Hadn't Norris known that IBM would overwhelm them with paper and legal expertise? Couldn't he approach IBM and beg to settle out of court? A few managers wondered aloud if the old man—Norris was now sixty-one—had lost his marbles.

Norris, however, showed no intention of backing down. Based on repeated conversations with Oppenheimer lawyer Elmer B. Trousdale, he held tight to the belief that Control Data would win. No matter the cost in legal fees, he would pursue the case. He would not extend a peace offering to IBM, or beg its executives to settle out of court. There would be no compromise. Norris was sure that he would beat IBM, and he was not about to back down now.

Les Davis knew Seymour Cray's technical capabilities better than anyone. Since his first day on the job at Engineering Research Associates in 1955, Davis had worked directly for Cray. He'd served as a technician on the Magstec project; then in 1959 he followed a wave of engineers migrating from ERA to Control Data. When Cray later announced his move to Chippewa Falls in 1962, Davis joined him again.

Davis didn't second-guess Cray's decision. He had enormous respect for Cray's leadership and was drawn to the air of excitement that always surrounded Cray's projects. For Davis, the best part of his job was the actual engineering—That was why he'd come to Chippewa in the first place. He didn't foresee himself as a corporate manager. He'd worked long and hard to become an engineer, finally finishing his degree at age thirty-two by going to the University of Minnesota at night. He reveled in the process of building new computers: formulating ideas, watching them take shape in hardware, struggling to make them work, carrying them to completion, sharing in the glory of meaningful new products. As long as he stayed near Seymour Cray, Davis knew he would always have a chance to do all of those things.

The Cray–Davis match-up also benefited Cray. Soft-spoken and likable, Davis possessed the people skills that Cray often lacked. He was tall and thin, with a gentle demeanor that contrasted sharply with Cray's more abrasive ways. A careful listener, Davis often acted as a sounding board for his colleagues, who came to him with problems, technical and otherwise. When they shuffled into his office, looking distraught, Davis always reached for a pen and a pad of paper. Quietly, he listened and took notes. He helped them whenever he could, often without their knowledge.

Sometimes their problems involved Cray. Most of the engineers were intimidated by him. Cray was so smart and logical that many were afraid to approach him with an idea. To have their ideas shot down by the modern-day Edison was more than they could take. If their concepts were going to be rejected, better to have someone do it gently, but Davis had an uncanny knack for keeping their ideas alive. At lunchtime he and Cray would disappear, usually driving over to their favorite spot—a dark, leathery hotel restaurant called The Flame. Often, after they'd returned, Cray would have adopted a new technical concept. Among the engineers, it was commonly known that Cray listened to Davis, mainly because Cray had such respect for his technical capabilities.

Ultimately that respect was what led Cray to walk down to Davis's office after making the biggest decision of his life. Cray and Davis seldom visited each other during the workday because of Cray's well-known penchant for silence, but on this particular day Cray had news to tell Davis: He was leaving Control Data to start a new company. He'd already worked out the business and legal details with a small group of former Control Data executives that included Frank Mullaney. They'd raised about $2.5 million in venture capital, about 20 percent of which came from Cray himself. Cray had accumulated several million dollars of his own, so he felt comfortable investing half a million dollars.

Cray knew that $2.5 million didn't go very far in the supercomputer business, and for that reason his plans were modest. At Control Data it took about $50 million to develop a big machine. If he could scrounge up some more money, he would build a whole machine, and if he could find support in the user community, he might even sell two or three machines. But there was no guarantee that he could build and sell machines on the money he'd raised. If he couldn't, the new company would have to survive by doing research for bigger computer manufacturers. That wouldn't be nearly so lucrative, Cray said, but it was likely to be more fun than what they were doing now.

Davis agreed. Much of the team enthusiasm had been drained from the 8600 project by Control Data's continuing cutbacks. Besides, the executives in Bloomington seemed to think that the scientific computing market was saturated. Davis thought that Cray's new venture had an air of electricity about it. It was simple, unstructured, nonbureaucratic, and completely open-ended. Of course, it was also scary—especially for an engineer who'd be giving up a good job with a growing organization—but that was part of the appeal. It was an adventure.

The prospect was beginning to look attractive until Davis went home that night and explained it to his wife. Les and Rosemary Davis were the parents of four children, ranging in age from five to eleven. They'd purchased a big new home on Lake Wissota a couple of years earlier. So money, while it wasn't necessarily tight, was still important. As he described the new business to his wife— and the prospect of money loomed suddenly larger—it dawned on Davis that his new salary wouldn't be enough for a family of six. Somehow, in the bubbly enthusiasm of their initial discussion, Cray and Davis had agreed to work for no salary, and it had seemed perfectly plausible. But in the light of a family budget, it looked ridiculous.

Over the course of the next several days, Cray and Davis discussed arrangements, such as real salaries, in greater detail. They handpicked a small cadre of engineers, which included Dean

Roush and a few others. They had to be careful about the number of engineers they hired, because they didn't want to create ill will between themselves and Control Data.

Ultimately Davis, Roush, and the others accepted substantial salary cuts to join the new company. Davis, who made $24,000 a year with Control Data, would be losing $6,000 a year—an enormous sum for a man with a young family. Roush, who would make less than Davis, would also absorb a 25 percent pay cut. Only Cray, who made a paltry $1.25 an hour at Control Data, would enjoy an increase.

At the Chippewa lab, staff members noticed the closed-door huddles and began to suspect that a change was brewing. Shortly after Cray decided to leave, Davis threw a weekend party for the Chippewa Falls crew at his home. The Davises regularly threw such parties at their home. The informal weekend affairs were attended by the engineers, technicians, support staff, and their spouses, and ordinarily the mood at the parties was light. Much of the staff had moved to Chippewa from the Twin Cities, and the common problems of adjusting to a new town had drawn them together. But this particular party had a nervous edge to it. It was January 1972, the air was bitterly cold, and it was dark outside. Staff members huddled in the living room, talking quietly. Although most of them weren't supposed to know yet about Cray's new venture, they all sensed a change. One engineer sat silently on Davis's couch, popping antacid tablets.

Most of the staff knew that Cray was working for minimum wage; they knew that funding for the 8600 had been cut; they knew that Cray had reached a dead end with his new machine. What they didn't know was what the Chippewa lab would do if Cray left.

About eight months after their last face-to-face conversation, Norris received a grim interoffice memo from Cray. The memo, titled "Emotional Problems" and dated February 14, 1972, outlined Cray's dissatisfaction with Control Data: He recalled the rapid growth of the early 1960s and his resignation from the company's board of directors. He described his revulsion over day-to-day corporate power struggles, saying that "the games grown men play in corporate life I find revolting, and I cannot personally participate." He thanked Norris for his support in the creation of the Chippewa Laboratory, and said that as a result of that support he had remained with Control Data, instead of starting his own small company. Then he dropped the bomb: The 8600 had problems that he couldn't yet solve, and he didn't know if he *wanted* to pursue them. He had reached the point where the idea of new work—maybe even outside the computer arena—appealed to him. To do that, he said, he would need to leave Control Data. "Ten years have now passed since moving to Chippewa, and two major products were developed and delivered to customers and to larger corporate development," he wrote. "The obligation which I felt in the 1960s has slowly been amortized, and I now feel a residual of zero."

Norris gazed at the memo and slowly laid it down. He had half expected this; he knew that Cray couldn't twiddle his thumbs for very long, but he hadn't thought it would happen so soon. Within hours he was visited by other Control Data executives who'd heard the news. "What are we going to do about it?" one of them asked breathlessly.

Norris gazed back at the executive. "Hell, there's nothing we *can* do about it," he answered. "It's his life. He's got every right to start his own company."

As he spoke, the potential problems of losing Cray began to run through his mind. Cray was, without doubt, the company's most valuable technical employee. His departure would leave a terrible gap in the engineering ranks. Norris suspected that Cray might be a competitor, despite his assertion that he might work outside the computer industry. Cray could build on the expertise he'd gained at Control Data, could take its best employees, and could even compete for a customer or two.

But Norris wasn't going to launch an effort to dissuade Cray or cut him off legally. For as long as anyone could remember, Norris had always insisted that the contract between a company and an employee was an inequitable one. An employee had only one life, he often said, whereas a company could go on and on. Besides, there was nothing to be gained by blocking Cray's efforts. He knew he had to let Cray go his own way.

Not long after Norris heard about Cray's new company, a luncheon was arranged to say good-bye to Cray and the six employees who were leaving with him. It was one of the few times that Norris was invited to Chippewa Falls. He and a couple of other Control Data executives drove out to a little restaurant on Lake Wissota called Reiter's Steak House. Reiter's was just about what they had expected: a blend of small-town charm and outdoorsman decor. It had a few big picture windows overlooking the frozen lake, a big stuffed trout on the wall, and a mirrored mural of a large-mouth bass over the bar. The group retired to a small room alongside the bar, where Norris and the others gave speeches, ate, talked, laughed, and shook hands.

Norris was so supportive that Cray later approached Control Data for funding. Cray even suggested that if Control Data wanted to share in the success of the new company, it might consider taking on this "small group of rebels" as a satellite operation. Norris, however, never received word of any proposed satellite operation; the idea was lost in the layers of bureaucracy that insulated him from Cray. Norris did consider the question of financial support for Cray's company, and decided to invest $250,000 of Control Data's funds in it.

Around the halls of Control Data headquarters, the company's managers whispered that Norris must be loosing his mind. *He's giving $250,000 to who? For what?* Most of the executives believed that Cray's little six-man company wasn't even worth Norris's consideration. At best, Cray's company would fold in two years; at worst, it would be a competitor. So why fund it?

Norris had always been a pushover for people with passionate ideas. He had a hunch about Cray, and he wanted to invest to show that there were no hard feelings. "Heart money," he called it.

To those who dared openly question his judgment, Norris was his typical blunt self. "Damnit, Seymour's made a great contribution to this company," he roared. "Besides, Seymour's gonna do what he's gonna do. If he's successful, we might as well get something out of it."

The issue eventually faded away. Within a few months the managers at Control Data didn't give Cray a second thought. His company couldn't possibly dent the armor of Control Data, everyone said. It was too small and vastly underfunded.

Control Data had more important matters to consider.

. . . .

SIX

The CRAY-1

The windowless thirty-by-thirty-foot room had no tile on the floor, no plaster on the walls. A single door served as its exit to downtown Chippewa Falls; a coat of white paint was splashed on the interior of its concrete block walls. Two metal desks and a drafting board were the room's only furniture. All in all, the new facilities of Cray Research befitted a company of modest goals.

Not that anyone talked about goals. From the outset the firm's objective had been so vague that it seemed pointless to talk about it. The engineers knew they wanted to build a machine and sell it, but no one was sure whether that was feasible. Even cloudier was the notion of a backup plan: What would the company do if it lacked the funds to build a computer? The firm's very name, Cray Research Corporation, had been a hedge against that possibility.

Despite the dubious sense of mission, everyone seemed to know what to do. On the first day, Dean Roush sat at his drafting board in the big empty room and began kicking around some ideas with Cray: If we use this kind of processor module, how much heat will it generate? Where will we put the cooling elements?

In some ways, the new effort seemed like a continuation of the 8600 program. Cray was seated in his chair in a sparsely furnished office in Chippewa Falls, talking about a new machine. It was vintage, bare-bones, no-nonsense Seymour Cray simplicity: The undistracted pioneer working in a room resembling an inventor's basement, surrounded by a few close friends, laying out the plan for his next technical masterpiece. His goals were the same—he still spoke of computing speed as if it were the Holy Grail.

In another time, in another place, Cray's seat-of-the-pants approach might have been ludicrous. To introduce a new product to a mature industry without so much as a marketing plan would be tantamount to corporate suicide. Auto executives, for example, typically surveyed potential customers, categorizing them by age, income, education, neighborhood, family size, geographic region, driving habits, political beliefs, and a hundred other little characteristics that composed a customer profile. *Then* they built their product. Never, in any mature industry, could an engineer singlehandedly target his market, then build a product around his own technical whims.

But this was not a mature industry. Cray understood that. He was creating a *revolutionary* product, rather than an evolutionary one, so he conceived it on simple gut instinct. His few competitors could do it any way they wanted. Let them survey it, study it, categorize it, analyze it, dissect it, and generally pick it to pieces. He didn't care. Cray knew his customers would pay for a big advancement in speed, and he was going to give it to them.

To achieve that speed, he made one technical assumption from the outset of the program: The machine's processor would not use discrete components. Though no one said it, everyone understood that discrete components—individual transistors, resistors, and capacitors soldered onto a circuit board—were the cause of the 8600's failure.

The new machine, not yet officially dubbed the CRAY-1, would use *integrated circuits*. The integrated circuit was not a terribly new idea, having been invented fourteen years earlier in September 1958 by Jack Kilby at Texas Instruments, but it represented an enormous step forward in the history of electronics. No bigger than a baby's fingernail, an integrated circuit incorporated transistors, diodes, resistors, and capacitors on a single chip of silicon.

Cray had avoided the use of integrated circuits, or chips, for nearly six years. As early as 1966, when he'd started on the CDC 7600, integrated circuits were commercially available at about five dollars each, making them roughly equivalent in price to a pile of discrete components. Even then, engineers understood the advantages of integrated circuits: They eliminated the need for careful hand soldering of individual components to a printed circuit board.

But Cray had always made a point of lagging a generation behind the technology curve. That was precisely what he'd done on the 6600—using the silicon transistor almost a decade after its introduction. That was also what he'd done on the 1604—employing the transistor about a decade after its introduction. By operating in this way, he said, he could let others make the first mistakes. Over time that approach had become a Cray hallmark, and no one in the supercomputer industry was about to question the design wisdom of Seymour Cray.

In 1972 Cray knew it was time to use integrated circuits. The U.S. military had employed them for nearly a decade, and the Apollo space program had purchased more than a million of them in the course of landing a spacecraft on the moon. Besides, the painful adventure of the 8600 had proven that Cray now *had* to use them. In the 8600 he had tried to shorten wire lengths by packing discrete components closer together on bigger boards, but the strategy backfired. Tens of thousands of soldered joints constituted a reliability nightmare. Even if a solder had a 99 percent chance of being reliable, as most did, the chance of one failure among ten thousand such solders was overwhelmingly high. The integrated circuit eliminated all but a few of the soldered interconnects. And with its tiny components, it lowered the power and heat dissipation in the processor module. So the decision was obvious.

In a way it was ironic that a packaging failure should have put Cray here in the first place. In the history of supercomputing, failures had far outnumbered successes, but most of the flops were failures of logic. The Livermore–Univac LARC fit in that category. So did IBM's Stretch and its paper machine, the 360/90. Control Data's Star-100, which had swallowed up $75 million in development funds, was now heading toward similar failure. Texas Instruments's Advanced Scientific Computer and Burroughs's ILLIAC IV computer also suffered logic and architecture-related problems, and were on their way to reaching the grand sales figure of four machines between them.

Cray's 8600 had failed in packaging, not logic. He had tried to carry the old technology a step too far, but his reputation for producing machines of elegantly simple logic was intact. Cray intended to maintain that reputation by writing the Boolean equations for his new machine. Unlike most of the engineers who headed supercomputer teams, he still wanted to do the basic calculations. A pencil and a pad of graph paper were still his most powerful tools. That was one of the reasons why Cray insisted on an ultraquiet work environment.

While laying out the plans for the CRAY-1, Cray also worked with his grade-school chum, Pat Durch, to design a lab for the new company. Durch had built the Control Data Chippewa Laboratory and Cray's home in 1962. In 1972 he would build another lab on the same property. All three buildings—the home, the Control Data facility, and the new Cray Research lab—would be located within a few hundred yards of one another. Despite its proximity to Cray's house, the new lab was located on the other side of the Chippewa Falls border, in a neighboring town called Hallie. As a result, it was informally dubbed the Hallie lab. With the construction of the Hallie facility, the laboratories of the world's two most powerful forces in scientific computing would now stand within walking distance of each other, and all three buildings would reside on Cray's personal property.

Cray helped with the layout of the new lab and asked Roush to select office furniture. By the time they occupied the new building in September 1972, more of the crew had joined them. Les Davis, who'd been asked to stay on board with Control Data for two extra months, was now in the fold, along with a few more engineers and technicians.

Because the goals for the new company were far more modest than those of Control Data, the new lab was considerably smaller. It was only about 10,000 square feet, making it less than half the size of Control Data's 24,000-square-foot Chippewa Lab.

No one, however, complained about lack of space. Nor did anyone dare to suggest that this tiny band of rebels might one day be the chief competitor to the large and powerful Control Data Corporation.

While Seymour Cray set the stage for his next great machine, Control Data Corporation prepared for the biggest moment in its history. Bill Norris had beaten IBM. Despite the whispering of Control Data executives and the wavering confidence of his executive board, Norris had stubbornly clung to his conviction that

IBM could be beaten in the courts. Late in 1972 it was obvious that IBM shared Norris's conviction. A few months earlier, IBM lawyers had begun talking about settling out of court. The subject had first been introduced in a tavern, over drinks, after one of the court sessions, but it slowly dawned on Control Data lawyers that it was more than cocktail talk. Although there hadn't been a "smoking gun" on either side, Control Data lawyers had found a collection of memos implying that IBM had marketed phantom machines. The documents also proved that they'd been willing to sell those machines at a loss in order to drive Control Data from the market.

The settlement talk trickled back to Norris. Control Data executives now urged him to call IBM president T. V. Learson. "Hell, no," Norris replied. "If Learson wants to settle, let him call me." Learson told associates that he would not call Norris at the office. Months passed again without resolution, before Learson finally got word to Norris that he would call him at home. The two talked, eventually agreeing to meet at a neutral site—away from the prying eyes and ears of the press—to hammer out the basic elements of a settlement.

Norris's first meeting with Learson took place at a second-rate, single-story motel in Omaha, Nebraska. Learson offered a financial package he valued at $150 million. Although the package included the sale of IBM's Service Bureau Corporation for a bargain-basement price, Norris turned it down. Norris badly wanted the Service Bureau Corporation because he believed it would strengthen Control Data's ability to sell computer time, but the entire package, he said, must be valued at $200 million rather than $150 million.

About two weeks later on December 21, 1972, Norris again met with Learson at a hotel in Bloomington, where they finally agreed on the settlement he wanted. IBM's payment to Control Data included $15 million in cash for legal costs and $26 million for fringe benefits for Service Bureau personnel. Norris later explained his demand for the cash payments by recalling the words of his father: "Always get cash when selling mules."

Norris was suddenly a hero. Newspapers in Minneapolis and St. Paul ran front-page business stories on the settlement, saying that Control Data had accomplished the impossible—it had beaten

IBM in a legal battle. In the process Norris had also significantly strengthened the company, adding an important business unit that would grow in value over the years. Norris, who was always good with the press, provided reporters with the proper tone for their stories, saying that the Service Bureau would be a "valuable and growing asset" and "a significant stride in our increasing emphasis on data services." All of the stories emphasized the broad vista of opportunities that now lay at Control Data's doorstep. The words *expansion* and *growth* were repeated over and over again.

Lost in the celebration was the diminishing role of the company's scientific computer manufacturing capability. Control Data's Chippewa Laboratory would soon close. It's Star-100 machine was struggling. The subtle message was that for the company to grow, it must now move into services, and away from the manufacture of scientific computers. Norris and the other executives still wanted to sell scientific computers, but that was a niche market; the real growth was in other areas.

And who could argue? The company was growing, creating more jobs. The stock was up. And IBM was now a more careful, if not less formidable, opponent. The executives at Control Data had seen the future, and their vision was paying off.

From the first day that they moved into the Hallie lab, all of Cray's engineers had a warm feeling for the new machine they were building. Almost immediately there was an inexplicable sense that everything was falling into place, that all of the parts would work right. The only sources of anxiety were on the business side, as the company's managers in Bloomington tried to raise more development money.

For the engineers—all of whom had worked on the CDC 8600—the CRAY-1 program was a cheery experience. Unlike the 8600, it had an upbeat, positive feel to it. Management issues were kept to a minimum. And funding, at least for now, was sufficient.

The real difference was that the engineers weren't overextending themselves. The 8600 had been a stomach-acid special, the kind of project that kept popping into mind day and night as engineers continually worried about making the next deadline. The problems on the 8600 had been numerous: In trying to endow it with an incredibly fast clock speed, Cray had employed bigger boards, tighter packaging, and a three-dimensional module configuration. *And* he tried to incorporate four processors. At best, one of the goals might have been achievable; together, they were impossible. A group at the Control Data Chippewa lab (which was only about three hundred yards away) was now finding that out. One of the CDC engineers had somehow convinced Norris that he could finish the existing 8600 project on a limited budget. That engineer was currently experiencing the maddening task of making several new technologies work in concert.

On the CRAY-1, there were no such worries, because its program objectives were far less ambitious. The first thing Cray did was *back away* from the 8600's clock speed goal; instead of eight nanoseconds, he aimed for twelve nanoseconds. Had anyone else backed off in this way, it would have been viewed as cowardly. Supercomputer technology was advancing in such great leaps that a speed improvement of 100 percent or 200 percent seemed inconsequential. To suggest that a machine should be *slower* than its predecessor was unheard of. But when Cray had proposed the 8600 in 1968, his goals had been so incredibly ambitious that no one, as of 1973, had as yet come close to them. So it was now possible for him to back off his earlier goals and still build the fastest computer in the world.

Reaching the new clock speed goal seemed, by comparison to the 8600, easy. Employing integrated circuits, the engineers shortened the wiring paths. The integrated circuit, by its nature, offered tighter packaging. Each of the little chips, or ICs, as engineers called them, incorporated the basic elements of a circuit. So by using ICs, an engineer could jam more circuits on a board.

Despite this tighter packaging, each CRAY-1 module was far less cumbersome than the earlier 8600 modules had been. Instead of a football-size unit, the CRAY-1's modules were nearly flat and relatively light. Each was smaller than a sheet of looseleaf paper and measured only about a half-inch deep. Engineers packed 144 integrated circuit chips on each side of the circuit board. About five hundred such modules made up the machine's entire processor. The resulting processor modules seemed impossibly dense. Each of the chips used two gates, or logic elements. So the entire processor, which incorporated 144,000 chips, had approximately 288,000 logic gates. Two decades later, when engineers would fit more gates than that on a *single* chip, the CRAY-1's density would seem trivial.

By comparison to its predecessors, the CRAY-1 was an extraordinary machine. When the CDC 6600 had come out a decade earlier, it incorporated a hundred thousand gates and was nearly the size of a small garage. The CRAY-1 would be far smaller, and its resulting compactness yielded shorter wire lengths and therefore greater speeds.

From the beginning Roush worked with Cray on the machine's cooling needs. This time they had no intention of being blindsided by unexpected heat problems. Because of its density, the CRAY-1 actually generated more heat than the 8600, but the CRAY-1's modules were flat rather than boxy, so it was easier to remove heat.

To cool the machine Cray and Roush devised a scheme in which they laid the modules horizontally, then stacked them in tower formations about six feet high. A "cold bar," which contained flowing Freon, ran from the top to the bottom of each tower, contacting each module along the way. As a result, the heat traveled from the modules to the cold bars, into the Freon, and finally into cooling equipment located at the base of the machine. Roush used a forty-ton refrigerant system—about twice the capacity of the 8600. In an unusual touch, Cray enclosed the cooling equipment inside a series of upholstered seats that looked like window boxes. The upholstered seats, he said, would provide maintenance technicians with a place to sit and warm themselves while they worked on the CRAY-1.

Years later when Cray Research opened a software facility in Mendota Heights, Minnesota, the company used CRAY-1 machines to warm the unheated building during Minnesota's frigid winters. To visitors, it seemed implausible that a building so large, without a working furnace, could be warmed by the operation of supercomputers, but it was no surprise to Roush, who had spent thousands of hours trying to get the heat out of the machines.

The biggest challenge to the new machine was the implementation of a concept known as *vector processing*, in which a computer performs mathematical operations on long strings of numbers, rather than doing each calculation individually. To perform a string of A + B = C calculations, for example, the vector machine would store all the As in memory, then store all the Bs in memory, then do all of the calculations at once. Vector processing was far faster than traditional *scalar* calculations.

The vector concept had already been tried on the CDC Star-100, and engineers had run into a rash of processing difficulties. The problem was that few tasks lent themselves to vector techniques. As a result, any engineer building a vector machine needed to include both a vector processor and the traditional unit known as a scalar processor. But coordination of vector and scalar processing had been a nightmare for CDC engineers, and many of the problems were never fully worked out.

Cray recognized the mistakes of the earlier program and made sure he learned from them. He openly admitted that he was lucky to have had someone else to blaze the trail for him. "The pioneer never wins," he said, referring to the Star-100. "It's always easier to be the one who goes second."

On the CRAY-1, Cray took full advantage of the work of his predecessors; in particular, he built on the efforts of Jim Thornton's Star-100 machine, created at Control Data. He vastly simplified the Star-100's vector processing, using less complex control schemes to pass signals and data between the memory, vector processors, scalar processors, and the controller. What's more, vectors were kept short—all had fixed lengths of sixty-four numbers.

His success with vector processing underscored Cray's particular genius in designing workable machines. For a man widely recognized as a brilliant inventor, Cray was remarkably conservative in his use of technology. He took great care in implementing new ideas, often waiting a decade, as he had with integrated circuits, and refusing to serve as the pioneer unless it was absolutely necessary. Cray invented when necessary and took the easy route when he could. His ability to balance theoretical underpinnings with remarkable practicality was what made him so ungodly successful.

The most prominent ingredient in Cray's success on the CRAY-1 was his gifted staff. Few times in the twentieth century had a staff worked with such technical harmony. In all areas where one engineer's expertise left off, it seemed that another's began. Cray had handpicked the best and the brightest from Control Data's technical staff as early as 1962, had brought them to Chippewa with him, and then winnowed the staff down further when he'd started Cray Research. As a result, engineers such as Davis, Roush, and Harry Runkel had hit the ground running when they'd arrived at the Hallie lab. Cray also added a small contingent of new, young engineers with the practical qualities he valued. These included Alan Schiffleger, a "young Seymour Cray" with an uncanny knack for designing a machine's control system, and Jerry Brost, who would one day rise to vice president of engineering with the firm.

The most prominent member of Cray's staff was Les Davis. Although Cray masterminded the architecture and showed the way toward innovation, it was Davis who made the machines work. In Chippewa the saying among engineers was "When Seymour drops the design out the window, Les catches it." Davis was always the first to identify the risks and the first to nudge the team forward when their course grew too conservative. After nearly twenty years of working for Cray, he had gained Cray's understanding of what worked. He oversaw the design for the memory, disk drives, input/output, cooling, and virtually every other aspect of the machine. In his soft-spoken way Davis blended talent, handled egos, and built confidence, and it was Davis, the street-smart engineer, who made the machines go.

By 1974 all of the early indications convinced the engineers that they'd created a winner. Nothing like the CRAY-1 had ever been built before. When they began to run tests, the engineers were measuring such eye-popping speeds that they could barely believe them. In the vector mode, the machine was regularly mowing through 80 million floating point operations per second, and engineers suggested that its peak speed could be twice that. In any mode—vector or scalar—it was the world's fastest computer.

Cray knew, however, that tests on stripped-down machines weren't enough. They needed more funding to finish the machine. They needed more space to carry out their growing effort. And they needed a customer.

While the engineers in Chippewa pieced together the CRAY-1, the company's missing ingredient sat in a barber's chair in Bloomington, Minnesota. John Rollwagen, a thirty-two-year-old salesman for International Timesharing Corporation, was getting his hair cut in the basement shop of an office building near the Minneapolis–St. Paul Airport.

Rollwagen, an affable salesman who'd started his career with Control Data, still knew many of the faces in the supercomputer business; however, Rollwagen could not recognize any of those faces when he removed his eyeglasses, as he'd done for the barber. Sitting in the big chair, gazing blankly at the blurry world around him, the nearsighted Rollwagen thought he sensed movement near the shop's door. From the man in the barber's chair next to his, Rollwagen learned that someone had waved at him—a former Control Data employee named George Hanson. Hanson, who had an office on the first floor of the building, had been a key figure in Rollwagen's life. He served as a scoutmaster in the St. Paul neighborhood where Rollwagen had grown up. He'd also helped Rollwagen secure a summer job at Control Data during his college years at Massachusetts Institute of Technology.

When he arrived at Hanson's first-floor office, Rollwagen was surprised to find the name of an unfamiliar company on the door: Cray Research Corporation. As a former employee of Control Data, Rollwagen had heard of Seymour Cray. In fact, he idolized Cray, although he'd never raised the nerve to talk to him. Rollwagen renewed acquaintances with Hanson and listened to a brief update on the status of Cray Research. Hanson suggested that the new company might eventually have a position for him, and implored Rollwagen to stay in touch.

For Rollwagen, the prospect of working for Cray Research was an intriguing one. Rollwagen was a bright, technically oriented, business-savvy salesman with an eye for growing companies, and he had the ideal background for Cray Research. A St. Paul native, he'd been an outstanding student in high school, a National Merit finalist, and an avid electronics hobbyist who built high-fidelity audio kits in his bedroom. At age sixteen he'd heard the beeping of the Russian satellite *Sputnik* on the radio, and answered the national call for engineers that were needed to win the space race. He graduated from Massachusetts Institute of Technology with an electrical engineering degree, then entered Harvard, where he earned an MBA. He later returned to Control Data and sold the machine widely regarded as the first supercomputer, the CDC 6600.

Rollwagen kept in touch with Hanson for nearly two years, and early in 1975 Hanson suggested that it was finally time to meet with Cray. Cray and Rollwagen met for lunch at the Minneapolis Club, a limited-member organization in downtown Minneapolis frequented by attorneys and wealthy businessmen. The two hit it off immediately. An easy conversationalist, Rollwagen was unlike most of the engineers Cray knew. A former college hockey player, Rollwagen was still trim and athletic looking. He was well dressed, technically knowledgeable, and had the smooth delivery of a salesman. And Rollwagen was impressed with Cray's wit and uncultivated charm. Despite the recluse label usually tacked on him, Cray could be charismatic. For three hours they discussed various issues without once touching on the subjects of Cray Research or a job. Then Cray offered to drive Rollwagen back to his office. As Cray drove out of the club's parking lot, he turned to Rollwagen: "Well, John, why don't you think about it for a few days and give me a call."

Rollwagen was bewildered. "Think about what?" he asked.

"I think you ought to join up," Cray replied.

Rollwagen agreed to consider it, although Cray hadn't yet mentioned money or position. He thought about it over the following weekend, then called Cray on Monday and accepted the offer. Cray was elated. "Terrific," he said. "Can you come over today and get started?"

"No," Rollwagen responded. "I think I have to give my bosses some notice first." With each word from Cray, Rollwagen was amazed at his own actions. Here he was, a thirty-four-year-old Harvard MBA who'd recently been promoted to vice president of his company, accepting an offer without knowing what he would do or how much he would be paid. But Cray seemed to expect his faith and that expectation was disarming, especially for someone accustomed to the ways of the corporate world. Cray's methods weren't planned or measured or intended as a test; they were simply the actions of a man who wanted to do business on the basis of sincerity, and who was unaccustomed to practiced corporate technique. Rollwagen's faith in Cray was rewarded when he was offered the position of vice president of finance.

Cray's hiring methods should have served as a precursor to the seat-of-the-pants, get-it-done nature of Cray Research, but for Rollwagen the Cray Way hadn't sunk in yet. He was still accustomed to the slower, more structured ways of the typical corporation. So when he joined Cray Research a few weeks later, Rollwagen was stunned to find himself thrown into a pressure cooker.

Though the Hallie lab team was unaware of it, management in the Bloomington office had been struggling to scrounge up enough cash to build the CRAY-1. The development team was spending about $42,000 a month—far less than they had spent at Control Data, but still enough to build substantial debt. Mullaney and the others in Bloomington had sold debenture bonds to raise additional cash, but were still coming up short. In August 1975 the company had enough money to last for only forty-five more days.

When Rollwagen had first accepted the job, Cray explained that he'd secured a $5 million bank loan. During his first management meeting, Rollwagen learned that the $5 million bank loan had fallen through. As Cray made the announcement, all eyes at the table turned toward Rollwagen. He was, after all, the Harvard MBA. The people at the table, experienced as they were, looked to Rollwagen to show them some way to keep the company afloat. Who better to save the company than the new financial officer? Eager to impress his new bosses, Rollwagen quickly set to work on the task of finding new funding. Within weeks he learned that some of the earlier debenture bonds had gone unsubscribed, so he found a list of Cray Research investors, picked up the phone, and started pitching. He ended up selling $600,000 worth of bonds, then he called a bank and lined up a $1 million loan.

If Rollwagen thought that Cray would be pleased by his performance, he was wrong. In October Cray walked into the Rollwagen's Bloomington office. "John," he said, as Rollwagen prepared himself for a round of compliments, "I don't want to borrow any money."

Rollwagen was astounded. "You don't want to borrow any money? We just set up this bank line so that we would have enough to make it through next year."

"Well, yes, I know," Cray replied. "But I just don't like to borrow money. I think we ought to take the company public."

Rollwagen was speechless. He was beyond the point of gentle persuasion. "You've got to be crazy," he said. "The market's all dried up. We're two million dollars in debt and we don't have a product to sell yet." Rollwagen said he would gladly fly to New York to talk to investment bankers about a public offering, but he doubted that any would go for the idea.

"You're probably right," Cray responded, "so why don't we just sell it ourselves?"

Rollwagen was appalled. That strategy had worked eighteen years earlier when Willis Drake had sold dollar-shares of Control Data stock out of the back of his station wagon. But in 1975, with the stock market on the skids, it was an unlikely prospect.

Seeing Rollwagen's concern, Cray tried to console him. "The public offering will work, John," he offered. "Next year is an election year. The market is always up during election years."

Cray's words did little to bolster Rollwagen's confidence. Because it was expected of him, he would go to New York and do his best to secure more capital. But he couldn't imagine why anyone would want to invest in a struggling supercomputer company at a time like this.

In 1975 there was little reason to believe that a public offering by a supercomputer company would be greeted with open arms by investors. Control Data, Texas Instruments, Burroughs, IBM, and the Univac Division of Sperry-Rand appeared to be searching for more lucrative markets. Tom Watson, son of IBM's founder, was now backing away from supercomputing, saying that he "couldn't compete with Control Data for the same reasons that General Motors couldn't compete with Ferrari in building two-hundred-mile-per-hour sports cars."

But Control Data was only slightly more enthusiastic about the high-end market than IBM. With its recent acquisitions, Control Data had grown overnight to become the world's largest supplier of computer *services*. In an ominous move for the future of super-computing, it had closed the doors of its Chippewa lab after engineers there had been unable to carry on Cray's work and finish the 8600.

Burroughs, Texas Instruments, and Univac were edging away from the supercomputer industry as if from a bad smell. The general feeling seemed to be that supercomputing was a risky niche market that was primarily controlled by Control Data. And even Control Data didn't seem anxious to deal with the risks.

The other view of the market—the optimistic one—was held by those who said that the apathetic approach of the computing giants was leaving a gaping hole for some ambitious newcomer. The key for that newcomer was to find a guru—a rare individual who knew how to build a supercomputer and make it work.

At Cray Research, of course, everyone felt that they'd already found the guru—Seymour Cray. What they didn't know was whether the rest of the industry shared their feeling. Chippewa Falls was so insulated, so far from its user base, that it was sometimes difficult for the engineers there to know whether they were practicing self-delusion.

The truth was that Cray may have been more revered *outside* of Chippewa than inside. One of the best indicators of that occurred in 1973 when Sidney Fernbach asked Cray to speak to "a small group of computists" at the Lawrence Livermore Laboratory. Because Fernbach was a critically important customer, Cray agreed to do it. As soon as word got out that Cray was speaking, the phones in Lawrence Livermore's computer lab had begun ringing. The calls came first from assorted departments around Livermore; then from Los Alamos, New Mexico; then from other government labs around the country. One engineer even called from Lucerne, Switzerland. All of the callers asked whether the programmers could squeeze them into the lecture.

Among programmers, Cray was still the unchallenged master of supercomputer design. Many programmers hadn't heard about Cray's failure with the 8600; of those who had heard, most didn't care. Users still described his machines as "symphonies of tight design." Anyone who truly understood the logic of software had only to look at the instruction sets of his machines to appreciate Cray's economy of thought. The performance of his machines—coupled with his well-known eccentricities—created an extraordinary mystique. Programmers wanted to attend his lecture not only to learn about supercomputing but to see Cray's face and hear his voice. They wanted to shake his hand, to share a moment, to offhandedly tell their colleagues—in casual conversation, of course—that, yes, they'd spoken with Seymour Cray.

When Cray arrived at the Lawrence Livermore lecture, he was stunned. He had expected to talk to a handful of local programmers. Instead he was greeted by dozens of programmers from around the country, some carrying tape recorders, others capturing the event on videotape. His reputation had grown to the point where he was generating the wide-eyed wonder and uncritical acceptance usually reserved for celebrities.

John Rollwagen, of course, had no way of knowing about that 1973 lecture when he flew to New York to launch Cray Research's public offering early in 1976. In New York, Rollwagen spoke to as many investment bankers as he could, relating the genius of Seymour Cray and the apparent gap at the high end of the market. To his surprise, investors expressed immediate interest in the new company. Many had followed Seymour Cray's career and were anxious to invest. In all, seventy firms agreed to underwrite Cray Research's public offering.

On St. Patrick's Day, 1976, Rollwagen and the rest of the company's employees learned how powerful a tool Cray's reputation was. Cray Research, offering six hundred thousand shares of common stock on the over-the-counter securities market, generated $10 million in a matter of days. The sudden infusion of cash enabled Cray Research to pay off its debts and start construction on a new development facility in another part of Chippewa Falls. Up to that time, the firm's growing employment rolls (Rollwagen was the thirty-eighth employee) had forced it to rent additional space in a shoe and boot factory.

Most important, the cash infusion enabled the engineers to finish construction of the CRAY-1. Everyone in the engineering staff agreed that they'd created the best and fastest supercomputer in the world. Now it was just a matter of convincing a customer of that.

Although John Rollwagen had earned an MBA from Harvard and was therefore expected to be a financial wizard, his real strength was selling. He enjoyed selling. And with his MIT background, he was unintimidated by the scientists and programmers at places such as Lawrence Livermore and Los Alamos. With customers, he was a master conversationalist—smooth, likable, and technically knowledgeable. Rollwagen's selling prowess, along with his desire to care for the investment of his new banking friends in New York, led him to step aside as vice president of finance. He personally hired his own replacement, John Carlson (from the giant accounting firm of Peat, Marwick, and Mitchell), and moved into the newly created position of vice president of sales.

There had previously been no need for a sales department, but as engineers put the finishing touches on the CRAY-1, Rollwagen prepared to sell the first machine. It was a role that he relished, having cut his teeth in the industry by selling CDC 6600s a decade earlier. One of Rollwagen's greatest assets as a salesman was his uncanny knack for plumbing the depths of his customers' egos and finding out what they needed—beyond the obvious circuitry and computing cycles. He recognized that supercomputer purchases were only partially driven by practicality.

Through his earlier experiences with Control Data, Rollwagen knew that government labs were always trying to collect status symbols to aid them in the battle against other government labs for funding and contracts. Hiring big-name scientists was one way for a lab to distinguish itself. Wide media coverage on a lab's story—especially in the *New York Times, Washington Post,* or *Time*—was another way. A third way was to garner the funding for a big technical toy. That was where supercomputers fit in. Supercomputers had developed into one of the great government status symbols of the 1970s. Having one enabled a lab to brag that it had the best and fastest computing capabilities in the world. It also served as a wonderfully scenic tour item when dignitaries walked through a building. The sight of the huge computers blinking and spinning their tape drives in a spotless white room created a science-fiction-like atmosphere.

For a clever salesman like Rollwagen, the fierce status competition between labs was a powerful tool. He exploited it by offering Serial Ones—the first machines of their kind—to as many customers as he could. Serial Ones were a tremendous status symbol; having one was a little bit like having the first Corvette to roll off the assembly lines. A lab manager who had a Serial One could show it off to customers and brag that his lab was the first in its field to have such a machine. In truth, owning a Serial One was also a financial risk, particularly if the machine flopped. But labs wanted them. Even a qualified Serial One—Serial One among the weapons labs or Serial One among the oil companies—was a status symbol.

When Rollwagen visited the dusty labs in Livermore and Los Alamos to sell Cray Research's very first machine, he had the *ultimate* Serial One. Customers at both locations jumped at the prospect. In a way that only the status-hungry government labs could comprehend, the issue of the ultimate Serial One became a top priority. Los Alamos programmers quickly decided to buy a CRAY-1, cleared their idea through the proper chain of command, then raced a purchase request to the Department of Energy. Programmers at Lawrence Livermore did the same.

The race for the ultimate Serial One seemed like a win-win situation for Cray Research, but it wasn't. The Energy Research & Development Administration planned to approve funding for only one of the requests, so the Serial One race grew into a competition. To ensure their victories in the race, the labs began working against each other. Both wanted the first CRAY-1 so badly that they were willing to do almost anything short of committing a crime to get it. Every time Livermore's case came before the Energy Research & Development Administration, someone from Los Alamos shot it down. Every time Los Alamos's case came up, Livermore shot it down.

Cray Research now had a new problem. In an effort to appeal to their status-hungry customers, they'd created a monster. Their two biggest potential customers, the two biggest weapons labs in the country, were at each other's throats, locked in viselike grips. Each prevented the other from buying the first CRAY-1.

Rollwagen finally appealed to Cray to loosen the logjam. Cray, Rollwagen, and Hanson flew down to Los Alamos. "Here's the deal," Cray told the top-level managers. "We'll *give* you the machine. You can keep it for six months, then you can decide whether to buy it or lease it or give it back. But we've got to get this machine installed." Cray's solution was almost perfect, because neither side could object to a machine that was being *given* away.

Los Alamos managers accepted the deal and installed the machine. But Cray's solution had loosened the logjam in a way that no one envisioned. Having a machine at a user site enabled Cray Research to get the word out in a way that no salesman could have. Word of Cray's new masterpiece circulated through the little user community, and the next customer *called them*. It was a salesman's dream: A product so good that the customers were lining up at the door. The first paying customer, the National Center for Atmospheric Research in Boulder, Colorado, heard about the CRAY-1 through programmers at Los Alamos, and it paid $8.86 million to use the machine for weather forecasting. Not long after that, Los Alamos reached its conclusion on the CRAY-1, which it disclosed publicly: The CRAY-1 was five times faster than its best computer—the CDC 7600—in the vector mode. The lab immediately signed a long-term lease agreement. It wasn't long before other customers began lining up: European Centre for Medium Range Weather Forecasts in Great Britain; United Computing Systems Inc. in Kansas City; Lawrence Livermore Laboratory in California.

For Cray, this latest success had an extraordinarily familiar ring: the tiny computer company, bootstrapping its way up through the strength of its engineering, struggling to gain a foothold against the industry giants—and winning. Suddenly Cray Research was the new high-tech darling of the Twin Cities. A *Minneapolis Star* cartoon depicted the CRAY-1 as a musclebound bodybuilder grinning at two tiny corporate weaklings struggling with barbells. On the backs of the corporate weaklings were the words *IBM* and *Control Data.* Cray Research was viewed as the industry's technical giant. When Lawrence Livermore chose the CRAY-1 over Control Data's Star-100A machine, Control Data executives even complained about unfair bidding practices. Their complaints signaled an extraordinary shift in the industry's status quo. *Minneapolis Star* headlines proclaimed "Cray bid victory unfair" and "Control Data edged out." It was a simultaneously bittersweet and ironic moment for Cray: His old company, bogged down by bureaucracy and struggling to finish a new machine, was crying that it had been unfairly beaten by a firm one-twentieth its size.

Sensing that a growth phase was imminent, Cray looked for a new president to run the company while he built the next computer. He chose Rollwagen. Some of the firm's board members mildly resisted the prospect of so young a president, but Cray's mind was set. Rollwagen, ever confident, was unsurprised by Cray's offer. "Of course I want to be president," he told Cray. "I went to Harvard. I'm supposed to be president." In a surprise move, however, he added that he would take the job for only ten years, and Cray could fire him if he wished in the interim. "I've noticed," he said in dead earnestness, "that companies tend to go sour if a president stays on too long." Cray agreed, and told his new thirty-six-year-old president that he would remind him of the promise in ten years.

Under Rollwagen's leadership, the company's success continued. Production jumped from four units per year to eight. The firm began building a new engineering building in Chippewa, moved into a bigger facility in the Twin Cities, and hired more engineers, assemblers, and software people. The plan was for continued growth. Cray's modest goal of selling two machines per year had long since been realized. Demand for the CRAY-1 was growing at an amazing rate. New machines were already on order for the British Ministry of Defence, Bell Laboratories, and Grumman Data Systems, in addition to more CRAY-1s for Lawrence Livermore and Los Alamos. The orders were coming in, and the salesmen couldn't very well turn them back. The company was growing bigger and more successful—whether Seymour Cray liked it or not.

. . . .

SEVEN

The Cray Way

Leaning against his stand-up desk, smiling cheerily for photographers, John Rollwagen looked like the consummate 1970s executive. Not yet forty years old, he was trim and athletic-looking, the antithesis of the plump, gruff bosses who ruled industrial America in the first half of the century. For the public image of Cray Research, he was perfect. He was a young man in a young industry. Standing at his desk with his sleeves rolled up and his tie loosened, he came across as energetic, casual, and intelligent. Reporters, in particular, liked Rollwagen. He wasn't much older than most of them, and he knew what they wanted. What's more, he genuinely seemed to like the press. He was a breezy, quotable personality who, unlike many high-level executives, didn't let his ego control an interview.

Rollwagen was smart enough to know how to use the media to promote his company. In that respect, he was the perfect complement to Seymour Cray. Rollwagen *wanted* to visit with reporters, mainly because he saw the value in positive publicity. He also knew that most reporters didn't want to write about packaging, cooling, processors, memories, wiring, transistors, diodes, capacitors, or any of the other electronic minutiae that made up a supercomputer. They wanted to write about people.

And Rollwagen wanted to help them. He understood better than anyone the profound impact of the genius image on Cray Research. Since his days as vice president of finance, looking for investors in New York, Rollwagen had grasped the importance of

Seymour Cray's reputation. In the early years Cray's reputation *was* the company. At one point Cray Research's founders even took out a $3.5 million life insurance policy on him. For a publicly held company, a reputation like Cray's was an invaluable asset.

Every time a reporter walked into his office, Rollwagen would subtly turn the conversation toward the issue of genius and the reputation of Seymour Cray. He sat there, gazing across the little table that he reserved for guests, calmly relating anecdotes of Cray's extraordinary genius and his eccentricities. The stories were irresistible and Rollwagen was a masterful storyteller. He relayed his tales so vividly, and with such rich detail, that reporters felt as if they were watching the scenes of a movie unfolding in front of them. In one of his favorite stories, Rollwagen told of Cray's meeting with a French physicist, a great admirer of Cray. Asked about his work habits, Cray told the physicist that he toiled mostly at his lakeside cottage, up on a sandstone bluff in Wisconsin. Normally, he said, he worked in three- or four-hour binges, with one-hour breaks in which he dug tunnels under his cottage. "Up in the woods of Wisconsin, we have elves," he said. "So I work for four hours, then I go down to the tunnels and dig. It takes me about an hour to dig four inches into the hillside, then I go back to my office. And the elves come in while I'm working on the tunnel, and they solve my problems for me. Then I work for three or four more hours until I come up with another set of problems for the elves to solve, and go back to my tunnels again." Rollwagen would spin his tales, seamlessly weaving them into his conversations, all the while knowing how his guests would respond.

Of course, no writer could resist such bizarre tales. Most business reporters spent their days neck-deep in the mundane world of stocks, bonds, and Treasury certificates. They didn't hear many stories about elves and tunnels. So the reporters sat there, scribbling wildly, trying unsuccessfully to look dispassionate, while Rollwagen calmly trotted out those and other tales of Cray Research's eccentric, reclusive genius. Suddenly the mundane world of scientific computing—which would have been otherwise ignored by the public—was a hot topic in the consumer press. The stories turned up in publications such as the *Minneapolis Star,*

Minneapolis Tribune, St. Paul Pioneer Press, Time, Newsweek, Business Week, Forbes, Fortune, and *Corporate Report Minnesota.* The public image of Cray Research became inextricably entwined with that of genius.

Some of Cray's friends and his neighbors in Chippewa Falls, however, were appalled by the "Seymour stories." Many felt it was a invasion of Cray's privacy; others said that the stories were fabrications of the press. But the vast majority of Rollwagen's stories were true. Cray *did* dig a tunnel in the hillside beneath his cottage. The tunnel was about eight feet high and four feet wide and braced by cedar timbers; it looked like a small version of a coal mine entrance. Cray dug deep into the hillside—twenty feet or more. There his shaft split off into a "T" and had a "skylight" on one end. The skylight had been an unintended addition; he'd been digging one day when the end of the tunnel had started to collapse. He hustled out of the tunnel just in time to look up and see a tree on the hillside disappear into his tunnel. Later he waded back inside, removed the tree, and braced the area around the hole, leaving it open and building a small bunker around it.

For those who knew Cray, there was nothing odd about his habit of tunneling. The tunnel didn't go anywhere; it wasn't supposed to. It was merely Cray's way of escaping a technical dilemma and letting his subconscious work while he engaged in mindless activity. Unlike many engineers and scientists who denied their artistic instincts, Cray had a good feel for his creative side. He used equations as tools to check the validity of his ideas, but he knew that his real job was to invent. Cray's parable of the elves, of course, wasn't meant to be taken literally; it was his way way of describing his creative process.

In Rollwagen's mind the Seymour stories showed that Cray Research possessed more than mere engineering talent—it was blessed with *magic.* And Seymour Cray was the magician. As the story of Cray trickled into the consumer press, Americans were inclined to agree with Rollwagen. Cray was a technical master in an industry that the average American barely understood. He *must* be a genius. His eccentricities only served to endear him to the general public. They made him sound as if he were a homebody, a man of such simple tastes that he wanted to do little more than dig a hole. Readers were charmed.

Rollwagen's use of the stories even went beyond the bounds of public relations. He used them to build a corporate culture. He wanted to mold the company in Cray's image, to build on Cray's philosophies. Like Cray, he believed in small, highly focused teams, and his goal was to nurture innovation. What better way to illustrate his philosophies than to do it through Cray? Innovation? One summer Cray built a boat, then burned it after purchasing a new one. The story demonstrated Cray's willingness to renew himself, to discard old ideas. Focus? Cray was so focused that he rejected a nomination from one of the energy labs for a National Medal of Technology, an honor for which he was a sure bet, and which would have taken him to the White House. But Cray couldn't be bothered; he was too busy building his next machine. He was too focused.

Before long the Seymour stories took on a life of their own. Engineers whispered them in the halls of the Chippewa facilities. Managers retold the stories at the new building in Mendota Heights. Magazine reporters used them to form lively leads for their stories. Tales of the reclusive genius slowly spread beyond the tight little user community, and Seymour Cray's name became nationally recognized. In the minds of programmers, engineers, investors, and now, the general public, Seymour Cray *was* Cray Research.

In his usual fashion, Cray dropped the CRAY-1 project before completion, leaving Les Davis and the rest of the engineering crew to finish the maddeningly difficult task of making the machine work. It was often said that the last 10 percent of the design was the toughest part. It was also the part for which an engineer received the least credit. Colleagues compared Davis's role to that of a streetsweeper after a Main Street parade: Cray rode at the head of the parade, smiling graciously as the crowds showered him with adulation; Davis silently swept up afterward, making the street usable on Monday morning.

That was the way it had been in 1976. While the others finished the CRAY-1, Cray began work on his new project, the CRAY-2. He had much higher aspirations for the CRAY-2: It would use four processors, and it would have a clock speed about three times as fast as the CRAY-1. If successful, the machine would have a clock speed of *four billionths* of a second.

To his dismay, however, Cray found that he was unable to devote himself fully to the new machine. A combination of work and personal problems tugged at him. Customers saw a need for a mildly upgraded version of the CRAY-1, so he and his staff began work on a machine called the CRAY-1S. His new company was growing rapidly and demanding more of his attention. He and his wife, Verene, divorced after nearly thirty years of marriage, adding personal distress to a chaotic business atmosphere. When Cray and his crew were finally able to return to the CRAY-2, more than a year had passed.

But by that time—early 1978—Cray's fertile mind had sprouted a new idea. He wanted to build a completely different machine. This new CRAY-2 would not use four processors and would depart from the vector scheme they'd successfully followed on the CRAY-1. This new computer was going to be a scalar machine—that is, one that does all of its calculations in series. But instead of one scalar processor, this machine would have *sixty-four*. For Cray, the new idea represented a stunning reversal. Throughout his career he had beseeched his troops to use proven technology, not to invent. Now he was entering the realm of the uninvented. Massive parallel processing was an architecture that wouldn't begin to gain favor in the industry for about five more years.

Cray assigned Steve Nelson, one of the company's best young engineers, to write a compiler for the sixty-four-processor machine. A *compiler* was a necessary software tool for supercomputers, and writing one for a sixty-four-processor machine was an extraordinarily complex task. Nelson had never designed a compiler before, but he threw himself into it, taking work home every night and struggling with it on his kitchen table until the wee hours.

Cray, Nelson, and a few of the others worked on the project for several months. Finally Cray and Nelson traveled out to Lawrence

Livermore to present some of their ideas to the programmers there. Nelson explained the logic behind the sixty-four-processor system, then the group sat down and discussed it for more than an hour. A few days later, Cray greeted Nelson as he walked through the door of the Hallie lab. "Steve, we're not going to do this. The customers are just not ready for a sixty-four-processor system." Cray didn't complain; in fact, he was totally unemotional about it. He simply believed that his idea was too far ahead of its time. And that was that.

From that day forward, he and the others reverted back to the original design goals for the team: four processors; four-nanosecond clock speed. But they had a new problem: With all of the fitful stops and starts, they'd lost almost two years. And Cray still didn't have a solution for a problem that had been nagging at him all along—how to cool the new machine.

Just as he had done on earlier machines, Cray wanted to shorten the wire lengths on the CRAY-2. Shorter wire lengths meant greater speed. On the CRAY-1, the longest wires had been four feet. On the CRAY-2, he wanted none longer than sixteen inches. So Cray devised a sandwich-type processor module. He stacked eight circuit boards, one atop another, then inserted seven cold plates between them. With the boards so close together, the wire lengths could be short. And the cold plates between the boards would absorb the inevitable heat and transfer it out of the module.

The problem was that engineers needed to run wires from board to board so that the boards could communicate with one another. To accomplish that, they cut holes in the cold plates, then ran the wires through the holes. They cut so many holes in the plates that they looked like Swiss cheese. With all those holes, the plates were less effective at removing heat.

The CRAY-2 project was now beginning to look like the 8600 all over again. Cray was again wrestling with a three-dimensional processor module, and circuit components were burning out because heat was building up inside. Cray tried throwing more engineers at the problems, building the team up to about twenty-five members, but that didn't work either. Then one dark day he turned to one of his engineers and said, "We need to do a purge." Frustrated by the whole ordeal—the stops and starts, the heat problems, the inability to maintain a schedule—he had decided that they needed to approach the CRAY-2 from a fresh perspective. Almost all of the people on the project must be purged, he said. They needed to be sent elsewhere, to do something else. Anything else. Cray kept only himself and a few other Chippewa engineers on the CRAY-2.

The move seemed logical to Cray. Throughout his career, he had always been intuitive about the design process. It wasn't that he was unwilling to work hard in pursuit of his hunches; on the contrary, he was willing to work long and hard at the most grueling tasks. He disliked prima donnas—engineers who wanted to hand the tedious work to technicians. But when it came to evaluating a machine, the technology either felt right, or it didn't. The CRAY-2 technology didn't feel right, so the logical course of action was to start anew.

In an extraordinary move, he concluded that the remaining Chippewa team needed competition. He talked with G. Stuart Patterson, manager of the computing facility at the National Center for Atmospheric Research (NCAR) in Boulder, Colorado, about joining Cray Research to lead a competitive effort. Patterson was a friend of Cray, an engineer with an extraordinary track record of academic and computational experience. He had a bachelor's degree in chemical engineering, a master's degree in nuclear engineering from Massachusetts Institute of Technology, and a Ph.D. in fluid mechanics from Johns Hopkins University. He had used computers to support his doctoral thesis and had remained in the computing business throughout his career, ultimately landing at NCAR. From his first dealings with Cray in 1976, the two had formed a fast friendship. Cray found Patterson to be smart, engaging, and likable. That was why Cray had called him in 1978 to offer a position on Cray Research's board of directors. Patterson had turned the position down because of a perceived conflict of interest, but in 1979 Cray called him again.

"I've got another idea," Cray told him. "How would you like to run a research lab for us in Boulder and serve on our board of directors?" Patterson was stunned by the offer; there'd been no indications that Cray Research had intended to do any such thing. He was also intrigued by the idea and eventually accepted.

For Cray Research's high-level management, the prospect of a new lab in Boulder seemed an ideal move. The Boulder lab could serve as a source of *revolutionary* technology, which would enable the crew in Chippewa Falls to concentrate on *evolutionary* products. Some Cray Research executives hoped that Cray himself would settle in Boulder. There, they believed, he could continue to focus on the revolutionary designs that lit his creative fires.

Cray Research's rank-and-file engineers, however, were dumbfounded when they heard about the new lab. Although Cray had talked to the company's other managers about the need to stimulate internal competition, the engineers were unaware of any such needs. They only knew that they were being pushed off the CRAY-2 project and were being replaced by outsiders.

But there was no room for protest. Within weeks, the new operation was suffused with optimism. Soon after management announced the formation of Cray Laboratories, Patterson began construction of a beautiful new thirty-thousand-square-foot facility in Boulder. The company's executives were so confident that they demanded the new facility be expandable to sixty thousand square feet. Patterson hired a top engineer from National Semiconductor, a world-renowned maker of integrated circuits.

The effort in Boulder was a calculated risk. It was true that Cray Labs's management was not particularly well versed in supercomputer design, but that was the way Cray wanted it. Both Cray and Rollwagen believed that there was a creative danger in building on existing designs. To veer away from such uninspired methods was, of course, the Cray Way—*burn the boat before beginning another.* Throw the old baggage overboard. Start fresh.

The leaders in Boulder were just far enough on the fringe of supercomputing to start fresh. Coming from NCAR, Patterson understood the world of supercomputing as a user. And the key engineer whom Patterson had hired from National Semiconductor knew supercomputing from a supplier's perspective.

With extraordinary speed, Cray Labs began carrying out a technical plan of action. It negotiated a technology trade agreement with Fairchild Camera and Instrument Corporation. It quickly staffed its engineering corps with the best available technical talent. And Patterson, together with his new technical crew, set out to improve on the CRAY-2. Their plan was to incorporate so-called VLSI (very large scale integration) chips into the architecture of a CRAY-1. To accomplish that, they first *reverse-engineered* a CRAY-1—that is, they tore it down and learned how its logic and architecture worked. Then they began incorporating the VLSI concepts.

In terms of pure density, Cray Labs's VLSI chips were far ahead of what Cray was using. On the CRAY-1 the chip of choice had been the simplest available—a design that employed only two logic gates. But the engineers in Boulder, many of whom had come from the semiconductor industry, knew that two-gate chips were now passé. Semiconductor manufacturers were building VLSI chips containing a thousand or more logic gates. They planned to eventually incorporate those VLSI chips, then cool them with a high-tech heat pump.

To successfully build the machine, however, they knew they would need to draw on the technical staff in Chippewa Falls. So Patterson and one of his engineers traveled to Chippewa, where they ran recruiting meetings for the engineers and technicians who were invited to Boulder. At the meetings they painted a beautiful picture of Boulder. Boulder was a mountain town, a youthful city, with a great university and an engineering school where they could continue their educations. It was also an outdoorsman's paradise: Skiing, hiking, bicycling, mountain climbing, and snowmobiling were all readily available.

From a professional standpoint, engineers who moved to Boulder would also enjoy the advantages of being at the cutting edge, technically speaking. Starting at the ground floor of the company, they would be first in line for promotions if the subsidiary proved successful. The problem was that most of the twenty-five engineers and technicians who'd worked on the CRAY-2 didn't want to move. They had wives, and kids, and homes to sell. And the cost of living in Boulder was far higher than that of Chippewa. But what would they do if they stayed? Would there be jobs for them? In the Chippewa engineering labs, engineers huddled in cubicles and offices to discuss their employment pros-pects. There was no way they could remain in Chippewa and work for another computer firm; Chippewa had no such firms.

When the office banter grew more frantic and temperatures began rising, Les Davis stepped in. One by one the engineers kept turning up at Davis's office for closed-door sessions. Ultimately only two people left for Boulder. The rest remained in Chippewa, reassigned to other projects. In many cases the projects weren't as exciting as their previous work, but the engineers had jobs. It was better than uprooting their families and moving to a strange town. They could live with this.

Their work on the CRAY-2, however, was finished. They could never go back to it. They could never again be inspired by it, or feel a sense of commitment to it, or share in the thrill of its success. Those opportunities were gone forever.

The man in the back of the room sat quietly, arms folded, listening to the company meeting that was taking place. There were about thirty people in the room, all employees at Cray Research's new suburban facility in Mendota Heights, Minnesota. The meeting was the kind that takes place ten thousand times a day across America, with employees quietly filing into a beige-walled conference room and waiting for a "state of the company" address from the president. Rollwagen stood at the front of the room, talking about the Cray Way of doing things: small groups, networking, diversity, personal contact. Rollwagen was big on those issues.

When the company had been small, there'd been no need for structured employee meetings like this one. But it was growing so fast that Rollwagen feared it was in danger of losing the personal touch. In the past year alone, employment had jumped more than 60 percent, from 321 to 524 employees. As he ran the meeting, Rollwagen could see obvious signs of growth: There weren't enough chairs in the room, so the last-minute stragglers stood in back, lining the wall.

For Rollwagen, the evidence of growth was both a blessing and a curse. Earlier in the day, he'd been paging through the *Wall Street Journal* and had seen a single-frame comic depicting a gruff-looking businessman seated in front of a complex organization chart with a tiny dot and an arrow on it. Next to the arrow were the words, "You are here." The drawing represented one of Rollwagen's greatest fears: a huge organization, layered with bureaucracy, and staffed by employees who didn't know where they fit.

He thought about that as he gazed across the conference room. After updating the employees on the state of the company, he made a move to end the meeting. "Any questions?" he asked. The man in the back raised his hand.

"Yeah, I have a question," he said. "Who are you?" Judging by the tone of his voice, Rollwagen could tell that the man wasn't challenging his authority or trying to be combative. The question was almost childlike in its innocence. He wanted to know who Rollwagen was.

Rollwagen was dumbfounded. He hadn't expected this to happen at Cray Research—at least not so soon. In small companies, employees know each other, and all of them recognize the president. This kind of miscommunication shouldn't be happening in a firm the size of Cray Research, he thought.

Cray Research, however, wasn't so small anymore. A year earlier, *Inc.* magazine had named it the fifth fastest growing company in America. In his first year as president, Rollwagen had increased the work force by 50 percent and tripled the manufacturing space. From 1978 to 1979, its revenues had jumped 149 percent to $42.7 million. Rollwagen expected a 50 percent revenue increase in 1980. He expected another 50 percent in 1981.

Investors couldn't help but notice that Cray Research now ranked among the nation's top ten computer manufacturers. Though its revenues were still only a small fraction of those of IBM and Control Data, it showed great strength for its size. It boasted the highest sales per employee of any computer manufacturer and the highest net income as a percentage of sales.

Among the Wall Street crowd, figures such as those were promising signs. Investors began buying more shares of the company, driving up the stock price. Seymour Cray worried that the company was growing too fast and actually warned investors through an article printed in the *Minneapolis Star.* "I would caution stockholders to take a hard, serious look at what they are buying," he said in a statement that amazed Wall Street. "I think the current stock price is greatly inflated over the value of the company."

Yet it was hard to discount the company's popularity among its customers. In four years since it had begun selling machines, sales grew every year—from four machines in 1978, to eight machines in 1979, to ten machines in 1980. Requests for the CRAY-1 were coming in faster than the company could build them: By the end of 1980, Cray Research had a backlog of five systems on order.

Rollwagen couldn't help noticing that the company was in danger of violating one of Seymour Cray's basic precepts. From the beginning Cray had wanted the company to operate in craftsmanlike fashion, building and selling a single machine at a time. Now the orders were coming in so fast—more than one a month—that it was growing more difficult to follow Cray's original pronouncements.

The problem was that no one had envisioned this kind of success.

Atop a sandstone bluff, in a three-bedroom cottage overlooking Lake Wissota, Seymour Cray wrestled with the design for the CRAY-2. Although few of the engineers in Chippewa Falls knew it, Cray had never stopped working on the machine. So while the crew in Boulder toiled away at their version of the CRAY-2, Cray continued to work on his.

In 1981 he spent most of his time at the cottage, trying to piece together the mix of technologies that was whirling around in his brain. To help him, he had set up his own design lab there: In one bedroom there was a big Data General mainframe computer, a real monster about six feet high, with several cabinets full of electrical racks.

Cray used the mainframe to run software programs that aided him in the design of the circuit boards for the CRAY-2. With the software he could lay out a complex array of electronic components and foil lines on the computer screen. Then, if he wished, he could shift the parts around on-screen without having to rebuild the hardware every time he wanted to make a change.

The mainframe helped Cray to improve the design process, but it was not without its penalties. In 1981 "computer-aided design," or CAD, was still in its primitive stages. So Cray needed to augment the mainframe with dozens of little personal computers, called SuperBrains, that he also kept inside the cottage. At any one time, Cray usually ran software on about half a dozen Super-Brains and on the mainframe. The SuperBrains were scattered all over the cottage—in the bedrooms, living room, and kitchen. Because personal computers were unreliable in 1981 and were constantly fizzling out on him, he stored extras in the garage and at the Hallie lab, where a technician was on call to fix the duds.

Cray liked the setup at the cottage. With Cray Research growing larger and more successful, the cottage was a safe haven where he could work in blissful isolation for days on end, away from inevitable corporate distractions, away from the concerns of a thriving business.

Still, the woods around Lake Wissota were a less-than-ideal locale for designing supercomputers. Power outages were commonplace. Cray never knew when the power might crash, causing him to lose hours worth of work, so he installed a utility power system in his garage. He also had to install a powerful air conditioner to cool the mainframe.

None of this deterred him in the least. Nor was he deterred when he decided that the operating system on the Data General mainframe wasn't right for his needs. He simply sat down and rewrote thousands of lines of operating system code. Ironically he did all of this—the mainframe, SuperBrains, backup power, air conditioning, and new operating system—to *save* time. Supercomputer design was such a complex process that an up-front investment like this could help in the long run.

Cray's emphasis on computer-aided design never prevented him from performing hands-on hardware work. When John Rollwagen climbed the steps leading to the top of the sandstone bluff in 1981, he found Cray on the front porch of his cottage, which faced the lake. Seated at a rickety card table, Cray was assembling the processor modules for the CRAY-2. In his right hand he held a large magnifying glass, the kind typically used for embroidery. The magnifying glass had a circular neon light around it, which illuminated the circuit boards in front of him. Aided by the white light, he inserted the electronic components onto the boards with a tweezers. Then he reached for his soldering iron, and with a characteristic tremble of the left hand, he attached the components to the boards as he squinted through the magnifying glass.

Rollwagen enjoyed watching Cray perform simple tasks like these. On one hand, there was great irony in Cray's use of such low-tech equipment. A man universally regarded as one of the world's great engineers, he was doing the kind of work that could easily be assigned to a sixteen-year-old kid in shop class. On the other hand, Rollwagen knew that this was what made Cray great: his willingness to do the most elementary work, to feel how his modules fit together. This helped etch the assembly process in his mind. It was an integral part of his famed intuition.

Rollwagen's visit, however, wasn't spurred by his desire to watch Cray work. Over the preceding year he had sensed in Cray a certain dissatisfaction. In subtle steps Cray seemed to detach himself from the company he founded. By 1981 most of Cray Research's management knew that Rollwagen ran the company on a day-to-day basis. In the past, Cray used to rear up and complain when he disliked something that Rollwagen had done, but not anymore. Cray's only corporate contact occurred when he drove into Mendota Heights for a board meeting. Beyond that, Cray didn't involve himself.

Rollwagen thought he understood the problem. When Cray had formed the company nine years earlier, he'd had a simple goal: to remain an engineer. Of course he could have remained an engineer at Control Data, but he would have had no control over his destiny. At Cray Research he hoped to control his destiny *and* remain an engineer, but with each passing day the company grew larger, and control of it was slipping through Cray's fingers. For his own personal reasons, Cray would have liked to reduce the size of the company, but he knew it wouldn't have been good for the stockholders or the new employees. And Cray was never one to confuse his own goals with those of the company.

There was an ironic lesson in all of this. As a young engineer, Cray had thought that by encouraging growth, managers were placing their own interests ahead of those of the company. As chairman he realized that by *blocking* Cray Research's growth, he would be placing his interests ahead of those of his company.

Of course, there was one obvious solution to that problem: He could leave. Rollwagen recognized this. A peek at Cray's track record made it obvious: He had helped to build Univac and Control Data, then left both places after the companies grew up around him.

Rollwagen didn't want the same to happen here, so he approached Cray. "Seymour, it's not really working out, is it?" he asked.

"No, it's not, John," Cray replied.

"You're going to leave, aren't you?"

"Yeah, I might."

"Well, Seymour, your name is on the door here," Rollwagen replied. "This is not Control Data. Maybe we can work out a way to keep you around."

Rollwagen and Cray broached various ways of keeping Cray in the company. Most of their discussions centered on the issue of supporting Cray's research. What would they do if the company wanted to follow one direction, and Cray wanted to go in another? Their solution was to make Cray an independent contractor, rather than an employee. Cray would step down as chairman, hand the position over to Rollwagen, and pursue new projects as he saw fit. That way, if Cray Research lost interest in the CRAY-2, or in any of his subsequent projects, Cray could move on and start another company. They agreed to pay him 6 percent of whatever he spent as a contractor; for example, if Cray spent $1 million in research money in a year, he would receive a $60,000 "salary."

The new arrangement seemed eminently logical to Cray and Rollwagen. Cray had already detached himself from the day-to-day operation of the company. The firm's engineers would understand the arrangement. Most knew that engineering was a religion to Cray. It wouldn't surprise them to learn that he had left management to focus more effort on engineering. Explaining the arrangement to the rest of the world wouldn't be so easy.

Newspaper reporters and stockholders weren't as likely to believe it. In view of the difficulty, the company's board decided to make the announcement in tandem with the introduction of the CRAY-2.

Cray Research wasn't in the habit of introducing machines that were still years from production, but during 1981 Cray had made giant strides with his new machine. The key was a stunning decision he had made about its cooling system. After repeatedly burning out circuits on the sandwich-style, three-dimensional processor, Cray had opted for a radical solution: *liquid immersion*. In liquid immersion cooling, engineers essentially build an aquarium, then immerse every chip and wire in a broth inside of it.

When Cray first suggested it, jaws dropped. Any child knows that electrical products aren't supposed to be immersed in liquid. Most liquids are good electrical conductors, and thus can quickly create a short circuit or even an electrocution.

Cray knew, however, that Control Data engineers had experimented with liquid immersion cooling of circuit boards a decade earlier, so he proposed using Fluorinert, a chemically inert liquid that 3M made for use in heart surgery.

Cray and the remaining CRAY-2 engineers in Chippewa built a prototype using Fluorinert cooling. Preliminary runs of the prototype convinced Cray that the concept would work. Their design called for a big coolant reservoir that pumped the Fluorinert across the electronic components at a rate of one inch per second. The passing coolant drew the heat off the modules and carried it back to a heat exchanger, where it was released. Late in 1981, however, their concept wasn't fully proven, nor did engineers know how they would eventually test the immersed modules.

The company's managers felt that the engineers were close enough, so they called a press conference at the Minneapolis Club, saying a day ahead of time that Seymour Cray would conduct the meeting. As soon as word of the press conference reached Wall Street, Cray Research's stock jumped. The prospect of the publicity-shy Cray leaving the seclusion of his Chippewa Falls lab heightened speculation that something big was about to happen. Analysts speculated that Cray Research would announce a new product or a tender offer for the company. A few analysts even suggested that Cray Research's wandering founder might be leaving the company. By noon on the morning of the announcement, trading of Cray Research stock was so furious that it was halted by the New York Stock Exchange after a three-dollar-a-share price run-up.

When Cray ambled to the podium the following morning, many in the room were slightly disappointed by the sight of him. Dressed in a sweater and sport shirt, his dark hair neatly combed, Cray looked absolutely normal. Now fifty-six, he was still trim and athletic-looking, a result of his passions for skiing and windsurfing. After years of hearing about his reclusive nature, some people had expected a Howard Hughes–like figure. But Cray was calm and even charming as he described the new machine. He told reporters that it would be six to twelve times faster than the CRAY-1. Then he described its four-processor design and pointed to the liquid swirling past the processors inside the "aquarium." The machine, he said, would be phased into production over the next three or four years.

Finally Cray explained his personal arrangement: In order to devote more time to developing the CRAY-2, he was stepping down as chairman. And, oh yes, he was now serving as an independent contractor to the company. Reporters questioned Cray and Rollwagen. Cray joked about it, saying that he was doing it so that he "wouldn't have to drive to Minneapolis for meetings every week." In fact, Cray was exaggerating: He rarely drove to Minneapolis anymore.

Most of the reporters in the room were satisfied with Cray's explanation. After nearly a decade of hearing about his reclusive style and his obsession with technology, it made sense to think that he wanted to divorce himself from management. The following day, headlines in all three local newspapers focused on the introduction of Cray's fast new machine, which was still three years away.

Cray stock, however, promptly dropped after the announcement, as analysts pondered the new arrangement. In the first day, it tailed off to $36 a share—precisely the level of two days earlier. It continued to drop, however, so Cray uncharacteristically agreed to do one-on-one interviews with reporters. Photos of him looking relaxed in his cardigan sweater appeared in newspapers, and slowly the company stemmed the tide of speculation.

News organizations had no way of knowing that the slow departure of Seymour Cray was beginning. Waiting quietly in one of Cray Research's labs was a computer that was more powerful and faster than the CRAY-1, but more conservative than the CRAY-2. This machine was not a Seymour Cray creation. Some of the followers of Seymour Cray had sarcastically dubbed it the CRAY-1½.

Cray felt no personal antipathy toward the new machine or the crew that designed it. He had always wanted competition. But he thought the new machine was unexciting, because the engineers who built it had had one eye riveted on the CRAY-1. That wasn't what Cray wanted to do. He wanted to "design from a clean sheet of paper," to start fresh, to burn the boat. That was the Cray Way.

The engineers in Boulder did not cheer over the apparent success of the CRAY-2. While Cray had been building his liquid immersion prototypes, the Boulder crew had struggled with its VLSI technology. And, as so many had before them, they found the task of designing a supercomputer to be a surprisingly complex one.

The first inklings of the demise of Cray Laboratories occurred late in 1981 at a board meeting in London. Board members staged the meeting abroad to allow input from Cray Research's European operations. They talked about the problem of supporting three research efforts: the CRAY-2, the "CRAY-1½," and Cray Laboratories. Board members agreed to support all three operations—at least for the moment—but G. Stuart Patterson sensed impending doom for his Boulder lab.

Late in 1981 there was still hope for the Boulder effort, but it seemed to be dwindling. In an interview with the *St. Paul Pioneer Press* in December, Seymour Cray had given a vote of confidence to the Boulder group. "The hope of the future is in Boulder and that's why we're making such a big investment there," he said. But the engineers in Boulder knew better. With the rise of the liquid immersion CRAY-2, they could feel the shift in focus at Cray

Research. No matter what the company's executives said publicly about Cray Labs's rosy future, the engineers suspected otherwise. All the promises of financial support were now just a memory. Engineers hammered "For Sale" signs into their front lawns in Boulder, and began scrambling to find new jobs in California's Silicon Valley. Morale plummeted; work ground to a halt.

In April 1982 Patterson had lunch with Rollwagen, who confirmed that Cray Laboratories was being disbanded. The company's institutionalized attempt at design spontaneity had failed. Management had followed the recipe for revolutionary product development—physical detachment, minimal intervention, and a fresh start—but for some reason, the ingredients hadn't jelled. They could not franchise the Cray Way. It was a little bit like ordering people at a party to have a good time. The outcome could not be preordained. And after a short time, Cray Research management had been unwilling to wait any longer for the right outcome. Now it was time to make a decision.

Cray Research would someday use the VLSI technology developed in Boulder, but the new hope for the future now lay inside a steel tank, immersed in a broth of chemically inert coolant. The new hope for the future, Rollwagen said, was the CRAY-2.

Or so he thought.

EIGHT

The New Genius

The natives of Chippewa Falls had never seen anything quite like it. About a mile from town, in an area where the loudest noise was the distant growl of an occasional farm tractor, locals could hear the steady thumping of a helicopter blade. The copter swung northeast of downtown Chippewa Falls, touching down near one of the three new Cray Research buildings that had risen, seemingly overnight, from the farmlands. A news crew from WCCO television in Minneapolis jumped out, joining a competing camera crew and a busload of print journalists who'd come in from the Twin Cities.

Over the preceding decade, Chippewa Falls locals had grown accustomed to visits by print journalists. The reporters came in, usually stayed for a day, asked a few questions, then exited as quietly as they'd come. Television crews with helicopters hadn't been part of the Chippewa Falls media scene. When they gaped at the TV helicopter gliding across the gray sky, the locals could only assume that Seymour Cray had again stunned the computing world by building another spectacular new machine.

Anyone who expected to see Seymour Cray on this day in April 1982, however, would soon be disappointed. As the reporters and camera crews shuffled into the lunchroom of the Development Building on Lowater Road, they were surprised to find a new face seated at the head table. Steve S. Chen, a slim, soft-spoken Chinese immigrant, was now playing the role that had been the exclusive province of Seymour Cray. Chen was the man behind the machine, and he quickly warmed to the role. He spoke to the entourage of about fifty people in heavily accented English, thoroughly and methodically stepping through the technical advantages of the new supercomputer that sat at the front of the lunchroom.

The new machine had a familiar look to it. It consisted of a C-shaped grouping of towers surrounded by the padded loveseat that had distinguished the CRAY-1. Inside, of course, it was different. It was the first Cray Research machine to operate two processors in parallel; its circuitry was denser; and it was speedier. Chen told reporters that the new machine was five times faster than a CRAY-1S. Its two-processor design was also a first of its kind. "This is the first supercomputer that can run two jobs on different processors, or one job on two processors," Chen said proudly.

For Rollwagen's purposes, Chen was the perfect spokesman. Throughout the press conference he answered questions with quiet poise and unshakable confidence. Reporters strained to pick out nuggets of understandable English, but that didn't matter. What mattered was that Chen was bright and pleasant, and he wasn't Seymour Cray. After Cray had shaken the public image of the company by stepping down and becoming an independent contractor, Rollwagen decided that Cray Research needed a new "face," a person who could be linked to the design of its computers. Many in the company had looked to Les Davis to fill that role. Davis seemed a solid candidate. Now fifty, he had been in the industry since 1955. He'd worked on Transtec, the CDC 6600, 7600, 8600, and the CRAY-1. The new machine, now called the CRAY X-MP, had been his idea. Davis formulated it, provided direction, chose technology, selected the team members, and gently guided them through the design, but he did not want to be its spokesman. High-profile activities weren't consistent with Davis's low-key style.

Chen had been perfectly willing to assume the role and he was a logical choice. Born Shyh-ching Chen in China in 1944, he was dedicated, industrious, and by most accounts, brilliant. The eldest son of a civil servant, his family had moved to Taiwan when he was two. He'd gone to high school and college on scholarships, graduated in electrical engineering from the National Taiwan University in 1966, and then had come to the United States to continue his education. In the United States he struggled with the language and culture. As a graduate student at Villanova University in the early 1970s, he took a job as a teaching assistant, only to have thirty-five of his forty students drop his class because they couldn't understand him. Chen persevered. To make his name easier to pronounce, he changed it to Arnold; when his students told him he'd made a bad choice, he changed it to Steve. Despite his difficulty with the language, Chen was a star student. He studied parallel processing and earned his Ph.D. in computer science at the University of Illinois, a school sometimes referred to as "the Jerusalem of the computing world." After graduation he worked on array processors with Burroughs and Floating Point Systems before ending up at Cray Research in 1979.

At Cray Research, colleagues immediately recognized him as brilliant, confident, competitive, and exceptionally hardworking—a real overachiever. Chen's self-confidence bred in him an extraordinary optimism; he believed that he could make anything work. As a result, he always seemed to be looking down the road for ways to stretch the technological envelope, to do the impossible.

Shortly after arriving at Cray Research, he was named chief designer of the CRAY X-MP. As the first parallel processing machine in the company's history, the X-MP was an ideal project for Chen. He felt he understood parallel processing as well as anyone in the company. Chen threw himself into the project, working nights and weekends. He forged ahead despite snide comments from some of Cray's followers, who dubbed the machine "the CRAY 1½". Within two years, Chen could see that the X-MP would be a gigantic success.

On this gray Monday in April 1982, Chen stood before the scribbling reporters, the financial analysts, the camera crews, the radio microphones, and the in-house closed-circuit TV, describing the machine that he considered his own pride and joy. It really didn't matter what he said—his mere presence was the most important factor. Financial analysts noted that the computer was the first to emerge from Cray Research without the help of Seymour Cray. The newspapers would note the same. And television stations would run clips of Chen proudly displaying "his" machine.

Even if Seymour Cray left the company, the public now knew that Cray Research had other talent. Cray Research was poised to dominate the supercomputer industry. And they were doing it without the help of Seymour Cray.

Deep inside the maze of labs and offices in the Lowater Road Development Building, the engineers watched a closed-circuit television broadcast of the X-MP introduction and scratched their heads. While they all acknowledged that Chen had been an important cog in the creation of the X-MP, many felt a certain discomfort with the events as they unfolded in front of them.

Most of the engineers knew that the company needed to establish the existence of technical talent beyond the realm of Seymour Cray. Cray's struggle with the CRAY-2, and his recent change in status, had made that necessary. But as Chen's face flashed across the screen, as his words reached their ears, one word in particular began to gnaw at the nerve endings of some of the engineers. Over and over again, the engineers thought they heard the word "I" as Chen described how the program's most important technical decisions were made. Whether it was because of his struggle with English, or because he thought he was expected to behave in this way, or because he *believed* that he'd done all the work, no one knew.

But all of them knew that the X-MP program had been launched, not by Steve Chen, but by Les Davis. Davis had dreamed up the idea for the X-MP in 1979 after watching nearly three years of fitful stops and starts on the CRAY-2 program. Having worked on unsuccessful projects, he knew what a major failure could do to a company's product line. Davis also recognized in 1979 that the company's mainstay, the CRAY-1, would soon run out of steam. If Cray Research didn't offer a new product soon, it would begin to lose business. He also knew that the CRAY-2, in typical Seymour Cray fashion, would not be compatible with the CRAY-1. That meant that its introduction would entail a "birthing process," as customers struggled to write all new software for the machine. In short, Davis foresaw customer frustration on the horizon, unless the company acted quickly to forestall it.

So Davis took it upon himself to start another program, one that would serve as a backup in the event that the CRAY-2 failed. He talked with a few of the best available engineers and outlined his plan: The new machine would be CRAY-1–compatible; it would use two processors instead of one; and it would operate off a ten-nanosecond clock. The faster clock cycle, Davis said, could be achieved by borrowing technology from the new CRAY-2 program. In the CRAY-2, engineers were incorporating chips with sixteen logic gates each. Those chips were eight times as dense as those in the CRAY-1, which had only two logic gates apiece. The new machine would use the denser chips, but not in the three-dimensional structure that Seymour Cray envisioned.

Approaching the project as he did, Davis was violating all of Cray Research's unwritten rules. Seymour Cray's design philosophy had always been to start fresh from a clean sheet of paper. Or, as Rollwagen might have said, Cray's Way was to burn the boat. Yet Davis had one foot planted squarely in the past as he stepped into the future. He was cherry-picking a combination of old and new, then blending those technologies into the X-MP. Without saying it in so many words, Davis understood that a subtle shift in supercomputing loomed on the horizon. Unlike the early years, when users had accepted little more than crude prototypes, they now wanted *products*. Programmers needed machines with operating systems, software, compatibility, and reliability. If all of that could be rolled into a revolutionary product, so much the better. But a revolutionary product was no longer their sole desire. For Cray Research, Davis's approach was a departure from the company's guiding principles.

On the other hand, Davis was clearly following Cray's lead in his use of a nonbureaucratic, small-team approach. Davis didn't ask permission; he didn't appear before the board of directors; he didn't form a committee. Davis knew what he needed to do, so he formed a low-visibility team, and encouraged them to go ahead.

Convincing the best engineers to join the X-MP program had been one of Davis's toughest tasks. Despite all the CRAY-2's public struggles, most engineers wanted to be where the action was, and at Cray Research that meant working with Seymour Cray. It was a natural tendency for any engineer to want to work on something important, and then to share in the glory of its success. And if supercomputer history had proved anything, it was that importance, glory, and success all resided in the camp of Seymour Cray. Nevertheless, Davis convinced some of the company's best engineers to join the project, partly on the strength of his own optimism, and partly because he caught some of them between projects.

The resulting team *was* exceptionally young. Chen, who was thirty-five when the project began, was the chief designer. The other key players—Alan Schiffleger, Jerry Brost, George Leedom, Rick Pribnow—were all under forty.

Months after they'd begun the X-MP, Davis told Rollwagen about it. Even then he downplayed it, saying, "It's just a follow-on to the CRAY-1, John. We're taking the CRAY-1, putting a couple of processors on it, speeding it up a little, and using Seymour's new circuits. It's no big deal." Rollwagen accepted Davis's explanation, and the project pushed forward in Skunk Works fashion—that is, with little or no corporate intervention.

From the beginning the team operated in classic Cray style. Chen didn't wait for corporate direction. He talked to customers to learn their likes and dislikes on the CRAY-1. He and Schiffleger drove together to the Twin Cities to visit the company's software engineers, who provided them with a wish list for the X-MP. The two engineers then returned to their lab in Chippewa where they hammered out the machine's logic and memory needs, based on the wish list. Years later, so informal a process would be impossible in the bureaucratized version of Cray Research, but in 1979 the Skunk Works approach enabled them to move freely ahead.

Within months the X-MP caught and passed the CRAY-2 program, which was still struggling after nearly four years. During the two years following their start-up, Chen's engineers solved the program's most difficult technical problems: how to control a memory fed by two processors; and how to jam two processors into the CRAY-1 chassis.

What emerged late in 1981 was a souped-up version of the CRAY-1. Its memory used multiple ports to pipe data back and forth more quickly to the two processors. The processors employed half as many modules, or electronic building blocks, as the CRAY-1 had. The engineers were thus able to fit two processors in the same space occupied by one on the CRAY-1, and the processors were better because of the dense new chips they were using. The X-MP had 2.3 million logic gates—exactly eight times that of the CRAY-1.

All of this translated to greater speed. Early versions of the X-MP routinely performed more than 200 million floating point operations per second. It was also compatible with the CRAY-1, a feature that the firm's growing class of corporate customers found useful. Unlike the weapons labs, which were staffed by scientists who wrote their own software, corporate customers didn't want to rewrite their programs each time a new machine was introduced. By 1982 Cray Research was serving a growing cross section of corporate accounts: The big petroleum companies now employed supercomputers to analyze the data they collected in their search for oil; auto companies were beginning to use supercomputers to simulate wind-tunnel and crash tests; aircraft companies found they could perform more accurate stress calculations on wings and fuselages by running them through supercomputers. All of these industries needed supercomputers to compete. Most could handle the initial cost, which ranged from $11 million to $14 million on an X-MP, but they didn't have a big enough programming staff to rewrite all their software. All of them wanted compatibility.

Prior to its introduction, the engineers who chided the X-MP program knew little about it. The project had low visibility within the company, and Davis had been extremely quiet about it. It was as if he feared that too much attention might cause someone to cancel the project. But when the X-MP was introduced on that Monday in April, the jokes about it being the CRAY-1½ quickly subsided. Analysts saw it and immediately recognized its value. The X-MP's performance benchmarks were so good, they wondered aloud how the CRAY-2 could possibly top it. Several financial analysts told reporters that they were giving immediate "buy" recommendations to Cray Research stock.

Within two months Cray Research began reaping the benefits of the speedy new design. Digital Productions, a company that had helped create the film images for the movie *TRON*, announced that it would lease an X-MP at the cost of $275,000 a month. Shortly afterward, a government nuclear research center in West Germany purchased a machine at a cost of $11.4 million.

Cray Research also found other ways to capitalize on the success of the X-MP. At an annual shareholders meeting Rollwagen introduced Steve Chen as the company's rising star. In interviews Rollwagen was heard to say that "other people had caught up with Seymour before, but nobody had ever gotten ahead of him." Davis meanwhile remained in Chippewa, happy to be out of the limelight as he pushed forward on the company's next machine, the CRAY Y-MP.

If Chen hadn't been sure about his stature before, his uneasiness with the new role had now disappeared. He believed that he was a master designer on a par with Seymour Cray, and that the two were in competition with each other. He made a point of telling associates that he never set foot in any of Cray's labs— proof that he was not stealing Cray's ideas. Chen installed locks on the doors of his own labs so that engineers from other projects could not pilfer his concepts. Chen even publicly uttered his disdain for Cray's designs on several occasions, saying "I can fix what Seymour made." He sometimes made it sound as if improving on a Cray design were something he could do while using only a portion of his prodigious brainpower. "I could see when I studied the CRAY-1 architecture that there were a lot of weaknesses there," he told the *Milwaukee Journal*. "I saw I could make up [for them] very quickly without a lot of exotic stuff."

Chen's reputation earned him a following within Cray Research. Many of the engineers who worked on the X-MP, and now on the Y-MP, began to feel the same kind of allegiance toward Chen that some of the older engineers felt toward Cray. Among Cray Research's veteran engineers, however, a deep form of resentment brewed. Some wondered how Chen could dare to think of himself as being on a par with Cray. Despite Chen's good fortune with the X-MP, they felt that he hadn't earned the lofty reputation he so readily accepted.

As the success of the X-MP grew, so too did Chen's fame. The *Wall Street Journal* referred to him as a "superstar." Newspaper articles identified him as the man who designed the X-MP, and

Chen graciously accepted that description. When it came to taking credit, the hardworking Chen was ever the overachiever.

Evidence was slowly growing that Cray Research management had unleashed an exceptionally powerful public relations vehicle. What management didn't know was that the vehicle would soon spin out of control.

Up in the dusty mountains of northern New Mexico, in the study center of Los Alamos National Laboratory, Bill Norris prepared to make Control Data's big announcement. Gathered for the 1983 Frontiers of Supercomputing Conference, 150 computing leaders from government, academia, and industry gazed at Norris from their cushioned theater seats.

In his gravelly, guttural voice, Norris announced that Control Data was reentering the supercomputing arena in a big way. It was launching a wholly-owned subsidiary called ETA Systems, which would build the fastest supercomputer in the world by 1986—a computer that would operate at the searing speed of 10 billion operations per second. Norris told the assembly that ETA Systems was not just another division of Control Data, but it was a separate entity, like the famed Skunk Works at Lockheed. "There is a need to sponsor smaller, entrepreneurial companies engaged in the development of supercomputers," he said. The announcement puzzled the audience. Hadn't Control Data *been* producing supercomputers for the past twenty-four years? Why were they spinning off a company *now?*

Norris's speech—and the very creation of ETA Systems—was an admission that Control Data had faltered. With the production of the Star-100, the Cyber 203, and the Cyber 205, they had never kept pace with Cray Research. The whole company had struggled. From 1968 to 1974 the company's stock nosedived from $159 a share to $10. In the late 1970s and early 1980s its mainframe and supercomputer businesses lost money and market share. Its peripherals division slumped. Now its computer services—which had performed so well since the IBM settlement—were struggling.

Wall Street analysts largely blamed Norris's personal idiosyncrasies for the problems. Now seventy-one, he was known for eccentricities that equaled those of Seymour Cray. Under Norris, the company invested in such dead ends as wind power and tundra farming. It also started a training and education group, then poured hundreds of millions of dollars into a project called PLATO, aimed at computerized teaching. Worse—in the eyes of the analysts—the gruff, tough-talking Norris had developed a social conscience. He frequently made speeches about social responsibilities of corporations. He invested in the revitalization of ghetto areas, and liked to tell and retell the story of Baltimore youths who'd broken into a school so they could play with the school's Control Data computers. Norris also was the force behind some of the company's forward-thinking programs, such as the establishment of day-care facilities.

Critics increasingly fired away at Norris for his investment in such programs at a time when the company was struggling. Norris responded by insulating himself from the criticism. He avoided the company dining room, spent more time behind closed doors, and walked the stairwells to his fourteenth-floor office for exercise. He unknowingly surrounded himself with adoring managers, some of whom called him "the pope." To analysts, Norris's idiosyncrasies had become the symbol of all that was wrong with Control Data.

Control Data's problems were in fact far more ordinary than the stories about idiosyncrasies indicated. Its real problem was that it had drifted away from its original strengths. In 1974 Norris had announced that "nobody can make money in the computer systems business. We at Control Data are going to make our future in computer services." Meanwhile Cray Research was establishing itself as a Fortune 500 company by building new computers. Foreign firms had grabbed the lead in peripherals. Computing services struggled following the explosion of personal computers on corporate desktops. A glut of companies squeezed Control Data's mainframe efforts.

Worst of all was Control Data's corporate culture. It was a beached whale—a bloated bureaucracy unable to move or change course. It had fifty-four thousand employees to manage, and its top managers were obsessed with their own little power struggles. The wave of success that the company had created fifteen years earlier was ending, and the company's managers were too bogged down with internal turf wars to restart it.

Those were the reasons that Norris was launching ETA Systems. His experience with the Chippewa Laboratory had reinforced what he'd already known: that innovation—*revolutionary innovation*—thrives when it's separated from the corporate bureaucracy. He knew that Control Data still had extraordinary technical talent; the trick was to create an atmosphere where that talent could bloom.

Norris hoped that if ETA was left alone, it could catch Cray Research. So he allowed the company's top people to start a separate facility at Energy Park in St. Paul, where they hired about 120 people, borrowed a few Cyber 205 computers, and began their odyssey.

Cynics wondered aloud, however, if St. Paul was far enough from the company's headquarters. To escape the corporate bureaucracy, they said, ETA might be better off moving to the moon.

By 1984 Seymour Cray's fertile mind began to drift away from the CRAY-2. It wasn't that the machine was finished—far from it. Cray simply felt that he had reached the limit of his usefulness on the project; at least that was what he told his colleagues. Most of the engineers suspected that he had another reason: Cray's real passion, the task that lit the fires of creativity in him, was the process of inventing from a clean sheet of paper.

So while the CRAY-2 engineers finished his machine, Cray spent his time on a new machine, the CRAY-3. For the CRAY-3 he'd taken a step in a dramatic new direction, one that many engineers openly questioned: He wanted to build the circuits from a new material called gallium arsenide. The move to gallium arsenide was somewhat un-Cray-like. Gallium arsenide had been used in satellites and military devices for years, but no one had employed it for anything as complex as a computer. For more than two decades, engineers had been building transistors and integrated circuits primarily from silicon, a material that had served Cray well ever since the development of the CDC 6600.

There was currently pressure in the industry to advance the state of the art in some new way. It had started in 1981 when the Japanese launched a project known as the Fifth Generation. The Fifth Generation was an exceptionally ambitious long-range program aimed at building supercomputers with artificial, human-like intelligence. In the United States, the Fifth Generation struck fear into the hearts of long-range thinkers who believed it would help the Japanese seize the world's supercomputer leadership. Defense and intelligence leaders were particularly anxious, because they had always believed that supercomputer leadership was analogous to world military dominance. Supercomputers were crucial to the design of nuclear weapons, defense aircraft, and intelligence systems.

The U.S. Defense Advanced Research Projects Agency (DARPA) responded to the Japanese challenge by funding companies in the area of parallel processing—computing with more than one processor at a time. Parallel processing was the hot new ticket in supercomputing, and most experts believed it was the future of the industry.

Cray knew that current technologies would soon bump up against nature's limitations. Nothing could be done, for example, to make electrons travel any faster through a copper wire. And tighter packaging (Cray's traditional solution) was reaching its limits. Of course, he could have followed DARPA's lead and joined the parallel processing race, but he wasn't ready for that radical step. While he conceded that parallelism was inevitable, he didn't believe in the concept of *massive* parallelism. For decades Cray had built machines with huge, powerful processors—*super*processors. In his early work at ERA a superprocessor had been roughly the size of a one-car garage. A processor in the CDC 6600 had been smaller, but still required thirty-four hundred circuit boards, each about the size of a looseleaf sheet of paper. The CRAY-1 processor was smaller still and it consisted of about five hundred module boards.

But the massive parallel machines used the *micro*processor, which first appeared in 1971. A typical microprocessor was about the size of a penny, but these powerful little devices were fueling the explosion of personal computers around the world. Cray, however, wasn't ready to use microprocessors in his machines. Microprocessors didn't offer enough computing power, he said. And he didn't believe that stringing hundreds of them together would solve that problem.

That was why Cray was now choosing a very different technology for the CRAY-3. There were only three ways an engineer could speed up a machine: The first was to pack the circuits closer together. Cray was reaching a dead end on that front, and he knew it. The second was to change the architecture. That was the solution of the massive parallel crowd, but Cray was rejecting that, too. The only avenue left to him was faster switching.

In a supercomputer the electrons streaked through the copper wires at roughly the speed of light, but when they encountered a switch, or transistor, they slowed down. That's because transistors were made from semiconducting materials, usually silicon. The only way to speed up the switching process was to use a different material. Cray reasoned that by using gallium arsenide he could speed the switching process. Tests showed gallium arsenide switched about six times as fast as silicon. And with hundreds of millions of switches taking place each second, Cray believed the new technology could dramatically speed up an entire machine. He estimated that by using gallium arsenide, he could lower the clock speed of the CRAY-3 to approximately one nanosecond.

The only problem was that no chipmakers manufactured the kinds of gallium arsenide circuits he needed. Unlike earlier years when he had simply purchased devices from Motorola or Fairchild, he would now have to make them himself. Cray was undeterred. He simply convinced Cray Research to build its own gallium arsenide fabrication facility at a cost of more than $20 million. The facility would be located in a forest area next to the Chippewa River. Engineers would take wafers—thin glasslike plates—and form the integrated circuits on top of them. Cray Research would be a chipmaker.

The very idea was a dramatic departure for Cray. He had always maintained that the pioneer never wins, that it is easier to be the one who goes second. But he had little choice: Computer technology had matured and competition was stiffer. If he still wanted to create revolutionary technology, Cray would need to change his approach. Now, he would be the pioneer.

☿

The CRAY-2, nine years in the making, finally rolled out in 1985. Even for industry veterans, it was a striking sight. The processors sat inside an aluminum tank with a red leather base and window openings milled into the side. Glass panels were pressed into the openings, the better for awestruck passersby to watch the machine operate. In its calculation mode the CRAY-2's circuits ran so hot that they literally boiled the Fluorinert coolant, causing bubbles to stream up past the glass windows. Programmers at Lawrence Livermore, the first customers to buy a CRAY-2, nicknamed it "Bubbles." For the uninitiated, it looked like something straight out of the television program *Star Trek*.

In the tight little programmer fraternity, few people knew how difficult the CRAY-2's birth had been. Among the general public, people knew only that the sight of it was awe-inspiring. Even after Cray had handed the project off in 1984, the struggles had continued. A young but experienced engineer named Jerry Brost, who finished the machine, had worked with his people to create custom test equipment for the liquid-cooled monster. When they had finally finished it, they too were glad to move on to other projects.

The CRAY-2 enjoyed some initial success, mainly on the strength of a vast new memory that Cray had added. The memory had actually come as an afterthought to the rollout of the X-MP. Cray wanted to ensure that the CRAY-2 was significantly better than the X-MP, in light of the fact that it was three years behind it.

In all, twenty-seven CRAY-2s were sold at costs ranging from $12 million to $17 million each. Cynics in the weapons labs, especially those now enamored with the idea of massive parallelism, claimed that many of the sales were spurred by a stirring description of the machine in the Tom Clancy book *The Hunt for Red October*. For any other supercomputer designer, the sale of twenty-seven machines would have been cause for major celebration, but twenty-seven was less than half the sales of the CRAY-1. And it was a mere fraction of what the supercomputer industry now expected from Seymour Cray.

By the time the CRAY-2 finally reached the marketplace, the engineers in the Development Building had already cranked out a four-processor version of the X-MP. The four-processor machine, which had taken more than a year to design, merely added to the X-MP's stunning success. Cray Research would eventually sell 126 X-MPs at prices approaching $16 million each. It was nothing short of a bonanza.

Management's view was that the X-MP had saved the company. The delay of the CRAY-2, they felt, would have been otherwise intolerable. It would have left a three-year gap in the company's product line, enabling three new Japanese competitors—Fujitsu, Hitachi, and NEC—to gain a foothold in the marketplace. Some managers felt that without the X-MP, there might be no Cray Research.

For that reason, the company now encouraged internal competition, so while Seymour Cray and his crew worked on the CRAY-3, Steve Chen and a separate group developed their next machine, the Y-MP. Chen had been handsomely rewarded for his role in the design of the earlier machine: He was now a senior vice president of the company, which was about as a high as an engineer could go and still have hands-on responsibility for a machine.

Chen's plans for the Y-MP were aggressive, but they would have been far more so without the guidance of Les Davis. Davis frequently walked the halls of the Development and Engineering Buildings, though his office was located on the other side of town. By doing so, he felt he could keep a finger on the subtle pulse of a project. He closely monitored morale, believing that engineers could never succeed in building anything if they lost their passion and optimism for a project.

The engineers for the Y-MP had again planted one foot squarely in the past as they stepped into the future. The Y-MP was regarded as a follow-on machine, aggressive in some respects but maintaining compatibility with earlier models. Its two biggest technical coups were its number of processors—eight—and the density of its integrated circuits.

For the engineers who'd lived through the ERA years, the Y-MP's circuit densities were absolutely mind-numbing. In the early years a logic element—consisting of a vacuum tube and circuit card—was too big to fit in the palm of a man's hand. When transistors had initially replaced vacuum tubes, a single logic element still barely fit in a person's palm. With the Y-MP's new chips, twenty-five hundred logic elements could fit in a child's hand—with room to spare.

The design process had changed, too. In the past Seymour Cray had always scribbled Boolean logic equations on paper. When Alan Schiffleger had written the Boolean for the X-MP, he'd also used paper. Computers were changing all that. For the Y-MP, Schiffleger typed his Boolean equations into a computer program, then transferred the files to a computer-aided design (CAD) system. The CAD system read the Boolean equations and helped Schiffleger determine how to connect the transistors on the chips. When he finished, Schiffleger turned over his CAD files to a Motorola facility, where the final layer of interconnects was deposited on preexisting chips. There was no other way to do it. With as many as ten thousand transistors on a single chip, to do it by hand would be far too time-consuming.

All this complexity had a dramatic upside. The new chips were so dense that an entire processor could fit on a single circuit board no taller than a three-month-old child. On the X-MP the processor had used 250 circuit boards, each about the size of a sheet of looseleaf paper. The Y-MP processor's smaller size meant that engineers could now fit *eight* processors in a chassis that had originally contained only one.

But Chen wanted more. Like many bright engineers, he was obsessed with speed, efficiency, and performance. Chen desperately wanted to endow the machine with multiple pipes—a feature that would enable it to read two "words" in each clock period. Processors had traditionally read only a single word in a clock cycle. If Chen were successful, he could once again dramatically increase the machine's speed.

Chen's engineers struggled with the multiple pipe concept and warned him that they would be unable to employ it without bulky hardware changes. Additional hardware, however, would prevent them from fitting eight processors in the original chassis. Chen persisted. He wanted to add the pipes. He also wanted to include other hardware features. When engineers struggled with all of his ideas, he told Davis that he would need more time.

Just as he had six years earlier with the CRAY-2, Davis thought he sensed that the project was spinning out of control. Davis knew better than anyone that completion of a project always looked easier than it really was. It was a complex, subtle process of testing, trial and error, and redesign. Yet engineers were forever keeping their projects unbuttoned to the last tense moment, claiming they were almost finished. Programmers had a name for this phenomenon: the Hartree Constant, named for a British physicist. Engineers afflicted with the Hartree Constant always said their project would take six more months; and when six months was finished, they needed six *more* months. Chen wasn't alone in this regard. It had happened to the great J. Presper Eckert—and to Seymour Cray.

Davis foresaw a problem on the horizon: If the Y-MP missed its window of opportunity, the furious efforts at Fujitsu, Hitachi, and NEC could catch those of Cray Research. So Davis met with Rollwagen. "The Y-MP isn't getting done," he said. "We're going to have to step in."

Davis suggested that they let Chen take his futuristic ideas to a new project that would be branded the "MP." The MP would be Chen's brainchild. Moving him there would serve two purposes: It would let him apply his inventiveness to a machine of the future; and it would get him out of the way. Davis said that he would personally see to it that the Y-MP was completed.

Rollwagen accepted the idea. Late in 1985 he proposed the long-range project to Chen. Chen eagerly agreed to it, and the MP program was born. Inherent in Chen's acceptance of the MP, however, was one unusual condition: Chen would not report to Les Davis. His project would be overseen by John Rollwagen. Though Chen clearly understood that he no longer answered directly to

Davis, colleagues weren't sure if he fully understood the implications of the arrangement.

Whether or not Chen realized it, the difference between Davis and Rollwagen was a significant one. Davis's approach was fatherly; he could manage a project by gently delving into the technical detail. It wasn't unusual for him to say, "Steve, I don't think that idea will work. You've got a better chance of success if you do it another way." All of the engineers at Cray Research respected Davis's judgment in these matters. For years he had done the same for Seymour Cray.

Rollwagen was far different. For all his personable ways and public charm, he could be a formidable opponent. He was every bit as intense as the hard-driving Chen. Rollwagen didn't possess the depth of technical knowledge of Les Davis, and didn't try to. And he was unintimidated by the prospect of directly managing a brilliant technician like Chen. Rollwagen would simply work with Chen to develop a budget, then force him to stick to it. Whether Chen knew it or not, the stakes were gradually inching upward.

While Davis oversaw the completion of the Y-MP, Chen ratcheted up his already high intensity a couple more notches. He quickly began recruiting engineers and laying out a schedule for the new machine, which he planned to finish by 1989, at a cost of $50 million. The snippets of news that trickled from Chen's camp revealed that he had soaring ambitions. Engineers talked about a raft of aggressive technical features: sixty-four processors, custom-designed logic circuits, multichip modules, multiple pipes, an optical clock. Chen even explored the possibility of using *optical* interconnects, so that the machine's electronic switches would be engaged by beams of light. He planned for the machine to have a one-nanosecond clock. Operating with sixty-four processors, it would be one hundred times faster than anything on earth. To some engineers it sounded like the project of a lifetime; to others, like science fiction.

In Cray Research's nonbureaucratic culture, management left Chen alone. As a senior vice president of the company, he could spend money as he deemed necessary, as long as he stayed within his budget. With fantastic speed, Chen built a big team, then kept adding to it. After a few months it included more than a hundred members.

Meanwhile, the unspoken spirit of competition between Cray and Chen increased. Chen's team worked in the Development and Engineering buildings near Lowater Road; Cray's worked in a forest area on the other side of the Chippewa River. In some cases, opposing team members refused to socialize. Cray seemed oblivious to any competitive spirit, but Chen and some of the members of his team took it more seriously. Some still felt they were working in Seymour Cray's shadow and wanted to prove themselves.

In 1987 Cray Research's financial position changed. The X-MP was running out of steam; the Y-MP was still a year from production; and the CRAY-3 was struggling. Meanwhile Japanese competition grew more intense. And Control Data, which had slowly drifted away from supercomputing in the late 1970s, was also back with its new ETA-10 machine. Management had to do something. It had three projects, all draining millions of dollars, and it had no new product. Rollwagen, in conference with other senior managers, decided that the company needed to cut spending—a general belt-tightening. As part of that, they asked Chen to cut $1 million from his 1987 budget.

In a series of phone conversations with Rollwagen, Chen agreed to the cuts, then changed his mind. Rollwagen grew uncomfortable. A year earlier, he and Chen and vice president of finance John Carlson had fattened Chen's $50 million allowance to $75 million over five years. In fact, Rollwagen and Carlson had privately agreed to allow for $100 million, but they had not told that to Chen. Chen was now saying that $75 million wouldn't be enough. With the project still at least two years from completion, Rollwagen feared that Chen would come back again and again, possibly running the tab as high as $300 million.

In August Rollwagen suggested that Chen meet with the company's executive committee to go over his plans and his budget. Chen drove to the Mendota Heights headquarters and met with Rollwagen, Carlson, Davis, and the rest. In a nerve-racking eight-hour session he explained his plans and his budget. He described the machine's sixty-four processors, optical clock, custom-designed integrated circuits, multiple pipes, one-nanosecond clock, and all its other technical features. His staff had reached 180 people—forty more than he was budgeted for.

The committee was stunned. Exceeding budget was one thing, but this was another. In the history of the company, no one had ever done what Chen was now attempting. Seymour Cray, who had sometimes stretched the technical envelope farther than he should have, had never come close to this. Cray had taken his components off the shelf. Chen was trying to invent *everything*. If the machine worked, it would undoubtedly be the greatest technical achievement in the history of computing, but no one in the room believed it would work.

A week or so after the executive meeting, Chen and Rollwagen met again. The MP project was being seriously cut back, Rollwagen said, and Chen's latitude, his ability to spend without supervision, was also being curtailed. Chen was incensed. He told Rollwagen that Cray Research could not expect to fend off Japanese competition with such a half-hearted effort. "If you scale it back, the machine becomes another me-too product," he argued. But Chen knew that there was little point in arguing. For some time he had felt that the deck was stacked against him. Management, he thought, was enamored with Seymour Cray. Chen believed that they'd never fully understood his contribution to the X-MP and couldn't see the potential in the MP. He thought that it was a battle based on emotion, rather than logic, so he fought back. If necessary, Chen said, he would leave.

Chen and Rollwagen both knew what that meant. For years Rollwagen had built the image of the company on the genius of Seymour Cray. For the past five years the public saw a shift in that image. Many recognized Chen as the new genius. His departure would send Wall Street into convulsions. Rollwagen, however, was unfazed. Go ahead, if you have to, he said.

On the following Saturday, Chen called a meeting of about six key engineers at his office in Chippewa Falls. Visibly shaken, he reported that Cray Research was scaling back the MP project, possibly even dumping it. He was leaving the company. If he formed a new company, would any of them want to join him?

The word was out. Panic ensued. The following week, Davis struggled with morale, trying to find new homes for the people displaced by the cutbacks in the MP program. He assigned Steve Nelson to lead the next new program, called the C90. Nelson met with groups of MP engineers, trying to convince them to stay with Cray Research. He was greeted with extraordinary, intense anger. Engineers in the room shouted at Nelson: "You just canceled our project! Why should we stay?" Nelson called several more meetings, sitting down with groups, small and large. Meanwhile Chen was doing his own recruiting: He began talking with engineers outside the MP project.

Early in September 1987 the press learned of the Chen situation. The already tense atmosphere grew more so. The *Wall Street Journal* described it as "the biggest trauma of the company's 15-year history." Cray Research had lost a superstar, they said. Company managers tried to backpedal, saying now that the loss of a single individual was not a catastrophe. *Teams,* after all, designed supercomputers. But the press, understandably, wasn't buying it. For years they'd heard about the genius of Seymour Cray; more recently they'd seen Steve Chen as Cray's successor. On the day of the announcement, Cray's stock dove $8.50 a share, to $96.

Within a few weeks Rollwagen received a call from a high-ranking IBM official. The official asked if he would be interested in co-investing in Steve Chen's new company. *Co-investing?* Rollwagen was appalled. He quickly rejected the idea. Later he received another call from the executive. "John, we're considering an investment in Steve Chen's company. What do you think?" Rollwagen explained that Cray Research based its MP decision on technology, rather than budgets, but he added, "Steve's a smart guy. If you want it, go for it."

IBM did. Shortly before Christmas 1987, IBM announced that it would invest in Chen's new company, Supercomputer Systems, Inc. Cray Research's market slide continued that day, with its stock dropping another $2.25 a share. If Cray Research management thought the worst was over, they were wrong. The states of Illinois and Wisconsin ultimately started a bidding war for Chen's company. Chen estimated that the company would employ between one thousand and two thousand people within five years, enough to put a small town to work. When Wisconsin won the bidding war by offering $42 million in incentives, Chen moved his company to Eau Claire. In the most painful move of all, Chen's company eventually hired forty-three Cray Research engineers and technicians. Chen had exacted some measure of retaliation on his former employer.

The Chen debacle had been a painful lesson for Cray Research. Inside the company, managers acknowledged that the problems had been self-inflicted. The genius image had gotten out of control, they admitted. To colleagues, Rollwagen confided that he would never again "put all his eggs in one basket." There would be no more geniuses, no more mysterious master architects. Supercomputer design was now a collaborative effort, a team sport. Henceforth Cray Research would no longer build its image on the shoulders of one powerful individual.

Little did they suspect how accurate that statement would be.

NINE

· · · · · · · · · · ·

Shakeout

The engineers at the Riverside Project Building in Chippewa Falls were dumbstruck. There, on a muggy August afternoon in 1988, the technical teams of the CRAY-3 project split into small groups and filed into conference rooms, where the leaders broke the bad news: The project was moving to Colorado Springs. And this time, unlike the Boulder venture of a decade ago, the *entire* project was moving out. This wasn't a parallel effort. It wasn't a way of fostering competitive spirit. It was the CRAY-3 program. *Seymour Cray was going, too.*

No one knew what to say. Groups of ten or so sat huddled around long conference tables, staring. The project leaders—most of them logic designers—played the management role. They explained that no one would be forced to go. For engineers who chose to stay in Chippewa Falls, Cray Research would find other jobs. But the project leaders were no happier about it than anyone else; most admitted that *they* were staying in Chippewa Falls.

Although there had been a few foreboding signs, no one had expected anything like this. The CRAY-3's manufacturing operation had moved out to Colorado Springs about five months earlier, but that was not surprising. For years Cray Research had talked about opening manufacturing facilities as far away as France. But no one had expected the *design* effort to move—design had always been done in Chippewa Falls.

The engineers' big question was Why? Why had Seymour, their mentor, their leader, decided to make this move? They felt as if they were being deserted. It didn't help that Cray was not there to explain it to them. Everyone knew that Cray wasn't fond of public speaking. He wasn't glib or smooth in the way that executives often are. When he spoke, he lowered his eyes, his lips curled into an impish grin, his voice trembled a bit, but he always came across as absolutely sincere. If there was ever a moment when sincerity was needed, it was now. Most of the engineers now believed that his absence meant something.

In truth, Cray's absence meant little. He was merely searching for the right recipe, trying to capture an elusive spirit from the early days of computing. Back then, it had been enough to change the locale, to detach the engineers from the morass of management, to infuse them with newfound enthusiasm. Now it was more complicated. The technology had matured. Larger teams, more money, and more coordination were needed. But Cray knew he needed to get the CRAY-3 program back on track, and this move seemed as good a start as any.

Whatever Cray's absence meant, the engineers weren't happy. The machine they had sweated over for five years was being plucked from their midst, and they didn't like it. Most engineers, particularly the good ones, were like artists in this respect. The creative process was addictive. They often spent nights and weekends in their labs struggling to solve seemingly insignificant problems, while their families sat at home wondering where they were. It was ironic, because engineers typically had little patience for artists, and vice versa. But both shared this same characteristic. It was typical for engineers to feel more devotion to their project than to their employer. At Cray Research there were stories about engineers who, after being laid off, begged to see their projects through to completion, even if it meant receiving no pay. The addiction was *that* strong.

Cray was now forcing them to choose between home and project. If they wanted to come, they could uproot their families, leave their friends, sell their homes, and move to an area where the cost of living was much higher. Or they could remain in Chippewa and say good-bye to the CRAY-3.

From the beginning, the engineers at Supercomputer Systems, Inc. (SSI) felt that everything would be different now. At last they would be appreciated. They thought they hadn't been appreciated at Cray Research. Most of them didn't understand how Cray Research could have cut the MP project. They considered it not only callous, but a bad business move. Cray Research had chosen Seymour Cray's CRAY-3 over the MP.

For most of the MP engineers, that had been a bitter pill to swallow, especially in light of Chen's success. It was Chen, after all, who had provided the lifeline for the company in 1982 by introducing the CRAY X-MP, they said. And it was Steve Chen, not Seymour Cray, who had unveiled the four-processor version of the already successful X-MP three years later. It seemed impossible that management, however enamored with Seymour Cray, could have ignored those facts. And it seemed impossible that any real business manager could have placed nostalgia or friendship or admiration ahead of the best interests of the company.

Yet, in the minds of most SSI's engineers, that was exactly what Cray Research had done. Most believed that Cray Research, and John Rollwagen in particular, had based their decisions on emotion rather than logic. Chen, upon leaving, had said so. By cutting himself loose from the firm, however, he believed he could now prove that Rollwagen and Davis and the company's board of directors had been wrong.

A surprising number of Cray's employees followed Chen. Cray Research's managers hadn't counted on that. Inside the company, the view of Chen had been mixed; some of the engineers had resented the way the firm conferred credit on him for the X-MP; others were downright resentful of Chen, believing that he had been overly ambitious in accepting the credit. But many engineers, particularly the younger ones, were fiercely dedicated to Chen. The firm's managers hadn't fully comprehended that dedication, nor had they understood the depth of loyalty that Chen's engineers had for their project. There was still an overriding bitterness among those engineers, who felt underappreciated anyway, and the death of the MP project had compounded it. That was why so many now wanted to join Chen.

At first, Chen's staff numbered just six, but the six were committed to the idea of starting a company. They were so committed that they left without any promise of salary, without any real business plan. For funding, they each kicked in a portion of their personal savings, from a few thousand dollars to one hundred thousand dollars. When they merged all their capital, it totaled about a quarter-million dollars, which was less than one-hundredth the amount needed to build a new supercomputer. So it was obvious from the outset that they would need much more money.

In September 1987 they began working, ironically, in the Hallie lab near Seymour Cray's old house. The facility was so small that Cray Research no longer used it, so Chen rented space there while he searched for funding. For Chen, working in the Hallie lab represented a strange sense of renewal. He had launched his career with Cray Research in the same wooded surroundings eight years earlier. Now he sat in the lab, renting space from his old company, while he tried with all his might to prove it wrong.

About a month after the company's founding, Chen received a stunning call from an IBM executive. IBMers had read in the *Wall Street Journal* about Chen's debacle at Cray Research and wanted to know if Chen was interested in teaming up with them. The executive told Chen that he had already talked to Rollwagen, who had given IBM his blessing. Chen quickly entered into negotiations with IBM. After two meetings, the firms had agreed upon an investment of $150 million in Supercomputer Systems. With that funding, Chen now had more leverage in his negotiations with the user community. In quick succession he secured smaller investments from Ford Motor Company, Du Pont, Boeing, Électricité de France.

Now more Cray Research engineers wanted to be a part of Supercomputer Systems. Slowly, the newcomers began trickling in, until they numbered forty-three. For Cray Research, it was an oddly competitive situation: Traditionally, their employees had been geographic captives. Now they had an option.

As the company grew, Chen transferred his firm to another facility near Interstate 94 in Eau Claire. It was a much larger building—maybe ten times the size of the old Hallie lab. The engineers soon learned that the building was incredibly dirty and parts of it were still unusable. Though it looked clean and new from the outside, it had previously served as a printed circuit board manufacturing facility for Memorex. And now the chemicals and dirt from the manufacturing operation needed to be cleaned up, so the new tenants set to work with brooms and mops.

By January 1988 the founders finally received their first paychecks. The dream was beginning to look like a reality. The engineers among them began drawing their periscopes down and focusing on the task of designing a computer. They decided that the new computer would borrow some, but not all, of the ideas of the MP. Most of the engineers now tacitly agreed that the MP's goals had been too ambitious.

More important, however, was the fact that the engineers were still together. They now had an incredible opportunity to prove that they were right—and to prove that Cray Research was wrong. Few individuals ever received such opportunities, but they had earned theirs by taking a risk and leaving their employer. Now it was time to go to work. Engineers in the supercomputer community were pessimistic about their chances, but they didn't care. They were young, confident, and energetic in the face of the odds, just as Seymour Cray and his colleagues had once been.

Tony Vacca couldn't help looking at the table. Vacca, one of the top engineers for ETA Systems, was supposed to be listening to his boss, but as he sat in the modern roomy office of Control Data's new chairman, Vacca's gaze kept returning to the table.

It was a big table. With its thick hand-carved legs and glass top, it looked like the kind of table that someone might have proudly displayed in the dining room of a 1950s bungalow—the type that family members passed along as an heirloom. Yet here it was in the office of Bob Price, the new chairman and chief executive officer of Control Data Corporation. Price, who had replaced Norris after his 1986 retirement, probably had no idea where the table came from. But Vacca knew. That was why his attention kept getting drawn back to it.

Vacca knew the table as well as anyone. For years he and other Control Data engineers had laid big drawings on that table. They'd done their design work on it. During countless lunch hours, they had played cards on it. While seated around that table, they had discussed the CDC 1604, Star-100, Cyber 203, and Cyber 205. They had laid their ham-and-cheese sandwiches on that table and set thousands of cups of coffee on it. Some engineers said it had been around since the days of Engineering Research Associates. In a sense, that table had been the design lab's family heirloom.

But all of that changed when Vacca had packed up the lab for ETA's move to Energy Park in St. Paul. He had ordered the movers to haul the table off to the new facility. Within weeks one of Vacca's engineers approached him, saying that the corporate offices wanted the table. "Why?" Vacca asked. "It's our table."

"I don't know," the engineer replied, "but we have to move it back there."

Vacca knew why they wanted the table. To someone in the corporate offices, it was a symbol of power. From the moment ETA had been announced in August 1983, some managers within the company had resented it. The prospect of a group of engineers departing *for the specific purpose of getting away from management* rankled them. "Forget it," Vacca told the engineer. "Tell 'em it's our table."

"We can't, Tony," the engineer replied. "They've got all the money." That's what it had come down to. Corporate had the money and power. So Vacca called a mover and sent the table back.

About a year later, having come to corporate headquarters for a meeting, Vacca turned a corner in one of the hallways and came face to face with the table. There it was, on the fourteenth floor of the main building, sitting idly. Someone in corporate had won, had flexed his political muscle, but didn't know what to do with his trophy. So the table sat in a hallway, while everyone walked around it.

Vacca, an affable, easy-going engineer who ordinarily avoided corporate politics, now grew obsessed with the table. To him it represented all of the corporate power plays, all of the usurpation of power that was taking place at ETA. He tried to work with management to get the table back. At one point, he extracted a promise: Corporate would return the table *after* ETA delivered its first big, multimillion-dollar system of 1988. But the multimillion-dollar machine was delivered, and the table never arrived.

Vacca had hoped it wouldn't come to this. When Norris had formed ETA, he had tried to insulate it from the corporate morass of Control Data. He had made it an autonomous business unit, a wholly owned subsidiary. He physically detached it from the rest of the company, but it had never really been a separate entity. The finances of Control Data and ETA increasingly became so tightly intertwined that it seemed like just another division of the parent company.

So now, as Vacca sat across the table from Price, he knew the end was near. Despite reassuring words, he could feel it coming. Price told him that ETA would survive, but each time Vacca looked down at the table, he was reminded of the constant turf wars within the company. The table had become a symbol of those turf wars: Corporate management had constantly badgered Vacca's boss, Lloyd Thorndyke. They continually challenged his decisions on the smallest issues, all the way down to such matters as the table. As Vacca listened to Price, he realized that when finances grew tighter, corporate management would again challenge ETA on the ultimate matter: its right to exist.

For Vacca, it was a slow but painful realization. He had invested five years of his life designing the ETA-10, an awesomely fast machine that threatened to give Cray Research a run for its money. In a technical sense, his engineers had come agonizingly close to achieving their goals. The ETA-10 was an inventive machine, using liquid nitrogen cooling and special kinds of chips that generated low heat.

The failure of ETA Systems would be a powerful blow for Vacca's crew. The engineers, technicians, and assemblers on the ETA-10 program were a highly committed bunch. They worked nights, weekends—whatever it took to get the job done. Vacca recalled attending a Saturday night dinner party, returning home, and telling his wife, "I have a feeling they're still at the lab." He packaged up a dessert and drove down to the Energy Park facility at 2:30 A.M. Sure enough, he found them there, wiring the modules for the ETA-10. Those crew members had believed in the machine and in the company. Now the company was dying, and their spirit was dying with it.

In the end no one could explain the reason for its impending doom. Corporate managers blamed late delivery of the machines. Engineers criticized management for their incessant petty intervention and continual shuffling of leadership. Whatever the reason, the company bled to death, eventually losing more than

$400 million despite installation of seven liquid nitrogen–cooled machines, and twenty-seven smaller air-cooled models.

Within a few months it was all over. Vacca received a telephone call late on a Sunday evening in April 1989 from Thorndyke. "They're closing it down tomorrow," Thorndyke said. Vacca could barely summon the strength to hang up the phone. He felt as if he'd lost a family member. The next morning, the eight hundred employees of ETA Systems found the doors locked at the Energy Park facility. Buses rolled up to the entrance and carted the employees off to a nearby theater, where they were told that ETA Systems was no more. Control Data was in such horrible financial condition that no one was shocked, but many had clung to the hope that ETA would find a way to survive. That hope was finally gone.

The death of ETA was especially painful for Vacca and Thorndyke. Both of them had worked as engineers during Control Data's heyday, when the company had dominated supercomputing. And they were the engineers whom Norris had chosen in 1983 to build ETA Systems and help Control Data regain its lost glories. But the plan had failed. Like Vacca's table, ETA Systems was now and forever lost to the tangled bureaucracy of Control Data Corporation.

For all of its north woods charm, Chippewa Falls had never been like this. The new facility in Colorado Springs was sleek, modern, and surrounded by breathtaking sights. In the morning employees could look out the building's front windows and see magnificent sunlit views of the Rockies' steep east face; in the afternoon they could watch the thunderheads roll beneath the peaks.

Seymour Cray had chosen the facility and the town himself. Cray's original intention had been to make a four-city tour and select the best locale for his new facility. Along with his second wife, Geri Harrand, and his handpicked manager, Neil Davenport, and Davenport's wife, Cray had planned an itinerary that included visits to all four cities. His goal was to find a city that wasn't overwhelmingly large, but was big enough to have surplus of talent in electronics and, particularly, robotics. The first stop in the four-city tour was to be Colorado Springs, followed by Austin,

Portland, and San Diego. But Cray, who had a passion for skiing and hiking, never made it past Colorado Springs. He liked the town so much that he didn't bother to visit the other cities on the tour. Cray Research quickly purchased an existing building from a British semiconductor maker, Inmos. It then began hiring and started moving the engineers from Chippewa into its picturesque new setting.

When the engineers arrived from Chippewa, they were appalled. They couldn't find their tools. Equipment was haphazardly stored in a dungeonlike area. The labs were incomplete. The offices looked as if some kind of high-speed Rocky Mountain gale had roared down off Pikes Peak and scattered every drawing, every memo, and every snip of paper. The new crew didn't know where to begin.

But that wasn't the worst of it. Cray Research was hiring a slew of new engineers, mostly in manufacturing. During tours of the building, company representatives told prospective employees that they were ready to build the CRAY-3. A so-called foreground processor had been completed, and it worked, they said. The plan was to deliver thirty new, multiple-processor CRAY-3s during 1989. That's why they were hiring manufacturing engineers, instead of design engineers. The CRAY-3 was nearly finished—or so Cray thought.

The truth was that they were nowhere near the manufacturing phase. The new technical staff quickly learned that *some* aspects of the foreground processor worked, but it didn't operate as a single entity. Worse, there was virtually no workable testing or manufacturing equipment. The "die attach" machines, which placed chips in electronic packages, didn't operate properly. The other automated manufacturing equipment—wire bonders and wire notchers and such—were also faulty. The tooling and jigs arriving from Chippewa Falls had to be rebuilt. Before long the engineers began to realize that they were at least two years away from delivering a finished product.

They couldn't get any help from the old CRAY-3 staffers in Chippewa Falls. Only about a dozen engineers and technicians had followed Seymour Cray on his trek to Colorado Springs. The remainder who'd stayed behind in Chippewa were bitter. So when the new crew called the Riverside Project Building to discuss the flaws in the equipment, they were greeted with stoic north woods mumbles and grunts. The message from the Riverside Project Building was clear: We may work for the same company, but there's no way we'll help *you* finish *our* project.

The big problem with the construction of the CRAY-3 was a familiar one. Like the CRAY-2 and the CDC 8600, the CRAY-3 used a three-dimensional board stack-up. In their assembly effort, the engineers were trying to cram more than a thousand chips in a three-dimensional module that measured about four cubic inches. To hold the module together, they needed to push about ten thousand tiny twist-pin jumpers through holes in the stack of printed circuit boards. The holes measured about five-thousandths of an inch wide, and no human being could consistently push the pins through them. It was like threading a sewing needle, except a lot harder. Consequently the engineers had to build machines to make the pins, then build more machines to insert the pins and trim them after they'd been inserted.

Before they could assemble the processor modules, they also had to test them. But they weren't yet able to do that, either. The clock speed goal on the CRAY-3 was two nanoseconds—the equivalent of five hundred Megahertz. No commercial vendor built 500 MHz test equipment of any kind, so the new Colorado Springs crew was forced to find a company that could custom-build the test equipment they needed.

By the end of 1988 it became obvious to everyone that the CRAY-3 wasn't ready for assembly. So the Colorado Springs division of Cray Research was forced into its first layoff. Assemblers and assorted other manufacturing people were targeted first. For Seymour Cray it was a highly distasteful step. Though he seldom hesitated to fire vice presidents, Cray felt he had an obligation to engineers, technicians, assemblers, and others who weren't part of management. As a result, he supplied generous severance packages, particularly for those who'd moved from Chippewa. Former Chippewa employees received one year's salary; those from Colorado Springs received six months' pay.

The engineers in Colorado Springs began to realize that Cray had never fully understood the status of the CRAY-3 program when he'd left Chippewa Falls. The engineers in Chippewa had been supplying cheery status reports on the manufacturability of the machine, and Cray had accepted them at face value. In the old days when Cray had built his machines piece by piece with his own hands, this wouldn't have happened, but in the era of auto-mated manufacturing, Cray was no longer in tune with all of the machine's facets. In addition, his exalted status and his lack of pa-tience made it unlikely that anyone would come to him with seri-ous problems.

In Chippewa Falls the company's veterans immediately recog-nized the problem: Cray needed Les Davis. No one had ever questioned Cray's brilliance, his commitment, his willingness to tirelessly devote himself to the most tedious tasks, but everyone knew that Cray's real skill was his creativity, his inventiveness. In an era when engineers increasingly cloaked themselves in the ra-tionality of mathematics, Cray was a rarity. Psychologists might have said that he was primarily a right-brain thinker.

Davis was the classic left-brain thinker. Much of his success had been built on Seymour Cray's architectures. In the X-MP and Y-MP he had borrowed Cray's ideas, expanded on them, and applied his own focus and discipline to them to make them work. His ability to ask the hard, logical questions was what enabled engi-neers to successfully finish the projects. Davis was one of the rare individuals who could ask those hard questions of Seymour Cray.

Cray needed someone to ask those questions. He needed focus and discipline. He needed someone to sort through the chaos of his program and find the nugget worth saving. He needed Cray Research to send him a Les Davis. Soon, however, that would no longer be possible.

When John Rollwagen boarded a Colorado Springs–bound air-plane early in 1989, he still didn't know what he was going to say to Seymour Cray. Rollwagen knew only that he needed to speak frankly with his old mentor. Rollwagen was, technically speaking, Cray's boss. He was the chairman and chief executive officer of Cray Research, whereas Cray was a consultant. That meant little to either of them, but it didn't make Rollwagen's visit to Colorado Springs any easier.

For more than a year Cray Research had been struggling. Its stock dropped when Chen left, then it plunged dramatically again during the national market crash of October 1987. Now it was declining again, along with the company's profits. Money for research and development was tighter than ever. Where once Cray Research had had room for three competing projects, it could currently support only one. That meant that one of the two existing projects—the CRAY-3 or a new machine called the C90—had to go.

A decade earlier there would have been little question about which project to back. Seymour Cray, master computer designer, would have won the day. But things had changed. The Chippewa Falls crew had proved that they could succeed on their own. Once their sadness and bitterness over Cray's departure had subsided, the crew banded together on the C90 project. By 1989 the young C90 team showed great promise. To pull the plug on their efforts now would not only be cruel, it would be bad business.

Cray, meanwhile, wasn't generating a lot of confidence among his management. It was obvious to many of the company's managers, from Davis on down, that the CRAY-3 program was mired in chaos. If Cray Research were forced to choose between the C90 and CRAY-3, the choice would be an easy one. From a purely logical standpoint, the C90 showed far more promise.

Still, this was *Seymour Cray.* The $1 billion-a-year company known as Cray Research had been built on his back. Although many wanted to believe that the company was succeeding without him, it was really just expanding on the architectural ideas he had pioneered fifteen years earlier.

As Rollwagen approached the sleek new facility on the south end of Colorado Springs, all of this ran through his mind. He sat down with Cray in the new offices and explained the company's financial condition. Cray Research simply couldn't afford to keep both projects alive, he said. Right now the C90 appeared to present a lower risk.

Cray understood. As he talked with Rollwagen, the two hit on an idea to split the company—break the CRAY-3 away from Cray Research and start a whole new company. It was one of the most unusual schemes in the history of American business. Cray Research would supply Seymour Cray with a $100 million promissory note and an additional $50 million in assets. In return, shareholders would be issued stock in a newly formed company to be called Cray Computer Corporation, and to be run by Seymour Cray. Seymour Cray would be a *competitor* of Cray Research, and the CRAY-3 would go head-to-head against the C90.

Oddly, this didn't bother Cray. Their conversation, a horribly difficult one for Rollwagen, was received in a very different light by Cray. Cray had always understood the risks of his business, and although supremely confident in his own abilities, he accepted the fact that others didn't always share his confidence. He held no animosity for Rollwagen; in fact, Cray's first move as chairman of the new Cray Computer Corporation was to try to hire the man who'd just let him go. With an impish grin, Cray looked at Rollwagen and asked if he would like to be the new chairman and chief executive officer of Cray Computer Corporation. When Rollwagen hesitated, Cray recalled their past glories, the excitement of starting anew, and suggested that they could live those days again.

The more Rollwagen listened to Cray, the more he liked the idea. That night, Rollwagen, Cray, Davenport, and their wives met for dinner and continued their discussion. Everyone at the table could feel the electricity—the combination of excitement and uncertainty that accompanies the start-up of a new firm. Their plan—hashed out right there at the dinner table—was for Cray to serve as chief technical officer, Davenport as president, and Rollwagen as chairman and CEO. They had it all worked out.

Rollwagen was so buoyed by the excitement that the next day he and his wife, Beverly, went out to search for homes in Colorado Springs. For the Rollwagens it was an enormous move, and a risk as well. They would have to uproot themselves from their Twin Cities community, and leave a Fortune 500 company for one that Rollwagen himself had deemed financially risky.

When they returned home a day later—away from the lofty mountain air and the entrepreneurial allure of Seymour Cray—Rollwagen rethought his decision. Colorado Springs' air of excitement was tempered by more sober observations. Rollwagen thought about the prospect of starting over, of building a company, of the heady experience that came with quick success, and he realized he'd done it all before. What he hadn't done was independently run a Fortune 500 company. Even when Cray had served as a consultant, his presence at board meetings had been formidable. It was said that he could still change the outcome of decisions with a nod of the head—no matter who was chairman. Now, that could all change.

Besides, Rollwagen thought, how would it look to have the founder *and* the chairman *and* chief executive officer take off, all at once? The company would have its hands full explaining that. So Rollwagen called Cray on the phone and said, "Let's go ahead with the split, Seymour, but you and Neil can take it from here, and I'll stay with Cray Research."

When Rollwagen publicly announced the new arrangement, it seemed that everyone in the company was appalled. Backers of Seymour Cray were shocked that Rollwagen would let him leave the company. Those who weren't among Cray's supporters were outraged that Rollwagen was *bankrolling a competitor.* Among investors, the reaction was similar. One day after the May 16, 1989, story appeared in the *Wall Street Journal,* the company's stock skidded downward $6 a share. Once valued at $135, it was now at $50.

Rollwagen also had to wrestle with the public relations problems caused by the loss of Seymour Cray. Investors, who had long heard about the genius of the founder, wondered aloud what the company was doing. First Steve Chen had left; now it was Cray himself. In the public's eyes, Cray Research had run out of technical talent. On the Monday after Cray Research announced the new arrangement, Rollwagen flew to New York and Boston to calm investors in those places. The company prepared a series of questions and answers on the topic and distributed them to Rollwagen, Davis, and several other top executives, all of whom were made available to the press on a one-on-one basis.

But the swoon continued. Cray Research's stock, which had been as high as $87 a share less than a year earlier, resumed its dive. Earnings were weak, and profits were down. Two small investors sued the company for what they believed to be a conspiracy to hide Seymour Cray's new status. In October Cray Research dismissed four hundred Chippewa Falls employees—about 18 percent of its manufacturing staff.

The company was increasingly under fire. Market analysts criticized it for letting its founder get away. Programmers, particularly those enamored with the idea of massive parallelism, described the firm as a dinosaur. Some implied that it would eventually go the way of Control Data. A raft of new supercomputer firms, born of DARPA seed money, took aim at the industry giant.

As far as Rollwagen was concerned, Cray Research's biggest competitor wasn't in massive parallelism; it was in Colorado Springs. Rollwagen's real worry was that Seymour Cray would work another miracle, and eventually make Cray Research as obsolete as Control Data.

A year after Seymour Cray moved to Colorado Springs, his new company was still in chaos. The employees, who at first thought the confusion was caused by the move, were now beginning to accept it as a way of life. The big difference between Cray Computer Corporation and other firms was the unbelievable lack of bureaucracy. Most of the engineers had been hired away from firms such as Hewlett-Packard and Digital Equipment Corporation, which had layers and layers of management. Low-level engineers in those places weren't allowed to make decisions. If they wanted to change a design or try something new, they approached a supervisor, who took the request to a committee. Formal meetings were a way of life.

At Cray Computer Corporation life was different. The engineers soon learned that Seymour Cray didn't want to be bothered with questions. He liked engineers who made their own decisions and didn't wait for direction. Meetings were kept to a minimum. The attitude seemed to be "sink or swim." Unfortunately, a lot of people were sinking, especially those at the higher levels of engineering. Vice presidents were coming and going at an extraordinary rate.

Every day at precisely 11:45 A.M., the firm's managers and top engineers donned their sport coats and began gathering in the hallway near Cray's office for the daily lunch routine. The group—usually about four or five of them—drove out to the restaurant at the Red Lion Hotel, where they all ordered corned beef hash, a dish that wasn't on the menu. Cray was fond of corned beef hash, and his managers, whether they liked it or not, voluntarily followed his lead. The routine went on like this, month after month. Over a period of about a year, however, the nonmanagers began to notice a curious thing: The people who gathered every day to eat corned beef hash at the Red Lion weren't lasting very long. The eager young managers joined the lunch crowd, and within months were replaced by new faces. The details of their departures differed, but for the most part, their problems universally involved a bad decision or a direct confrontation of Cray. Cray didn't like to be confronted. If someone confronted him, he seldom argued. It simply wasn't his style to lose his temper. But soon the offending engineer was shuffled off to an inconsequential position, or he simply disappeared from the company.

It didn't take long for employees of Cray Computer Corporation to regard an invitation to join the lunch crowd as a kiss of death. People who joined it, or those whose photos appeared in the annual report, didn't last very long. In general, it was far safer to keep a low profile. Cray rarely fired lower level engineers or technicians. In fact, he took pains to provide good care for them. He set up a "stock grant" program so that they could share the wealth if the company was wildly successful. And he protected them from layoffs, unless there was absolutely no other alternative. Inside the company it was known that Cray had several times dipped into his own pockets to meet the payroll, rather than lay people off.

It didn't take long for most of the engineers to realize that working for Seymour Cray was unlike anything they had experienced previously. Cray was not the typical chief executive. He made himself known to his employees, not through meetings or speeches or public utterances, but through nuts-and-bolts activity. At sixty-five, Cray was still the lead designer on the CRAY-3 project. He wrote the Boolean equations, designed the board interconnects, and defined the so-called wiring masks. It wasn't unusual to see Cray sitting at a bench in one of the labs, doing the microprobing of the tiny circuits on the modules, testing for signal errors. In the beginning, technicians and assemblers were stunned to see this wealthy genius hand-wiring the modules. Cray did the most monotonous and tedious tasks, partly because he felt it made him understand the machine better, and partly because he felt that *no* engineer should be above it.

Cray detested prima donnas. He wanted his managers to understand engineering as well as the engineers who worked for them. One day, as the lunch crowd began congregating prior to corned beef hash, Cray approached a vice president of engineering who was well liked and easy to work with, but whom Cray suspected didn't know his stuff. Cray handed him a computer simulation of a waveform—a graph, essentially—with a big spike on it. "I have a question for you," he said to the vice president. "What's this big spike on this waveform? It looks like an inductor, but there are no inductors of that size on our die. So what do you think is causing that spike?" When others tried to volunteer their answers, Cray quieted them. "I want to hear it from the vice president of engineering," he said, turning to the man. "You don't have to tell me now, but by the time we get back from lunch, I'd like to know." None of the other engineers witnessed their exchange after lunch, but a few weeks later, the vice president of engineering disappeared from the company.

Other managers vanished just as quietly, albeit under different circumstances. Whatever the reasons—bad decisions or disagreements with Cray—their disappearances only added to the feeling of corporate chaos.

At the same time, the engineers wrestled with the problems of using gallium arsenide for the circuits. The problem was that there weren't many vendors who made gallium arsenide circuits, and their vendor, Gigabit Logic, was struggling. So every time the engineers designed new chips, it took three or four months for Gigabit to get a finished product back to them. A pattern formed, where the engineers hurriedly designed the chips, then twiddled their thumbs while they waited for the chips to be fabricated. If the engineers wanted to make changes, they again waited another three or four months.

Cray alleviated the problem by negotiating a deal with his struggling vendor. In exchange for several of Gigabit Logic's production lines, he offered shares of stock in Cray Computer Corporation. The company delivered the production machinery, which Cray installed in a new 30,000-square-foot facility adjacent to his building. By the end of August 1990, Cray Computer Corporation produced its first gallium arsenide wafers.

Still, the atmosphere in Colorado Springs was frantic. Everyone knew that the CRAY-3 was behind schedule. To compensate,

Cray worked longer and harder than at any time in his career. At one point, he turned down a National Medal of Technology, an honor that would have taken him to a Rose Garden ceremony at the White House. Although the bronze medal was already cast, he told Commerce Department officials that he was too committed to his project to take twenty-four hours off. It wasn't a lack of appreciation, he said. It was more a matter of his employees depending on him, and he didn't want to let them down. It was rumored to be the second time that Cray had been nominated for the medal, but there was no time for honors now, even if those honors meant a personal visit with a United States president.

All throughout this complex and difficult process, Cray Computer's prime customer, Lawrence Livermore Laboratory, was kept apprised of the delays. Once the gallium arsenide foundry was up and running, both sides felt ready to sign a contract for the delivery of a machine. Cray Computer sent its West Coast salesman, Howard Watts, to Lawrence Livermore to hammer out the details. What emerged was a contract calling for delivery of a sixteen-processor CRAY-3 no later than June 1992.

Cray Computer suddenly had a schedule and deadlines. Special milestones had been written into the contract, calling for the company to show proof of progress at various points along the way. By the first quarter of 1991 it was supposed to show a working foreground processor—the part that acted as the machine's "traffic cop." By June engineers had to prove that the machine's memory worked. Cray's engineers successfully passed both milestones.

As the year wore on, however, plans began to unravel. By Thanksgiving, the company's engineers realized that they were not going to meet a December 9 deadline to demonstrate a working floating point unit. Watts, who had been selling supercomputers to Lawrence Livermore for more than a decade, relayed the information, believing that the lab would understand.

But the supercomputer business had permanently changed. Government labs were being squeezed; budgets were slashed. There was no room, no patience, no financial means to deal with failure. Lawrence Livermore could not wait, even for the likes of Seymour Cray.

Watts, sensing that something was dreadfully wrong, tried to maintain contact with the lab. He called, sent daily progress reports, but heard nothing. From the perspective of Cray Computer's executives, it was as if Lawrence Livermore lab had slid off the face of the earth. Finally, on the Friday before Christmas, as the sun was setting over the mountains, Cray Computer received word: Lawrence Livermore was exercising an option in the contract that allowed it to transfer its order from Cray Computer to Cray Research. It was buying a C90 instead of a CRAY-3.

The company's executives were devastated. In the space of one short telephone call, they'd lost $29.3 million. Worse, Lawrence Livermore was *the* leader among industry users. When Livermore purchased a new machine, the other government labs took notice. When Livermore backed away from a contract—as they were doing now—everyone was bound to notice that, too. From the opening bell of trading on the following Monday, Cray Computer's stock slid hopelessly, eventually coming to rest at about $5 a share. Four days earlier, its value had been $10 a share; several months before that, it had been $20. In the meantime, the company continued to spend $4 million a month on research and development.

Weeks after the Livermore debacle, the company's tailspin continued. When Davenport and Watts prepared to bid on a contract at NASA-Ames, Cray advised against it. The machine still wasn't ready, he said. Cray could see that his machine was missing its window of opportunity. He announced that he no longer intended to build a sixteen-processor system. When the company's board of directors advised employee layoffs, Cray nixed that, too. He wasn't about to cut any jobs, he said. If the company was going to hit the wall, they would all hit it together.

Davenport, however, wasn't waiting for the crash. The company's president and chief executive officer resigned in April. He didn't want to sit and twiddle his thumbs any longer, he said, while he waited for the technical crew to get the CRAY-3 up and running.

The firm's morale was scraping bottom. Engineers wondered aloud about the security of their jobs. Four years had now passed, and *still* they had no working prototype. For anyone who cared, the job was an emotional roller coaster: One day, it seemed the company was building an empire; the next, it looked as if they wouldn't last another week. The mood was decidedly dour, funds were dwindling, and the CEO was leaving.

For those who stayed, the decision usually boiled down to one key factor: Seymour Cray. He had struggled at other times in his career, but had usually succeeded. Somehow, he had solved the technical problems. And when it came to money, there always seemed to be another pocket. Even with all the setbacks, that seemed to be the consensus. Yes, the machine was a mess. Yes, they were running out of cash. Yes, the executives were jumping ship. But Seymour would find a way. He always found a way.

When Supercomputer Systems' mission began to unravel, the changes were at first so subtle that they were almost unnoticeable. Most of the engineers, after all, had their heads down, buried in a tangle of CAD drawings, equations, and test results. All engineers were similar in that way; they tended to ignore the subtle political signs that foreshadowed change.

Besides, the crew at Supercomputer Systems was immersed in an uncommonly complex task. Steve Chen's new machine, the SS-1, incorporated a wide array of new technologies. Chen departed from Cray in that sense. Whereas Cray implored engineers to remain a decade behind, to use established technologies, and to configure them in novel ways, Chen's team *invented*.

Even for experienced engineers, a demonstration of Chen's new technologies was awe inspiring. His team spent five years perfecting a technology loosely referred to as a multichip carrier. The *multichip carrier* enabled them to vastly increase the machine's packaging density because it allowed them to put, not one, but *four* chips in a ceramic package. Because each of these chips contained 30,000 gates, the multichip carrier enabled them to pack 120,000 gates in a single package. Suddenly, the size of a processor had shrunk beyond anyone's wildest dreams. Chen could now carry a processor in one hand—a circuit board measured just six by eight inches. It was far smaller than Cray Research's Y-MP processor, which was about the size of a suitcase, and a far cry from the days when a single central processor had been as big as a one-car garage.

The multichip carrier wasn't the company's only far-reaching technology, however. Because the packaging density was so great and the circuits developed such tremendous heat, Chen's engineers devised an innovative cooling system that was a variation on earlier immersion techniques. But instead of merely immersing the circuit boards in a bath of liquid coolant, SSI developed a special "liquid jet," which looked like a showerhead. The liquid jet sprayed pressurized coolant through the immersion bath, enabling the liquid to more effectively remove the heat. It was a little bit like placing a showerhead inside a full bathtub: The liquid removed the heat; the showerhead circulated the liquid.

Chen's machine incorporated so much new technology that the employment ranks ballooned to 320, most of whom were engineers. Some engineers were creating a new compiler, others were developing new software. His teams designed 130 different types of new chips and 100 different types of chip carriers. The machine's mother board incorporated seventy-eight layers of electronics. Only a decade earlier, supercomputers had used single-layer boards.

Despite all this technological success, it was hard to ignore the political changes. In 1991, IBM's managers started to show up more regularly, and a few lodged themselves in permanent management positions at SSI. Early reports had indicated that the SS-1 would be ready in 1992, but IBM officials were concerned now that the end was not in sight. So they began creeping in, examining the product, its procedures, and costs. Then they recommended changes.

To Chen's engineers, IBM's very presence was a violation. They responded by quietly digging in their heels. As much as was reasonably possible, they resisted change. They believed they could still build the machine and grow the company without help from New York. In their eyes, the SS-1 was coming alive. In 1991 they successfully ran one module. In 1992 they successfully ran an entire processor. They planned for at least four different versions of the machine—Models 226, 327, 428, and 529—with the number of processors ranging from four to thirty-two. They believed that this was not, to use the words of John Rollwagen, "too many three-point shots." By the end of 1992 they ran their first prototype and beamed with pride.

Still, their machine was a prototype. It was not yet a product. And as a prototype, there was no guarantee that it could be manufactured and assembled at reasonable costs or that it would work repeatedly and reliably. For that, the engineers needed a different kind of experience. And Les Davis, Chen's old mentor at Cray Research, was not there to help. Even with Davis's guidance, it had taken them more than a year to push the CRAY X-MP from prototype to production. Without Davis, they could only guess how long it might have taken for the SS-1.

But they would never find out. In December 1992, Chen attended an SSI board meeting in the Twin Cities. There, he learned that IBM would not support him through his planned initial public offering (IPO) scheduled for the first quarter of 1993. Suddenly, the end was in sight. Chen had planned to raise nearly $50 million in the IPO, but he knew that all his underwriters would now back off. He needed IBM's support for survival. Worse, he knew that he could not change their minds. IBM itself was struggling; it had just realized its first quarterly operating loss in its seventy-eight-year history. Outside investments, particularly shaky ones, were in a precarious position.

Chen crisscrossed the world in search of additional funding, but found none. His one customer for the SS-1, the U.S. Department of Defense, was not enough to save the company. The old rule of thumb—that the first machine pays for all development costs—was no longer true. A supercomputer maker now needed to sell many machines just to break even.

Chen knew it was over. On a frigid Saturday morning in January 1993, a dozen or so employees showed up at the front door of the SSI facility and slid their security badges past the card readers, but nothing happened. They stood there for a moment, waiting for the familiar click of the door, gazing vacantly at one another, before they comprehended the truth. *No one's* card worked. The building was closed. The company was dead. Still convinced of their ultimate success, a group of engineers drafted a letter to President Clinton, begging for help so they could finish their machine, but help never came.

Two months later, one of the company's engineers was driving the back roads of Wisconsin, miles from Eau Claire, when he spotted a familiar object: the SS-1. There, on the grounds of a small farm nestled in the northern Wisconsin forest, sat the machine's outer frame. He slammed on the brakes, veered the car to the side of the road, and jumped out. Examining the machine's skin, he spotted boxes containing more parts from the SS-1. He gently ran his hand over the parts. His heart sank. Whatever hope they'd had for resurrecting the machine was now gone. He knew there was no turning back. The SS-1 had been sold for scrap.

By the time Seymour Cray *gave* away his first CRAY-3 early in 1993, he was almost sixty-eight years old. His hair was a bit thinner and nearly all white, but he still had the same trim, athletic build, the blue jeans and the flannel shirts, the spring in his step, the sparkling blue eyes, and the general appearance of a younger man.

Cray had changed far less than the industry around him. In 1993 it was growing more difficult to build a machine that was five or ten times faster than its predecessor. It was no longer like those do-it-yourself, pioneer days when engineers had built their own test benches, swept the floors, soldered the boards, and sent the state of the art soaring beyond everyone's imagination. Back then it had been enough for an engineer to fight the corporate bureaucracy, to avoid the childish power struggles, and to fend off the efforts of marketing managers who wanted to turn the machines into some kind of convoluted *kludges* that satisfied everyone. When it had come to fighting the corporate urges, Cray had been a master among engineers, and that had been one of the keys to his success.

But it wasn't enough anymore. In 1993 supercomputer users no longer talked of pure performance. They talked of *price-performance*. In the wake of the Cold War, with the energy labs struggling, users didn't have the time or the staff to write their own operating systems, nor did they have the funds to rewrite their software for every new machine. They wanted compatibility, reliability, software, and on-time delivery. Looking back at the 1960s, it seemed ludicrous that the *customers* had written hundreds of thousands of lines of operating system code at the snail's pace of seven or eight lines a day—all in the interests of creating their own perfect machine. They had been willing to pay any price to acquire more speed.

For an engineer like Cray, there could be no more grand and glorious time than that. It had been more like pure research than pure engineering. The engineers didn't answer to marketing or manufacturing. They stretched the technological envelope in ways that no marketing-based operation could ever hope to. They were the best in the world; the highest of high-tech industries; they knew their customers, and because of it they could tell the marketers to take a flying leap if they wanted.

But those days were gone. People were talking about *flops* (floating point operations) per dollar, and the industry was learning about hard economic realities in the most ignominious ways. Steve Chen had been among the first to learn those realities in 1993. Chen's new company, which seemed to be forever on the brink of introducing the world's fastest computer, had watched investors suddenly scatter when it had run out of funding. The engineers at Chen's firm had been confident—absolutely *convinced*—that nothing in the world could touch the performance of their pending machine.

One year later, Thinking Machines and Kendall Square Research, firms that had pioneered the use of microprocessors in supercomputing, suddenly found themselves out in the cold. DARPA, the government agency that had provided them seed money, had changed its name and veered away from its commitment to massive parallelism.

It wasn't that the supercomputer industry didn't want to innovate—far from it. Thinking Machines had set a goal for itself to build a computer *a thousand times* faster than anything on the planet, but such revolutionary innovation took revolutionary capital, and no one in private industry had it.

It was now more effective to take a conservative approach: Study the market, ask the customers, design by committee. It was safe and it offered broader appeal. Cray Research was now doing a large percentage of its development work this way. The hardware engineers worked with manufacturing, marketing, accounting, finance, and software departments to reach a consensus that

would satisfy everyone, that would offer lower cost and less innovation—an *evolutionary* approach.

Supercomputing wasn't dead, but it was different. Most computer makers couldn't afford to build the costly custom-designed
superprocessors that had once ruled the industry. Only Cray
Computer and Cray Research still built such machines. Even Cray
Research foresaw a need for an alternative on the horizon, so
along with several other firms, it now offered smaller, sub-million-
dollar machines. For customers who wanted more, Cray Research
could scale up, piece by piece, until it created a high-perfor-
mance computer. It was a little bit like building a luxury car on a
subcompact platform—the result was never *quite* the same as a
real luxury car—but it was in line with economic reality.

No one in the industry could possibly fail to recognize the economic realities, but that didn't make it easier for the industry's
veterans. Many of the best engineers were now retiring from Cray
Research—not because of age, but because of the company's
changing needs. The most prominent of those was Les Davis, now
sixty-two. For the engineers remaining in Chippewa Falls (most of
whom worshiped Davis), his departure was particularly difficult.
A few followed him, some still in their forties and fifties, choosing
to retire rather than to accept the diminished role of the hardware engineer.

All of this signaled a sad and subtle shift away from the industry's pioneer days. Gone were the times when an engineer could
isolate his crew among the pine trees and build revolutionary machines without corporate intervention. It was a team game now.
There would be no more engineer's paradise. Companies were
setting their sights lower and building machines that offered
more performance per dollar. The end of the Cold War had
changed everything. Supercomputer firms no longer struggled to
develop revolutionary technology; they struggled for survival.

When the CRAY-4 program began early in 1994, most of the engineers were amazed by the speed and relative smoothness of it all.
For those who had joined Cray Computer in 1988, it didn't seem
possible that so many things could go right, all at once.

Although the CRAY-3 hadn't yielded a single sale, Cray Computer Corporation had learned several valuable technical lessons from it, mainly about automated construction of the processor modules.

In a sense, the CRAY-4 was a simpler machine, because it used chips that were packed with about ten times as many logic gates as the chips in the CRAY-3. The CRAY-4 needed only five modules; the CRAY-3 had employed forty. This added up to unexpectedly easy success for the engineers. It seemed that a new internal technical report came out every week saying that the CRAY-4 team had just finished another set of tests on the foreground processor, or the background processor, or the memory. The reports always pointed out that these tests were completed in three weeks, or a month, whereas the same tests on the CRAY-3 had taken eighteen months.

The chaos that had enveloped the team two years earlier was now dwindling away. By mid-1994 most of the engineers knew their jobs and didn't require much direction. Management shuffling had slowed to a crawl. Cray was working extraordinary hours in an effort to get the machine out the door by the end of 1994. He worked at the facility during the day, then the engineers would deliver boards and test equipment to his home so he could keep working at night. At home Cray kept a computer workstation, a plotter, and various test stations and scopes. Surrounded by that equipment, he could work late into the night, just as he had for so many years at Control Data and Cray Research.

Concerns over money never ceased. Every few months a spate of articles would appear in various publications around the country, saying that Cray Computer Corporation was on its last legs. The articles were accurate: The company was constantly seeking more capital to offset its huge development costs. The print media were so loaded with colorfully depressing descriptions of the company—a Ferrari running on fumes, a three-legged stool with a missing leg—that most of the engineers simply refused to read about it. Many of them, buoyed by the success of the CRAY-4, avoided the finance department as well, because news from there was so bleak. Cray himself had to concentrate on blocking the money troubles from his mind. Increasingly, he performed the most tedious wiring chores, saying that such tasks were "good therapy. They keep me from thinking about money."

Despite all of this, morale in the engineering ranks was soaring. By fall of 1994 the Cray Computer's engineers were staging diagnostic tests on single-processor models of the CRAY-4. After only a year, they had reached a point that had taken nearly a decade for the CRAY-3. Preliminary tests revealed that the new machine had a one-nanosecond clock cycle (1 Gigahertz)—the fastest in the world. The company's executives were talking publicly about delivering four- and eight-processor systems early in 1995. The new machines offered twice the performance of the CRAY-3 at one-fifth the cost, they said.

For those who could manage to keep the blinders on long enough, it looked as if Cray had worked another miracle. The legendary tunnel-digger had succeeded again. And why not? He was the genius who had built the first transistorized computer. He was the intuitive wizard who had engineered an extraordinary string of four colossally successful supercomputers in the 1960s and 1970s. *His* architectural ideas served as the foundation for the stunningly successful CRAY X-MP, Y-MP, and C90. Once again Cray was beating the odds.

The technical staff was so enthralled with the apparent success of the CRAY-4 that it began planning for two new machines: the CRAY-5 and CRAY-6. The first, they said, would have a half-nanosecond clock; the second would operate at a quarter of a nanosecond. Engineers were already looking into techniques for eliminating all of the metallic connections in the firm's next-generation machines. Cray Computer was cooperating with Massachusetts Institute of Technology, Hewlett-Packard, and Honeywell to put the proper technologies in place. The executives also planned for Cray's retirement. He would finish the CRAY-5, write the Boolean for the CRAY-6, and announce his retirement some time after that. The company's executives could already see that far down the road.

That was why the morning of March 24, 1995, was so bitterly disappointing. Some of the engineers had been descending the steps to the lower-level entry doors early on that Friday morning when they saw the yellow police tapes. At first they thought that the door's plate glass had been broken again, but then the truth dawned on them: The blinds were drawn; a plainclothes security guard stood sentry; and a white flag waved on the pole out front. The white flag had been intended as a slightly sarcastic touch for the media, who kept hanging around, eager for the crash.

In the cafeteria one of the company's executives laid it all out. To the sound of snuffling gasps and the sight of stunned, pale faces, president Terry Willkom explained that the company had been unable to secure its most recent round of funding. They were closing. It was over. The employees of Cray Computer Corporation could clean out their desks and go home.

Cray issued a memo saying, among other things, that their effort had been "a contribution to science." Although he attended the meeting in the cafeteria, he did not address the assembly. He couldn't. He walked the halls of the building, shaking hands, thanking his employees, barely speaking. But the employees didn't need to speak with him; they could see the sadness in his eyes. To those who had watched him pour his soul into the CRAY-4, he looked lost.

Cray had known failure before, but not like this. He had always assumed that they would all hit the wall together, but he knew that he would not endure the economic hardship now facing some of his young engineers and their families. He wanted to reward those who had persevered to the end, but there was little left to give.

In the building's vast lower level, a member of the technical staff shut down the forty workstations. The monitors blinked off; the fans stopped. In the silver-mirrored tank room, the technician turned off the coolant pumps and blowers that cooled the CRAY-4, enveloping the work area in an eerie silence.

As the employees shuffled out the door for the last time, carrying their personal belongings in boxes and coat pockets, no one knew what to say. There had been so many warnings and so many close calls that they'd all grown oblivious to the predictions. Besides, this was *Seymour Cray*. They had all expected him to pull money from another pocket. They had all believed that he would make it work.

A few of the engineers remained optimists to the end. Seymour Cray would continue his search for funding, they said. Ultimately, he would reopen the facility, and when he did, they would rejoin him. They would gladly accept the chaos, the craziness, the long hours, if it meant they could be part of this electrifying, oddball culture. Their families might cringe, but yes, they would do it again.

Cray and a few of the executives stayed until July, frantically trying to scrounge up enough cash to stay in the game. But with each day, the goal slipped farther away. By July the CRAY-4 had missed its window of opportunity. Cray Research meanwhile introduced its own powerhouse machine, the T90. The energy labs, with their limited funds, would surely opt for that machine.

When Seymour Cray shut the doors for the final time, the rest of the industry barely noticed. A few competitors noted that it was an inescapable fate; they'd believed all along that gallium arsenide wouldn't work. Others felt it was a sad conclusion—an inappropriate way for Cray to end an illustrious career. Those who were close to Cray, however, suspected he would be back. "Seymour will never quit," they said. "He's not the retiring type." Indeed, they were right.

For the rest of the supercomputer industry, the demise of Cray Computer Corporation was an asterisk—an interesting human story in an otherwise inhuman market. The gap it left was more in the heart than in the mind or pocketbook. Cray Computer was, after all, not a major player. It had never sold a machine.

In the end, however, its fate was no different than that of ETA Systems, Kendall Square Research, or Supercomputer Systems. They were all dead.

Cray Research, meanwhile, was extending its dominance. The company founded by Seymour Cray in 1972 was still producing machines loosely based on his architecture. Early in 1995, it rolled out a powerhouse superprocessor machine known as the T90, which operated at speeds approaching sixty billion floating point operations per second. That machine had been the last built under Les Davis, prior to his 1995 retirement. At the same time, the supercomputer giant also made a concession to the microprocessor, introducing the new, so-called massively parallel machines. The very idea had been a reversal for Cray Research; Seymour Cray had never liked the idea of using microprocessors.

He believed in "balanced" machines—machines that smoothly integrated the operation of the processors, memory, and input/output systems. So now, even as Cray Research entered the massively parallel market, its competitors jeered. But their jeering was soon quieted. Shortly after Cray Research introduced the machines, the market began snapping them up, and suddenly Cray Research was a leader in the massively parallel market.

Still, being the leader of the supercomputer industry was no longer the regal position it had once been. Even while dominating the industry, Cray Research reported staggering 1995 losses of $226 million. In light of the company's financial condition, some of its customers now hesitated to purchase a $30-million supercomputer, fearing that the company might not always be there to offer support. The maturing technology, the end of the Cold War, the reign of the personal computer—all of it now seemed to work against Cray Research and the rest of the industry's players.

In February 1996, Cray Research announced that it would seek shelter against the market storm: Silicon Graphics, Inc., a California-based company best known for workstations, acquired it. To those in the industry, the deal was no surprise. The *New York Times* said that Cray Research "was seeking the refuge of a large corporate parent with deep pockets . . ." Industry insiders acknowledged the necessity of the deal, but wondered what it would do to the now-famous Cray Research corporate culture.

In truth, however, they needn't have worried. Cray Research's charmingly eccentric culture had grown increasingly corporate long before the Silicon Graphics deal. Out of financial necessity, the flannel shirt had been gradually replaced by the business suit.

By this time, most of the industry's technical gurus had fled elsewhere, to more stable areas of the computer industry. Steve Chen formed a new company to market computer servers. A segment of the massively parallel crowd moved into software. A few top engineers landed in places like Microsoft and Digital Equipment Corporation; others simply retired. The long-awaited shakeout had reached its peak, and the industry's best talent was fleeing.

When Seymour Cray looked at the flagging supercomputer industry, however, he saw a different picture. Cray still foresaw a need on the horizon for someone to carry on the industry's legacy of revolutionary technology. He firmly believed that the industry, the country, would someday need it. Yes, Cray knew that this wasn't the best time to start a supercomputer company. But the difference between Seymour Cray and the rest of the industry's players was that Cray simply would not quit.

From the moment Cray Computer Corporation collapsed, Seymour Cray never stopped thinking about his next machine. Just as he had after the failure of the 8600, he felt a sense of liberation. Now, he was once again free to "start from a clean sheet of paper."

Early in 1996, Cray investigated ideas that interested him. Technology's grand planner was at work again, examining all possibilities. By mid-year, he had chosen a new technical path. Working with Terry Willkom, former president of Cray Computer Corporation, he found investors for a new company, to be called SRC (Seymour Roger Cray) Computers. Then he contacted engineers from his now-defunct firm. At age seventy, forty-five years after accepting his first job at Engineering Research Associates, Seymour Cray was starting anew—again.

But, for Cray, it was not to be. On Sunday afternoon, September 22, 1996, as Cray drove home after purchasing software at a local store, his sport utility vehicle was struck by a car. Cray's black Grand Cherokee rolled three times, finally coming to rest in the middle of Interstate 25. Emergency crews spent the next ninety minutes extricating him from the vehicle. At a local hospital, doctors found that Cray's neck was broken. He had undergone massive head trauma and would never again regain consciousness.

A day after the accident, Cray's five-man engineering crew was crestfallen. They sat idly in the company's office, waiting for medical updates, unable to work. Most had been on the job less than a month. For those who had been with Cray Computer Corporation, it was as if March 24, 1995, was happening all over again, only worse.

This time, however, the company would not collapse. Cray had seen to it. He had handpicked his crew and laid out his technical vision: His plan was to create "a typical Seymour Cray computer with Intel inside." For Cray, it was an extraordinary change of heart, an admission that the microprocessor was ready for super-computing. His new supercomputer would be a parallel machine, employing as many as 512 microprocessors. In his mind, Cray had already seen how the machine would work. He had preached the gospel of balanced design, laid out his plan for the computer's architecture, and described the company's anchor product: a supercomputer that would operate at a trillion floating point operations per second—about 12,000 times the speed of a CRAY-1.

Two weeks later, Cray died of injuries sustained in the car crash, and the supercomputer era was permanently changed. But even with his untimely death, his vision had been preserved. Now, it would live on in another form, strangely paralleling his earliest efforts. SRC Computers would follow his lead. Working in a tiny office, its small, focused staff would go head-to-head against the big firms, just as Cray Research had a quarter-century earlier. It would defy the risks and try, against the odds, to build the world's fastest computer, the Ferrari of the industry.

That was the Cray Way.

NOTES

• • • • • • • • • • •

1. The Codebreakers

7   "For six days . . ." Kahn, *The Codebreakers* (New York: Macmillan, 1967), 504.

7   "Kapitänleutnant Gerhard . . ." *United States Submarine Losses* (Office of the Chief of Naval Operations, Naval History Division, 1963), 168.

7   ". . . on the moonlit night . . ." Roscoe, *United States Destroyer Operations* (United States Naval Institute, 1953), 306.

7   "Refueling impossible . . ." Kahn, 504.

8   "A tidy, red brick . . ." Ibid.

9   "By now . . . fifteen hundred vacuum tubes . . ." Burke, *Information and Secrecy* (Scarecrow Press, 1994), 299.

9   ". . . *Allan Jackson* . . ." Hoyt, *U-Boats: A Pictorial History* (McGraw Hill, 1987), 135.

10   "Through a series . . . *USS Buckley* . . ." Roscoe, 307.

10   "The *Buckley* was about twenty-five hundred yards . . ." Ibid.

11   "His bedroom was strewn . . ." Worthy, *William C. Norris: Portrait of a Maverick* (Ballinger, 1987), 16.

16   ". . . Commodore Hotel . . ." Parker oral history (University of Minnesota, Babbage Institute, 1985).

16   ". . . part-owner of Toro Company . . ." Ibid.

17   "Parker did, and was stunned . . ." Ibid.

17   "Aye, aye, sir . . ." Ibid.

17   ". . . After they finished, Parker still knew . . ." "The Birth of an ERA," *IEEE Annals of the History of Computing* 1, no. 2 (October 1979), 86.

18   "Parker liked to tell . . . symphony orchestra . . ." Ibid.

18   ". . . loss of jobs for all the machinists . . ." Ibid.

18   "They and their wives met for dinner . . ." Ibid.

2. The Incubator

21   "Its main compound on Minnehaha . . ." "Engineering Research Associates, the wellspring of Minnesota's computer industry" (Sperry Corporation, 1986), 15.

21   "A corner of one of the buildings . . ." Mullaney oral history (University of Minnesota, Babbage Institute).

21   "Creasor carefully watched . . ." Ibid.

21   ". . . 'hrrumphs' . . ." Ibid.

22   ". . . drab pea green decor . . ." Lundstrom, *A Few Good Men from Univac* (MIT Press, 1987), 1.

23   "... 'self-emptying ashtray' ..."
     "Engineering Research Asso-
     ciates, the wellspring of Min-
     nesota's computer industry"
     (Sperry Corporation), 11.

23   "The interviewer ... Bill
     Windget ..." Drake oral his-
     tory (University of Minnesota,
     Babbage Institute).

30   "... crude word processor."
     Butler oral history (University
     of Minnesota, Babbage Insti-
     tute).

31   "How much for the magnetic
     read/write heads?" Ibid.

32   "... Selective Sequence Elec-
     tronic Calculator ..." Watson
     and Petre, *Father, Son & Co.*
     (Bantam Books, 1990).

33   "... so on a chilly afternoon
     in December 1951 ..." Drake
     oral history.

34   "... founding partners would
     make *eighty-five times* ..."
     "Engineering Research Asso-
     ciates, the wellspring ..."
     (Sperry Corporation), 16.

34   "Well, now, we've answered
     your questions ..." Mulllaney
     oral history.

35   "... was so incredible that
     CBS executives balked ..."
     Lukoff, *From Dits to Bits*
     (Robotics Press, 1979), 131.

35   "... Christmas tree lights."
     Ibid.

38   "In mid-1953 ..." Drake oral
     history.

38   "... floor-to-ceiling glass walls
     ..." Lukoff, 139.

38   "There were no input or out-
     put ..." Drake oral history.

39   "Gee, the card-to-tape ..."
     Ibid.

39   "'Either this equipment' ..."
     Ibid.

39   "... Ping-Pong table." Ibid.

40   "You're wrong." Ibid.

3. Seymour

41   "Well, Seymour thought this
     ought to be changed." Mul-
     laney oral history (University
     of Minnesota, Babbage Insti-
     tute).

48   "... circular slide rule had
     given him social problems."
     "What's all this about gallium
     arsenide?" Supercomputing
     '88 speech by Seymour Cray,
     Orlando, Florida.

53   "In Philadelphia, J. Presper
     Eckert ..." Lukoff, 137.

53   "... Harry Vickers, an old-
     time engineer ..." Mullaney
     oral history.

55   "As frustration built in St. Paul
     ..." Ibid.

56   "... executives frantically
     approached Mullaney ..."
     Drake oral history.

56   "You don't have any products
     ..." Ibid.

57   "... he sat in his station
     wagon ..." Supercomputing
     '88 speech.

58   "*Now what do we do?*" Drake
     oral history.

59   "The walls ... Desk lamps
     and phones were prized ..."
     "Preparing for the 21st Centu-
     ry—40 Years of Excellence,"
     brochure published by Law-
     rence Livermore National
     Laboratory, 1992, 5.

60   "... *tens of billions times* atmos-
     pheric." Mackenzie, "The
     Influence of Los Alamos and
     Lawrence Livermore National
     Laboratories on the Develop-
     ment of Supercomputing,"
     *IEEE Annals of the History of
     Computing* 12, no. 2 (1991), 186.

60   "'Never let the lab' ..." Sid
     Fernbach Memorial Sympo-
     sium, 1992.

61   "... the wives against the punch-card machines ..." "Weapons Simulation Leads to the Computer Era," Los Alamos National Laboratory, 1983, 132.

61   "... shake of a lamb's tail." Mackenzie.

62   "Instead of calculating one hundred cells ..." Ibid.

63   "... the lab ordered a string ..." Sid Fernbach Memorial Symposium.

66   "They also considered building digital gasoline pumps ..." Drake oral history.

4. Engineers' Paradise

73   "... Thomas Watson, was on the cover of *Time* ..." Watson and Petre, *Father, Son & Co.* (Bantam Books, 1990), 239.

76   "'Five-year goal: ...'" *Wall Street Journal*, 3/15/93.

89   "... the 6600 would need ten to twenty times ..." Thornton, "The CDC 6600 Project," *IEEE Annals of the History of Computing* 2, no. 4 (October 1980), 339.

89   "... 'cordwood' package ..." Ibid.

91   "... sixty-seven hundred cordwood packages ..." Ibid., 341.

92   "... 'salt lick for the deer' ..." *Business Week*, 8/31/63, 28.

93   "Last week ... most powerful computer." Watson and Petre, 383.

5. The Hog Trough

103   "... 1,500 employees ... 9,000 worldwide ..." Control Data Corporation: Organization, Facilities, and Experience, January 1963.

104   "He asked his fifty top ..." *Minneapolis Sunday Tribune*, 1/12/64, 8.

104   "... Holley Computer Products ..." *Minneapolis Tribune*, 4/17/66.

105   "... Meiscon Engineers." Worthy, *William C. Norris: Portrait of a Maverick* (Ballinger, 1987), 67.

106   "... $40,000-a-year ..." Ibid.

106   "In 1966 four top people ..." *Minneapolis Tribune*, 7/22/66.

106   "... 'prestige matter' ..." Trousdale, "The 360/90 Series," 69.

109   "'I think it's a bad idea.'" Worthy, 69.

118   "... *eighty million* documents ..." Trousdale, "The Suit Begins," 33.

118   "... *fifteen million* documents ..." Ibid.

119   "... 'I don't know' ..." Trousdale, "Depositions," 44.

6. The CRAY-1

129   "... Burroughs's ILLIAC IV ..." *Speed and Power*, TIME-LIFE Books, 34.

131   "... he would not call Norris at the office." Worthy, *William C. Norris: Portrait of a Maverick* (Ballinger, 1987), 70.

132   "... 'valuable and growing asset' ..." *Minneapolis Tribune*, 1/16/73.

140   "... 'couldn't compete with Control Data' ..." Watson and Petre, *Father, Son & Co.* (Bantam Books, 1990), 384.

142   "On St. Patrick's Day, 1976 ..." *Corporate Report Minnesota*, December 1982.

8. The New Genius

168   "'This is the first supercomputer . . .'" *Milwaukee Journal,* 1983.

168   ". . . born Shyh-ching Chen . . ." *Minneapolis Star-Tribune,* 9/14/92.

169   ". . . Villanova . . ." Ibid.

169   ". . . he changed it to Arnold . . ." Ibid.

173   ". . . *TRON* . . ." *St. Paul Pioneer Press,* 7/30/82.

174   ". . . 'superstar' . . ." *Wall Street Journal,* 11/28/88.

175   "'There is a need' . . ." *St. Paul Pioneer Press,* 8/19/83.

176   ". . . tundra farming." *Wall Street Journal,* 6/27/85.

176   ". . . Baltimore youths . . ." Ibid., 7/19/89.

176   ". . . 'the pope' . . ." Ibid.

180   ". . . 'Bubbles'" *Time,* 6/17/85.

185   "In a nerve-racking . . ." *Corporate Report Minnesota,* January 1988.

9. Shakeout

202   ". . . company's stock skidded downward $6 . . ." *Wall Street Journal,* 6/17/96.

202   ". . . conspiracy to hide . . ." Ibid., 8/4/89.

ACKNOWLEDGMENTS

. . . .

This book could not have been written without the invaluable help of many individuals.

I am particularly grateful to those who generously shared their recollections of the supercomputer industry in lengthy interviews, both on and off the record. They include Jerry Brost, Bill Butler, Steve Chen, Arnold Cohen, Seymour Cray, Seymour Cray Sr., Les Davis, Rosemary Davis, Willis Drake, Jon Huppenthal, Carol Kersten, David Lundstrom, Mike McDonald, George Michael, Norman Morse, Frank Mullaney, Dick Nelson, Steve Nelson, Bill Norris, Rex Rathburn, John Rollwagen, Dean Roush, Lou Saye, Alan Schiffleger, Charlie Slocumb, Tim Tewalt, Lloyd Thorndyke, Gloria Thornton, Jim Thornton, Tom Thorson, Dolan Toth, Tony Vacca, Eric Varsanyi, Howard Watts, Terry Willkom, Jack Worlton, and numerous individuals in the Twin Cities, Chippewa Falls, and Colorado Springs who asked not to be named.

Special thanks also to Kevin Corbitt and Bruce Brummer at the University of Minnesota's Babbage Institute, for helping guide me through numerous historical searches.

Lastly, thanks to my editor at *Design News,* Paul Teague, for his tolerance while this book was being written, and to Mike Bartlett, for encouraging me to write it, and to Emily Loose of John Wiley & Sons for patiently guiding me through the entire process.

INDEX

• • • • • • • • • • • •